THE ART
OF
OFFICIATING SPORTS

THIRD EDITION

THE ART
OF
OFFICIATING SPORTS

John W. Bunn

Emeritus Professor of Physical Education,
Colorado State College, Greeley, Colorado;
Editor, Basketball Rules.

PRENTICE-HALL, INC., Englewood Cliffs, New Jersey

PRENTICE-HALL INTERNATIONAL, INC., *London*
PRENTICE-HALL OF AUSTRALIA, PTY. LTD., *Sydney*
PRENTICE-HALL OF CANADA, LTD., *Toronto*
PRENTICE-HALL OF INDIA PRIVATE LTD., *New Delhi*
PRENTICE-HALL OF JAPAN, INC., *Tokyo*

COLLABORATORS

Volleyball and Handball

Marshall L. Walters

Professor and Chairman, Department of Health, Physical Education and Recreation, Appalachian State Teachers College, Boone, North Carolina; Editor, USVBA Annual Guide and Rule Book.

Wrestling

John W. Hancock

Director of Athletics and Varsity Wrestling Coach, Colorado State College, Greeley, Colorado. (Retired)

Soccer

Irvin R. Schmid

Soccer Coach, Springfield College, Springfield, Massachusetts; Past President, National Soccer Association.

Swimming and Diving

Warren "Bud" Best

Swimming Coach, Associate Professor of Physical Education, Colorado State College, Greeley, Colorado.

Skiing

Robert Rock

Section of National Ski Patrol System, Springfield College, Springfield, Massachusetts.

INTRODUCTION

Officiating is an important phase of athletics that has been very much neglected until recently. Because poor officiating detracts so much from the enjoyment of spectators and players, and results in dissatisfaction and bitterness, efforts to improve it have increased in recent years.

To produce better officials, amateur and professional sports organizations have studied and conducted research in the officiating of the various sports and have organized schools and clinics for officials. These efforts have done much to improve officiating. However, until recently, an additional, definite need in the field of sports was an authoritative and up-to-date book on sports officiating. Such a textbook, experts agreed, should bring together all of the data that had been developed on officiating the different sports. Material on the techniques and mechanics of officiating was also needed in this volume, since this very important aspect of officiating had never been adequately stressed.

Fortunately for everyone concerned, such a volume on officiating has been prepared by John W. Bunn, with the assistance of a group of authorities in different sports. THE ART OF OFFICIATING SPORTS is an outstanding contribution to physical education literature and will be welcomed by officials in the various sports as well as by the instructors of professional courses in officiating at teacher education institutions.

ARTHUR A. ESSLINGER
*Dean, School of Health, Physical
Education, and Recreation*
University of Oregon
Eugene, Oregon

PREFACE

This book has been planned primarily for use in courses on officiating. However, it is also written to serve as a handbook on officiating for those who are engaged in administering sports programs. It brings together the best information available for the administration of a large variety of sports. The material in each sport has been compiled by experts in coaching and officiating that sport. For many years such a treatment has been needed to fill the gap in a field that has been growing in importance with each season. Students, teachers, coaches, and officials will find this information indispensable in their work.

The book is divided into three logical parts. Part I lays a foundation for the job of officiating in general. It states a point of view, it discusses the qualifications for an official, and it lists some general principles that are necessary for the efficient and successful administration of a sport. This part is designed to cover all sports and proposes to build a pattern by which the greatest uniformity may be attained. Parts II and III apply the theses developed in Part I to specific sports.

The activities covered in this book have been divided into two groups according to the nature and type of officiating required by each. Some sports, for the most part, require a decision on every single action that takes place. The officiating required in this type of sport may be likened to a true-false test. Baseball, track, and tennis are typical of this group of activities. In baseball, for example, a decision must be made on every pitch. It is a strike or a ball. The ball, when hit, is fair or foul. The base runner is either safe or out. The umpire must make a declaration on every action that takes place. The official is usually stationary in such a game. He must, however, be alert every minute. He is under constant tension. For convenience, the sports that fit into this category are grouped together in Part II.

The sports that generally require discriminating judgments by the official—sports in which his decision depends upon the effect created by the players and the rules that permit him to exercise discretion—are grouped together in Part III. Football, basketball, wrestling, soccer, and lacrosse are typical of this group. The officiating techniques for each of these are treated in exactly the same fashion as those for sports in Part II.

Each sport is treated separately and the techniques required of the official in each are explained in detail. In addition, those play situations that cause the official the greatest concern, those that are likely to create a divergence of judgments, or those that need the special attention of officials are given particular treatment.

By this comprehensive coverage of many sports the necessity for a large and expensive library of the many pamphlets and guides in various sports has been eliminated. And, much valuable material that has not been recorded previously is also presented.

No attempt has been made to present the rules *in toto*. These change too often to justify their inclusion in a volume of this kind. The reader has been provided, however, with the foundations necessary for the proper interpretation and administration of rules in general.

The unique feature of the book is the emphasis on the guiding philosophy that forms the basis for the judgment and decisions by the official in each sport. This philosophy helps the official to orient himself with respect to his activity. The reader should acquaint himself thoroughly with this phase of the book (Part I) before proceeding to the study of the techniques of each of the individual sports.

The author is deeply indebted to those who have so willingly and generously contributed to, and assisted in the preparation of, that part of the manuscript which deals with the individual sports, and to those who have permitted the use of materials from other publications. Without their co-operation and expert knowledge in the field of their specialties, this book would not have been possible. To all of them, my warmest thanks.

JOHN W. BUNN

CONTENTS

PART ONE

Chapter 1   The Job, 3

Chapter 2   Qualifications of an Official, 8

Chapter 3   A Basic Philosophy, 23

Chapter 4   General Principles of Officiating, 28

PART TWO

Chapter 5   Baseball, 37

Chapter 6   Guides to Special Play Situations: Baseball, 50

Chapter 7   Softball, 58

Chapter 8   Track, 60

Chapter 9   Field Events, 77

Chapter 10   Swimming and Diving, 88

Chapter 11   Tennis, 100

Chapter 12   Volleyball, 111

Chapter 13   Badminton, 130

Chapter 14   Handball, 135

PART THREE

Chapter 15   Football, 143

Chapter 16   Football: Guides to Play Situations, 171

Chapter 17   Basketball, 177

Chapter 18   Basketball: Guides for Administering the Rules, 227

Chapter 19   Soccer, 246

Chapter 20   The Techniques and Art of Wrestling Officiating, 281

Chapter 21   Hockey, 314

Chapter 22   Lacrosse, 321

Chapter 23   Organization of Ski Meets, 335

FIGURES

Number		Page
1	Basketball officials in official uniforms	20
2	Baseball officials in official uniforms	21
3	Umpire-in-chief in proper position to call balls and strikes on a right-handed batter	41
4	Signals commonly used by umpires to convey decisions	43
5	Starter with gun up, ready to start race	64
6	With watch poised and ready, the timer watches for the flash of smoke from the starter's gun	70
7	Judge watching the approach of a runner	74
8	Judge sighting along the finish yarn to pick the winner	74
9	To detect any foot faults by the discus thrower, the head judge must have his eyes focused on the feet of the contestant and upon the ring	85
10	The judge of the javelin throw checks the thrower's position	85
11	Umpire in umpire's chair, ready for duty	103
12	Four types of foot faults, and two legal serving positions in tennis	106
13	Linesman's signal indicating ball is in play	114
14	Linesman's signal indicating ball is out of bounds	114

Number		Page
15	Referee's signal to stop play	120
16	Referee indicating that a net violation has been committed by a player to his right	121
17	Referee's signal to indicate a net violation by each team	122
18	Referee's signal to indicate that a player has touched the net	122
19	Referee's signal to indicate the ball has been carried	123
20	Referee's signal to indicate that a player has pushed or shoved the ball and has not batted it	124
21	Referee's signal to indicate the spiker has thrown the ball and not batted it	124
22	Referee's signal to indicate a player has hit the ball twice before it has been hit by another player	124
23	Referee's signal to indicate 4 hits by a team before batting ball across net	125
24	Referee's signal to indicate a point has been scored	126
25	Referee's signal to indicate side out—no score	126
26	Referee's signal for time-out	127
27	Referee's signal to indicate a player has touched the opposite court across the line of the net	127
28	Referee's signal to indicate a substitution	127
29	Referee's signal to indicate players are out of position on the serve	128
30	Referee's signal for a technical foul	128
31	Referee's signal to call attention to good sportsmanship by a player	128
32	(33, 34) The official football signals used to indicate actions taken by officials	169-71
35	Two methods of fastening whistle to hand by a rubber band or ring for ready use	186
36	Position of official when tossing ball for a jump	199
37	Position and attention of officials on a shot from out in court	214
38	Trail official watches ball as it approaches basket while lead official continues to direct attention to players	215
39	Lead official demonstrates a common error of watching ball on a shot	216

Number   Page

40   The official basketball signals   227
41   Positions of wrestlers and referee for starting or resuming
       a bout from standing position   288
42   Referee's position to begin "wrestling on mat"   290
43   Referee in position to check a possible hold to prevent an
       injury   290
44   Referee's position when wrestlers are on the edge of the
       mat   291
45   Referee's signal to indicate wrestler who has the advan-
       tage   292
46   Referee's signal to stop wrestling   292
47   Referee blows whistle and signals "stop wrestling" when
       all supporting parts of wrestlers are not on the mat   293
48   Referee awarding points with finger signal and upraised
       arm   294
49   Referee points to player who has the advantage   294
50   Referee signals no advantage—neutral position   295
51   Referee indicates neutral position standing   296
52   Position of referee to judge a near fall   298
53   Referee awarding points for a near fall   298
54   Referee in ready position to declare a fall   299
55   Referee giving the warning signal for stalling   300
56   Referee declaring a fall by slapping hand to mat   300
57   Referee awarding a decision   302
58   Referee indicating time-out   306
59   Referee indicating rule infringement—interlocking hands   307
60   Official signals for lacrosse   335

DIAGRAMS

Number		Page
1	Position of umpires at start of inning or with no one on base	45
2	Field umpire in position to make a decision on play at first base	46
3	Field umpire behind pitcher with runner on first base	47
3A	Field umpire behind pitcher and infield when bases are filled and infield is drawn in	48
4	Position of umpire-in-chief on a fly to right field with a runner on third	48
5	Positions of base umpire with a runner on base in a soft-ball game	59
6	The correct point of measurement for the high jump	81
7	Method of measuring distance in the broad jump	82
8	Method of measuring distance in the shot put	83
9	Position of linesman for a tennis match	105
10	Position of linesman and umpire for a badminton match	131
11	Positions for the chainmen and linesman for a scrimmage play	147

12   Positions of officials at the kickoff in a four-official game   149
13   Positions of officials for scrimmage play   154
14   Positions of officials for a kick from scrimmage   154
15   Positions of officials for a goal line play   160
16   Positions of officials during a try for field goal   162
17   Positions of officials during a try for field goal from a free
         kick   162
18   Positions of officials during a time-out   164
19   Procedures and positions of officials between quarters   165
20   Positions of officials when a measurement is taken   166
21   Position and movement of referee and umpire at center
         jump to start a period   197
22   Positions and movement of lead and trail officials when
         the ball is in play at one end of the court   200
23   Movements and initial positions of lead and trail officials
         when the ball goes from one end of the court to the
         other   201
24   Positions and movements of the officials on a jump ball at
         the free throw line   203
25   Areas from which play is resumed after a held ball   204
26   Positions and movements used by some officials for jump
         balls at the free throw line   205
27   The lines between the arrows show the boundary lines over
         which each official has jurisdiction for out-of-bounds
         balls   207
28   Method of handling throw-in and subsequent play   208
29   Positions and movements of officials during and following
         the throw-in   209
30   Positions of officials during a free throw   211
31   Positions of officials during a free throw for a technical
         foul   212
32   Starting positions and movements of each official in a 3-
         official game during a jump ball and as play moves
         to one end of the court   221
33   Positions of officials after tip to cover play in front court   222
34   A continuation of play from diagram 33 to show how of-
         ficials rotate positions when play moves back to end
         of court as shown in diagram 32   223

Number		Page
35	Positions of officials during a free throw	224
36	Positions of officials for a throw-in when play is to move to opposite end of court	225
37	Legal and illegal contact in a contest for a loose ball	232
38	Legal and illegal screening movements	235
39	Offense is moving in a different or opposite direction to the defense	236
40	Roll screen movement	237
41	Preventing a player from gaining a desired position on rebounds	240
42	Legal screening movement	242
43	Legal screening movement	242
44	Blocking by the defense	243
45	The diagonal system of control	253
46	The position of the referee at the start of play	254
47	Position of referee during a corner kick	254
48	Position of the referee during a penalty kick	255
49	Area of responsibility of each official in dual referee system	256
50	Positions of the referees during a kick-off	257
51	Positions of the referees during a corner kick	258
52	Movements of referee and assistant referee along the boards in a hockey game	317
53	Positions of officials at face-off in a lacrosse game	328
54	Positions and movements when ball is in play	329
55	Positions of the officials when the play is around the crease	330

FORMS

Number		Page
I	A sample form for recording the results of a continuous type of field event	80
II	A sample form for recording the results of a limited trial event	82
III	A sample score card for tennis	109
IV	A sample score sheet which shows the running score	116
V	The Official USVBA score sheet	117
VI	Umpire's score card for keeping a record of Hand In and of continuous score in a badminton game	133
VII	A sample score card showing two methods of keeping score	137
VIII	A card for rating and reporting the work of the soccer officials	250
IX	Instructions to and duties of Timekeepers (wrestling)	303
X	A plan for rating and reporting the work of the officials	311
XI	Wrestling referees' signals	312
XII	Officials' check list	313
XIII	Form for rating lacrosse official	325
XIV	Lacrosse game record sheet	327

THE ART
OF
OFFICIATING SPORTS

PART ONE

FUNDAMENTAL
PRINCIPLES

chapter 1

THE JOB

The primary job of an official is to cause the game or contest to progress with as little interference as is necessary on his part. Officiating is an art. The individual who can develop this art can become a successful official. He must consider the following if he is to perform his duties successfully.

The Potential of Presence

The official has attained the perfect relationship to the game when the influence of his presence causes players to avoid rule

Be felt, not heard, as much as possible

violations. His influence is felt, but he himself is not noticed. Probably no single rule or set of personal characteristics can be listed that each official must have in order to approach this perfect relationship. Neither is there necessarily a set pattern. Many men reach the same goal, but usually by entirely different routes. Likewise, no two games or situations are the same.

The successful official, by some combination of characteristics and through some pattern, which may vary from game to game, creates an influence that causes the players to avoid rule infractions. Confidence and cooperation are established. The players somehow sense that here is a man who is on the job; he is in the right place at the right time; he is fair; he is consistent; he has understanding; and he senses the significance of each situation.

Time or several experiences with the same official are not primarily necessary to establish this relationship. It may happen the first time an official works a particular game. Recently, the author had occasion to recommend an official for a very important basketball game. The man recommended was in no way known to any of the parties concerned. He was chosen as the official for the game.

The game was a hard fought one. However, it was not five minutes old until it was evident that the players had complete confidence in the official. The game—bitterly contested—was played in the smoothest fashion. Seldom have more complimentary remarks been made concerning the work of an official. Somehow, this man made his influence felt at the outset, and the game was played smoothly and fairly.

The opposite results have been attained at times by the same official. On occasions, it seems that in spite of his efforts, the game goes badly. Much whistle blowing is necessitated. The play is not smooth. It may be the players, the official, that particular game, or a combination of factors. Somehow the official never seems to gain control. He has not hit upon the right formula or correctly sensed the situation.

The author's basketball teams have traveled throughout the country and have experienced many kinds of officiating and many types of officials. It has been interesting to note that the officials either established their influence, or failed to establish it, right at the

Win friends but don't violate principles

beginning of the game. The initial reaction is seldom changed. The players invariably reflect in their play the influence of the officials on the game. The same may be said for officials in other sports.

Official—Player Rapport

A personal relationship that breeds friendliness and trust and not antagonism is essential to successful game control.

Several years ago, a friend presented my wife with a dog, a registered schnauzer. The pup felt strange, looked sad, and remained aloof when it was put into our automobile to be taken away. However, as soon as the car was out of sight of the dog's former home and she was cut off from the other pups and her mother, she accepted her new mistress with complete devotion. She crawled close and laid her head in my wife's lap and looked trustingly up into her face. From that moment, there was complete understanding. The dog would have given her life henceforth for her new mistress.

What brought about this relationship? One can speculate endlessly. All that is definitely known is that perfect rapport was established between dog and mistress. Likewise, one sees a harmonious relationship between players and officials without knowing exactly how it is brought about.

Some officials have attained it by extra-strict tactics at the beginning of a game. Others, by a stern, but courteous attitude. And still others by a warm, pleasant, friendly, and helpful approach. The approaches which are used must fit the occasion. Also, each individual must follow that tack that best fits his own personality. No one method will fit all situations or all officials. The art of being one's self and being able to sense the correct approach to each situation is the secret of establishing the correct rapport.

When one sees a game in which the players are in conflict with the official, one may be sure that the official is either incompetent in the rules and mechanics or that he lacks those personal qualities which help create mutuality between himself and the players. Sometimes he lacks both essentials.

Use your strong points to win respect

chapter 2

QUALIFICATIONS
OF AN OFFICIAL

The art of officiating is largely dependent upon human variables. The more important personal qualities that most authorities agree are necessary in a good official will be discussed in this chapter. These are the factors that will help provide "the potential of presence," "official–player rapport," and "good public relations" if developed and applied artfully.

At the outset, the young official should be advised that he be himself in all cases. He may have an older and more experienced official as an example, but unless he has all the characteristics of his model, he should not try to mimic him. The tyro can gain much valuable information by watching the techniques of his idol,

Be yourself

but they should be adopted only to the extent that they fit his own personality.

The following qualities are listed in the order of their importance and in the reverse order of the control the individual has over each quality. These qualities may be used as factors in a rating scale, so that one may give himself a self-test of his personal qualities. By use of a point system in which 5 is excellent; 4, above average; 3, average; 2, below average; and 1, inferior, he can get a quantitative estimate of where he stands in relation to his fellow officials. The qualified officials average 4 or better.

Reaction Time

This quality is placed first on the list because one either has quick reaction time or one does not have it. Likewise, by a little practice, one reaches the maximum of one's potentialities in this quality. Additional practice does not change the results materially. A person who does not possess above-average reaction time has little chance of becoming a top-grade official.

Split-second decisions must be made. The tempo of games is such that unless the official can react quickly enough to make his decision at the moment the action occurs, subsequent play will have confused the situation. A deliberate, slow-reacting official will let play get out of hand. The best method of gaining the confidence of players is to make decisions at the time a player is going through his maneuver. A player is often unconscious of the fact that he is committing a foul or violation. If, for instance, a player is pushing or holding illegally and the act is called to his attention while he is pushing or holding, he is likely to have the greatest respect for and confidence in the official in the future. In addition, he is often surprised to find that he has developed a habit which is contrary to the rules. By good officiating with respect to reaction time in this instance, the official is making a player conscious of mistakes and thus helping him to correct them.

If, after considerable experience in officiating, the aspirant finds that he is always late in making decisions, he has rather conclusive evidence that he is not likely to become a successful official. Without this first essential—fast reaction time—he has little favorable prospect.

React quickly

During the war, the author was refereeing a basketball game in which the great St. Mary's preflight team was participating. One of the outstanding players on that team, a former college star, had unconsciously developed the habit of pushing an opponent who was in front of him then jumping to rebound the ball. In quick succession, three personal fouls, all for this type of pushing, were called on the player while he was still in the act of pushing. He was embarrassed when he was made conscious of his foul and realized that he had his hands on the small of his opponent's back.

As a result, every time thereafter, when he was in a rebound position, he deliberately restrained himself. He did not commit another foul during the game and corrected a habit that he had developed unconsciously.

Confidence

1. There are many factors that reflect the confidence of an official and gain the confidence of competitors, coaches, and spectators. Probably the most effective characteristic is the manner in which he comports himself in carrying out his duties. A movement that denotes sureness—even a degree of cockiness, when not carried to the stage where it causes resentment—transmits a feeling of confidence to others.

2. Decisive action that is not hasty but has no element of hesitation is highly desirable. It leaves no doubt in the minds of others. It portrays positiveness that wins acceptance. For example, balls or strikes in a baseball game should be called instantly and with conviction. To be apologetic or hesitant conveys uncertainty. It even leaves the suspicion that the umpire by his delay is being influenced by the catcher or other players. Certainly the time to make the decision is the moment when the ball passes the plate. The after-image may be distorted.

A resonant, strong voice is a great asset to an official in those sports in which vocal announcement of decisions is necessary. By means of a clear, strong voice, the official is able to convey to all, particularly the participants, the exact decisions he has made. His voice properly pitched, carrying conviction, and displaying firmness can do more to breed confidence and give poise than any other

Spread confidence—not distrust

factor. A baritone quality is probably best; a high-pitched voice is poorest. Tennis is an example of a sport in which the voice is all important. Not only the decisions on play but a running account of the game and match must be given repeatedly. It is the only means whereby both players and spectators can be kept informed of the progress of the play. In this sport the voice becomes of primary significance.

The use of the voice supplemented by pantomime for clarity in signaling decisions is desirable. Only a few of our officials have mastered the acting stage of their art. Most of our officials have not developed the techniques of using their voices and motions effectively.

Officials tend to be too timid in this phase of officiating. They display indistinctness and indefiniteness in conveying their decisions to the players and spectators. As a result, they sometimes create a lack of confidence toward themselves.

On the other hand, it should be emphasized that dramatics carried to the extreme of putting on a show or of entertaining are definitely frowned upon. Such tactics take attention from the game and the players and focus it upon the official.

If a whistle is used, it can do much to give a feeling of certainty. The whistle should be blown to produce a sharp, staccato sound— not a slow, feeble, extended wheeze. The whistle blown sharply has the effect of saying "attention please" and alerting everyone to the fact that an important decision is to be announced.

Calmness

The excitable official contributes more than the players to a raggedly played game. As a matter of fact, a highly nervous official usually upsets the equilibrium of a team and even induces jumpiness among the players.

Players, particularly the younger and more immature ones, are usually nervous, and they play under considerable tension. Consequently, any actions that will produce calmness and emotional control should be employed. The better official will inject sufficient pauses and quieting maneuvers to create a steadying effect upon the contestants. He will do this throughout the game and particu-

Make decisions clearly

larly toward the end, when a closely contested affair might otherwise become disorganized and players become so overwrought that pleasing performance would be impossible.

There are many play situations when the official can employ tactic to relieve the tension. They are actions that are seldom noticed and yet are tremendously effective.

As an example, a warm friendly attitude on the part of the official has a disarming and relaxing effect upon players and even upon spectators. An official who makes his decisions with a show of belligerency or intensity or with a "there, I caught you that time" expression often arouses the animosity of the players (and the spectators) and thus heightens tension. On the other hand, the official who makes his decisions just as firmly, but with a smile and a friendly manner that says, "I'm sorry, but unfortunately you made a mistake and I have no alternative," tends not only to inject a bit of relief into an otherwise hectic scene but also to create a cheerful atmosphere between opponents, which makes for a better game—certainly one that is easier to officiate. The oft quoted expression, "A soft answer turneth away wrath," applies perfectly.

The best officials are those who remain human and approachable. They are always most warmly received; usually they are accepted even when they are wrong. At least, everyone is more charitable toward them when there is disagreement with their judgments. The players invariably react favorably toward such an official. They respect him and cooperate with him. On the other hand, the official with a chip on his shoulder is disliked and quite often distrusted. It is surprising how frequently he engenders the ill will of everyone at a game. He may be feared by the players, but he is seldom rated above average by them. It often appears that he is presenting a brusque exterior as a cloak to hide inferior ability. It is surprising that an official who has developed unfortunate mannerisms or who presents negative personality traits does not realize that they reflect adversely upon his effectiveness. If he were aware of his weakness, he could work to correct it.

Deliberate movements are sometimes indicated in the progress of a game. In basketball, for instance, when handling the ball out of bounds, the official can restore poise by even, unhurried action rather than hasty, impatient motions. Likewise, hesitation on free throws, to permit adjustments at the free-throw lines and to give

Be calm at all times

clear, complete information on the number of shots, tends to ease the situation considerably. It may even steady the nerves of the free thrower.

Quietly reporting a penalty to the referee in football, oblivious to the mounting fury of the guilty player, usually avoids a heated scene. Holding one's gaze on a play in baseball, after a decision is made, seems to reduce the pressure developing in opposition to the decision.

A pause before announcing a decision, after blowing the whistle to stop play, is effective in keeping play under control. It also causes the players and spectators to hesitate and turn expectantly to the official to get his decision. Timing the announcement of decisions in this way tends to carry the crowd along in a more cooperative fashion. If the voice is also steady, the result is doubly effective.

As has been stated, the subtleness of tactics of this kind hides the intent, but nevertheless produces the desired results.

Consistency

Consistency is the greatest virtue an official can possess. He may have a warped interpretation of a rule; he may practice techniques contrary to those to which a team is accustomed; his judgment on some play situations may vary from the commonly accepted pattern —but with it all, if the official's practice and decision are exactly the same under the same or similar circumstances, players can readily adjust their play to fit the official. They may be surprised and confused momentarily, but when they discover that the official is unwavering in his procedures, they can reorganize their play and continue the game with confidence.

On the other hand, if an official is vacillating in his methods and decisions, he will disrupt the play of a team. He will keep the players in a dither and upset them emotionally, so that their effectiveness is lost entirely. Situations have occurred in which players have become so wrought up that they had to be removed from the game.

A few examples of these two situations will more clearly point up the importance of consistency and the disaster that accompanies the absence of it.

Do you excite or soothe?

In baseball, some umpires have the habit of giving the batter the benefit of the doubt on all low balls. When pitchers learn this and find that the umpire is consistent, no difficulty arises. But if one time the call is a ball, and the next time a similar pitch is a strike, then both the pitcher and the batter become disturbed and much bickering results.

The football linesman who becomes hypertechnical on offside play at one time, and extremely lenient the next, can throw the timing of both lines into a frenzy.

The development of trends in games necessitates rule changes or changes in the interpretation of rules. There is often a lag on the part of officials in adjusting to changes in rules or interpretations. This lag creates inconsistencies that are frustrating to players and confusing to spectators. Sometimes the lag is deliberate because of a disagreement with the change. There is no excuse for the lag in such cases. The rules legislation by the national rules bodies is binding on everyone. If the rulings are wrong they may be changed. They should never be ignored. Recent developments in basketball present excellent examples of a lag in adjusting to a change in interpretations. In order to create a better balance between offense and defense, the action of the offense has been restricted while the defense has been given greater freedom of movement. In spite of the fact that guides for making decisions were so definite that the officiating could be mechanically accurate, there was a long lag in adjusting to the change. In many cases this lag was deliberate.

There is a tendency to officiate with a different degree of strictness at different stages of a game. Such a pattern of officiating can be upsetting to players and to the rhythm of play. For example, to be lenient with respect to contact in post play and rebounding during the early stages of a basketball game and then to become very strict and technical when as a result of leniency the contact is permitted to develop to a vicious stage of roughness, is not indicative of high-grade officiating. It is not fair to the players. They are unable to adjust readily to the change in officiating and as a result more fouling and more disqualifications occur and dissatisfaction increases. It is sounder practice to set the pattern for officiating at the beginning and maintain it throughout. Players will adjust quickly at the beginning, less fouling results, a better attitude and spirit is maintained, and everyone is more satisfied.

Be consistent

Lack of emotional control can cause inconsistency. The official who is bothered by the crowd, or who is nervously affected when he moves from the high school game to the college game, or from the regular season play to the championship tournament is not likely to perform consistently.

Conscientious, intelligent effort coupled with experience will develop consistency for most officials. Some, because of a combination of the factors just discussed, may never be able to attain a high degree of consistency. Officials who are unable to attain a high degree of consistency should be eliminated from games, just as the incapable players are gradually weeded out of the squad and do not get a chance to play with the first team. However, much can be done to help set guides by which all officials can arrive at uniformity and consistency. The presentations in later chapters are intended for this purpose.

Judgment

Judgment and consistency go hand in hand. If basic principles are established that will be the guide for determining the legality of play and the responsibility for acts committed, the foundation upon which to develop judgment has been laid. If these basic principles are thoroughly understood, then sound judgment will be built up through experience in handling contests. One needs to practice the art of officiating in order to become proficient, in the same way that a player must practice the techniques of play in order to develop his skill. It is not absolutely necessary to have played a game in order to qualify as an official. To have been a player, however, gives one an understanding of and a background for officiating that is invaluable.

The young official is likely at first to feel lost and incapable of discriminating between legal play and violations and fouls. Play may even appear as a blur of movement from which he is unable to distinguish any pattern whatever. Under such circumstances, he will probably be hesitant to act. Such a state of confusion need not deter him. With continued practice, the picture will gradually clear. Good judgment will develop with experience. If the official possesses the qualities already mentioned, he should not be discour-

He who hesitates, loses control of the game

aged by any temporary difficulties that present themselves during his early training period.

Practice in officiating under intelligent supervision and guidance is the surest method for attaining consistency and sound judgment. There is no short cut to becoming a top-grade official. It requires work, conscientious study, self-analysis, patience, persistence, and real dedication. A person should not expect to be chosen to officiate the national championship contests or the bowl games immediately after passing the preliminary tests, winning the right to wear the official uniform, and being placed on the official rolls as a registered official. He will reach this goal eventually, however, if he has a burning desire to officiate and persists in his efforts.

Cooperation

In contests that require more than one official, the ability to team with fellow officials is absolutely essential to a well-handled game. The men should gauge their decisions so that they are as uniform as possible. If they diverge to any great extent, the game will be conducted in a very erratic fashion.

Each must have faith in the other, and harmony must exist between them. Any tendency for one official to attempt to dominate the game may cause a poorly administered game. Likewise, if one official is so sensitive that he resents the other for making decisions on plays that he feels are his responsibility, harmony between them may be destroyed. Rather, each should welcome the support of the other. Each should realize that he is not always in an advantageous position to see all the action, even though he is close to the play. Each should be ready to cover play for the other when one is momentarily caught out of position.

There are occasions when the personalities of officials clash. Their temperaments, mannerisms, tactics, seem to conflict rather than blend. Their general analyses of play are often antithetic. When these differences become evident and seem to be fundamentally difficult to resolve, then these officials should not work in the same game. Each may otherwise be an excellent official in his own right.

Be dramatic but don't grandstand

Integrity

The integrity of an individual is always subject to scrutiny whenever he has the responsibility of serving as a judge or arbiter. Sports are no exception. Those who would officiate sports contests must guard this personal quality zealously. No action, no association, no situation should arouse even the slightest suspicion concerning the honesty or integrity of the official. Not only the reputation of the official but the life and value of sports contests is at stake. The attempts of crooked gambling interests to control the outcome of contests by influencing officials, even blackmailing them, is a bitter, unforgettable experience.

Knowledge of the Rules

Knowledge of the rules, the mechanics of movement, and the duties of the officials prior to and during a game are discussed near the end of this chapter on qualifications of an official because any individual with even average intelligence can learn the rules and duties and can practice the mechanics of officiating. The development of these qualities is one of the functions of the officials' organizations.

An official should know the rules perfectly. He should review the rules many times before each season begins. But this alone is not enough. A perfect knowledge of the rules does not in itself guarantee good officiating.

It is also essential that the official know the relationship of one rule to another. Further, it is most important that he understand the background for the rules: If the reason a rule has been inserted into the official guide is understood, if the evolution and development of the rule in connection with the progress of the game is known, and if the official interpretation of the rule in its application to play situations is clear and properly related to the literal wording of the rule, he is most likely to administer the rules intelligently during a game. It is the job of the officials' associations and athletic conferences and leagues to furnish this information to

Assist, don't resist fellow officials

officials. Through their delegated officers these organizations should continually work at informing officials about the rules.

Many sports, such as football, soccer, and basketball, do not permit a literal interpretation of the rules. Rather, the official must make his decisions largely on the effect a violation of the rules has upon the play in a particular situation. An official who insisted on a literal construction would ruin the play. In these sports the official must make judgments and decisions within his discretion.

Many rules are stated in general terms to cover all possible situations. This procedure is followed deliberately in order to prevent exploitation. Because of this fact it is the duty of the rules legislative body to provide the official with a guide, which will assist him in administering the rules in the best interest of the game. The different rules bodies have provided play situations and interpretations to indicate the intent for implementing the rules. A sound philosophy to guide the official may be stated as follows: Those actions on the part of players, which would constitute an infraction of the rules if interpreted literally, but which do not adversely affect an opponent or the progress of the game, should be classed as incidental or technical infractions and should be ignored. The next chapter will deal with this point in greater detail. It is mentioned here as a guide for the official in a proper understanding of the rules.

In football, many rule violations in use of the arms in blocking have no effect whatever on the play. Consequently, the violations are ignored or the violator is quietly warned of his practice before he commits an offense that really places his opponent at a disadvantage. In basketball, essentially a noncontact game, there are no end of instances of contact. However, only that contact which materially affects the play is recognized.

On the other hand, baseball, track, tennis, and swimming require exactness in practically all decisions. In addition, a decision must be made on each play. The official, while largely stationary, must be constantly alert and poised, ready for every single play. In baseball, every ball thrown to the plate by the pitcher when in position, must be called a ball or a strike. Every hit ball is fair or foul. The baserunner is either safe or out. In tennis, the serve is in or out of the service court. The ball hit was in the court or was outside.

Guard your integrity

A decision must be made. Likewise, in track or swimming, one competitor finishes first, another second, and so on. A choice must be exercised. There is not the opportunity to make decisions about the action as a whole; each situation is separate and distinct and should be ruled literally.

It is an understanding of these differentiations that distinguishes between the competent official and the incompetent one. Knowledge of the rules is not complete without this understanding. Various play situations and background for interpretations of rules are presented in Parts Two and Three.

Duties of Officials and Mechanics of Officiating

Rules for different games vary in their instructions concerning the duties of officials. For the most part, only general directions are given for the administration of the rules. For example, the Basketball Guide, with the exception of describing the relation between the scorers and timers and referee, presents only two specific directions for the guidance of the officials in controlling the actions of the players during the game. In only one instance is there any mention of officials in the tennis rules. In contrast to this, the Track Guide has developed a detailed pattern for the officials in both the track and field events.

[. To implement the rules, manuals for officiating have been created by various groups under the auspices of authorized conferences and associations. These manuals present complete patterns of action for all the officials for all situations prior to, during, and at the conclusion of actual play. Some of them go so far as to designate which official should arrange transportation for the other officials.

2 It is the duty of every official to know exactly where he should be, what he should look for, and how to support and cooperate with his fellow officials on every play situation.[7] These are the mechanics of officiating. An official who is in the right place at the right time and looking in the correct direction will at least look efficient. He will be where he can make decisions when necessary.

The techniques contained in these manuals represent a develop-

Know the intent and purpose of a rule

ment that has evolved through years of experience in handling athletic activities. There is great uniformity throughout the country. A few differences in practice do appear, so that it is the job of the official to acquaint himself with the fashion in the locality where he operates and with the requirements of the organization which he represents. References will be made to these officiating manuals in the chapter where specific sports are discussed.

The essential features of the various habits in officiating will be presented in this text, and a background to justify the practice will be discussed. It is hoped that by such a logical and reasoned development the official will have a more intelligent understanding of his duties.

Appearance and Condition

No man has any right to pose as an official who is not willing to dress the part and to get into good physical condition. Almost every

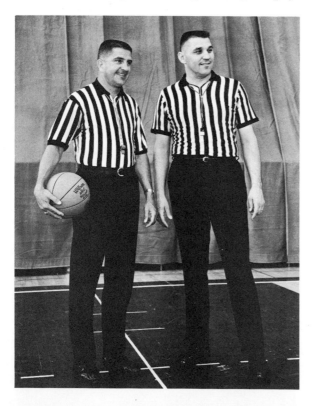

FIGURE 1. Tom Benich and Rudy Marich modeling the official basketball uniform. Marich is an international official.

FIGURE 2. Nick Reveille displays the official American League baseball umpire's uniform while Guy Reiff of the University of Michigan wears the field umpire's uniform.

sport has a distinct uniform for the official. Some sections of the country adhere to special fashions. Each official should secure the proper uniform and should be sure that it fits. He should at all times present a neat, clean appearance. Figures 1 and 2 show two sets of officials properly attired. The men in Figure 1 are dressed for basketball and those in Figure 2 for baseball. Their neat, tailored, athletic appearance is evident.

Some men who officiate wear glasses. The fact that an official wears glasses should not disqualify him. If he needs glasses for perfect sight under normal circumstances, he should wear them when he officiates.

Officiating requires the best physical condition. It will not be possible for a man to be alert and to perform successfully at a high level throughout a game unless he is in top condition. He should, therefore, start strenuous training before his first assignment. Leg strength and endurance (heart power) should receive his attention. Some practice officiating before the season opens is just as essential to the official as play practice is to the athlete. Even those

Be neat

sports, such as baseball, in which the official is comparatively stationary, demand an alertness and a concentration that necessitate top physical condition for the best performance.

Endurance is by far the more important quality for the official to develop in his conditioning program. For this reason a simple, practical, and physiologically sound routine is presented for the convenience of that official who may be pressed for time. To build endurance one must increase his circulation, extend his circulation to the minutest muscle fiber, and develop his heart power. This can be done quickly by activity performed intensely, at as rapid a rate as possible, for a short period of time and repeated every other day.

Three simple exercises, performed in the bedroom in the morning will suffice.

> 1. Run in place for ten seconds, lifting the feet just enough to clear the floor and attempting 80 steps per ten seconds. Rest ten seconds. Repeat ten times.
> 2. Do sit-ups for two minutes, hands clasped behind head, touching elbow to opposite knee each sit-up. Attempt 100 sit-ups in two minutes.
> 3. Do push-ups for 30 seconds as rapidly as possible. Attempt 25 push-ups in 30 seconds.
> Gradually work up to the ten innings spot running, two minutes of sit-ups, and 30 seconds of push-ups.

This program requires less than ten minutes, but it will help one to build and maintain a fit body that will sustain him through the requirements for officiating of sports contests.

It is surprising how neatness of dress and a conditioned athletic appearance will make a favorable impression on the spectators and players.

The foregoing emphases on qualifications are worth the most serious attention by officials. Since, to a certain extent, officiating is a profitable business, it is not too much to expect each official to come to a game fully qualified and prepared to meet the highest standards. Many officials earn as much as $2,500 during a season in one sport; scores of them will pick up $250 to $500. This money represents extra earnings, since most officials hold regular jobs. Officiating is their side line, an avocation.

Get fit—keep fit

chapter 3

A BASIC
PHILOSOPHY

Each official should have a clear conception of his over-all responsibility when he reports for duty. If all officials possessed the same conception, there would be uniformity in administration of all contests.

Some years ago, Mr. Oswald Tower expressed an opinion on the application of the basketball rules to the game by the official. No other individual is better qualified to speak on this subject. He was a member of the Basketball Rules Committee from 1910 to retirement in 1958. As editor and official interpreter of the Basketball Guide since 1914, he has watched the game develop and the rules evolve. He has been able to view the work of officials from a detached, objective vantage point, since he was neither coaching nor

It is not only what happens, but also what effect it has on the play

administering athletics. His opinions are entitled to serious consideration and evaluation by coaches and officials.

The essence of his utterance is: *It is the purpose of the rules to penalize a player who by reason of an illegal act has placed his opponent at a disadvantage.*

Here is the most realistic approach by which a common but intelligent application of the rules may be made. It puts a tool into the hands of the official for his use in implementing the rules during the game. Tower's statement was applied to basketball, but it represents the underlying principles which guide the judgment of officials in making decisions in all sports where the effect upon the play is the factor in determining whether or not a rule violation has occurred.

The following examples chosen from the football, soccer, and basketball rules are presented to substantiate the application of this philosophy. In football, at least seven players of the team in possession of the ball must be on the line of scrimmage when the ball is snapped. The same rule states that no player of either team may be ahead of his line of scrimmage when the ball is snapped. Yet, anyone who has ever acted as a head lineman knows that, on many occasions, one or more of the players of the team in possession of the ball may be behind the line of scrimmage, and the fact is ignored. Immature linemen seem to form a "V" with the ball as the apex, so that all the linemen except the center and guards are not legally on the line. Such a situation operates to the detriment of the team violating the rule and, therefore, seldom if ever, draws a penalty. Similarly, players may line up slightly off side with only a warning from the official. In such cases no real advantage is gained by using these innocent tactics, and, likewise, the opponents are not placed at any disadvantage.

The football rules state that each player of the team in possession of the ball, except the runner or passer, must have his hand or hands in contact with the body when contacting an opponent with said hand, hands, or arms. The purpose of the rule is, of course, to prevent a player from reaching out with the hands to interfere for a teammate with the ball. It is also to prevent striking with the hands or fists. Blocking is supposed to take place with the body, and only the arms under the limitations mentioned above are allowed.

If one were to apply the rule literally, a foul would have occurred

The rules are a guide for intelligent administration of the game

if a space could be detected between the player's body and his hand when he was blocking with that hand or arm. However, no capable official will administer the rule in this literal fashion. Instead, he judges the act in terms of the total situation and the effect any deviation from the exact rule may have on the play.

The basketball rules say in part: "A player shall not contact an opponent with his hand unless such contact is only with the opponent's hand while it is on the ball. . . ." If one were to administer this part of the rule literally, the game would be one of continual fouls. Even the most technical officials do not go to that extreme in their whistle blowing. The more outstanding officials realize that contact not only in this instance but in other phases as well must be viewed in the light of the effect it creates. If there is no apparent disadvantage to the opponent, then, in reality, no rule violation has occurred. The official must use discretion in applying the rule. The comments and play situations that accompany the rules verify this procedure.

The 3-second rule in basketball is another example of the application of the Tower philosophy. The purpose of the 3-second rule is to prevent a player from parking in the restricted area. When an official notices that a player is exploiting the intent of the rule, he will apply the rule.

In soccer, a player may be off side, but if in the opinion of the official such player is not interfering with the play (that is, the opponents are not placed at a disadvantage), a violation need not be called. The decision is within the discretion of the official.

The soccer rules also provide that when a player is tripped or charged from the rear, it may be intentional. The referee shall not penalize the offender but shall permit play to continue if the offended player recovers his balance and control and continues towards the goal for a shot.

These examples (and there are others) taken from the rules themselves, should furnish sufficient evidence to establish the logic of our basic philosophy. They should convince even the most skeptical that here is the only realistic solution to the hue and cry about too much whistle blowing.

In essence, this philosophy states:

It is not the intent that the rules shall be interpreted literally. Rather, they should be applied in relation to the effect which the action of

Weigh the effects of all acts

players has upon their opponents. If they are unfairly affected as a result of a violation of the rules, then the transgressor should be penalized. If there has been no appreciable effect upon the progress of the game, then the game should not be interrupted. The act should be ignored. It is incidental and not vital. Realistically and practically, no violation has occurred.

This whole philosophy presupposes that the official has a thorough understanding of the game. It further assumes that he has been employed to officiate the game because he has sport intelligence. He is expected to exercise mature judgment in evaluating each play situation in the light of this basic philosophy.

Some officials will be confused by an officiating procedure of this kind. They are the ones who are looking for a mechanical device that may be used for making decisions. They are the literal-minded individuals, the strict constructionists. They have no faith in their judgment. Consequently, they feel insecure when presented with this kind of responsibility. They are the inveterate whistle blowers, who are ruining our games. They want a rule for every little detail to replace judgment. They are the robots of sports who should be weeded out and replaced by human beings.

Officials and coaches can be too concerned over minor details about play situations. Much time is wasted in digging up technicalities that are of little or no significance. Unfortunately, officials' meetings, rules clinics, and interpretation sessions get sidetracked too often by heated discussions over many of these nonessentials. Some situations might happen once in a lifetime. If they did, and no ready solution was at hand, no great harm would be done. From the officials' standpoint, it would be better to have overlooked the situation than to have worried unnecessarily beforehand. More profit can be gained by concentrating on the basic, fundamental issues. These should not be lost sight of by letting the technicalities cloud the picture.

This basic philosophy is the starting point from which a set of general principles has been developed and guides to specific play situations have been established. These are intended to supplement the primary tool and to give the official some handy devices by which he may implement the basic philosophy. They should also

Are you realistic or hypertechnical?

help him to develop a pattern by which he can be consistent in all his judgments.

The general principles follow in Chapter 4, and the guides to specific play situations appear in Parts Two and Three, where the techniques of officiating the various sports are discussed.

chapter 4

GENERAL PRINCIPLES
OF OFFICIATING

A basic philosophy of officiating has been stated. Its validity has been established from evidence and precedents that have been taken from the official rules. This philosophy has been developed in the interest of greater uniformity and consistency in officiating. The need for the elimination of excessive whistle blowing and for a reduction in the number of game interruptions has been clearly demonstrated.

To accomplish these goals, the following basic principles are presented. These are *six* principles chosen because it was felt that they were primary. They are given emphasis because they are the ones most often neglected. Failure to employ them gives rise to

The goal—uniformity in interpretation

many of the wrong decisions made and to many of the unfair situations that develop during a game.

1. *Coaches are obligated to accept the official interpretations of the rules for their sport as issued by the national rules committees.* Coaches must attend the rules clinics conducted for this purpose, so they may keep apace with the interpretations and so they may receive the same directions as the officials. If this procedure is not followed and if there is not a common understanding and acceptance of the rules and the interpretations, the official has little chance to work satisfactorily for both teams. Whatever pattern he may follow in his work is likely to be in conflict with one of the teams.

Fortunately much progress has been made to secure uniformity. Representatives of the college and university conferences hold master clinics and then each conference follows up with a clinic for its coaches and officials. When competition begins, supervisors observe the play of teams and the work of the officials for the purpose of checking on the implementation of the rules and interpretations as presented at the earlier meetings.

The state high school athletic groups hold similar meetings for their coaches and officials. These meetings are supplemented with film and literature.

In some sports, the coaches have taken the leadership to create uniformity. The wrestling coaches have conducted training programs and demonstrations for officials for many years. Their procedure has been to discuss rules, to instruct officials in the techniques of officiating, and to conduct tryouts for qualifying officials. As a result, a mutual understanding exists between the officials and the coaches, and there is great harmony and confidence during the progress of their contests.

The soccer coaches have been carrying on similar programs, although not on quite so extensive a basis.

2. *The officials have the responsibility of administering the rules according to the official interpretations and of following the manual of officiating as adopted by the organization for which they are working.*

If the officials and coaches are given the same interpretations and both use them consistently, the greatest harmony and satisfaction will exist between these two groups.

A necessity—close collaboration between coaches and officials

In general, the rules do not provide a plan for officiating a contest. Therefore, each sport organization has worked out a manual of officiating procedures. The purpose is to provide a uniform plan for the officials to follow, and in those sports which require more than one official, to lay out a plan for the cooperative effort of the officials. There are some differences in these manuals. It is, therefore, incumbent upon the official to follow the plan adopted by the organization for which he is working.

The officials are employed by the organization they represent. Consequently, they have no alternative but to work in accordance with the desires of their employers.

This obligation on the part of the officials further emphasizes the necessity for a uniform, nationwide interpretation of the rules by the coaches. It also assumes that this interpretation shall conform to that of the official interpreter for the national rules committees of the various sports.

3. *The official must observe play from close quarters in order to make accurate judgments.*

In spite of the fact that the spectators at games do considerable second guessing, it is not possible to make correct judgments on most play situations without being within a few feet of the action. It is necessary to be close enough to determine the effect of maneuvers of all kinds. From a distance, the picture presented may have all the earmarks of foul play, while at close quarters little or no effect upon the play or on the movement or freedom of players has taken place.

In wrestling, for example, when a fall appears about to occur, the official must get his face close to the mat and sometimes use his hand to measure the situation in order to be able to rule correctly. It would be impossible for anyone from a distance to render a just decision. Holding in close line play in football requires that the umpire be within two or three yards of the total scene in order to give a fair ruling. Unless the umpire in baseball is right on top of the play when a runner slides into a base he cannot be sure whether the runner is safe or out.

The one exception to this rule is in judging the finish of a running event in track. The finish judges in a track event are able to judge more accurately from a distance than from close quarters.

Keep close to the play

From a distance they are able to encompass all runners in their visual fields and thus gain a better evaluation of the relative positions of each.

4. *The official must see the total scene in order to be able to make a just decision.*

Three situations will clearly illustrate this principle. A player, with his back to an official, is dribbling a basketball. An opponent comes up from the rear, thrusts at the ball, and either knocks it away from the dribbler or misses it. The view of the official who is directly behind the dribbler is partly obscured so that he cannot see the arm of the defensive player as he reaches in front of the dribbler for the ball. There is no apparent charging or contact from the side. Since the official in the rear is unable to determine whether or not an illegal act has occurred, he is unable to make any decision. If he rules on suspicion, he may be doing an injustice to the defensive player, who may have performed a clever legal maneuver.

Unless an overt act is committed and is seen in its entirety by the official, he should refrain from acting. In this case, he should defer a decision to his colleague who is in front of the play. It is better to do nothing when all the facts are not available.

Jockeying for position on the center pivot play in basketball usually causes contact. Quite often the end court official, who is primarily responsible for this play, does not see the preliminary movement before the contact occurs. He must, of necessity, divide his attention between the ball and the action of players around the basket. Therefore, when he is attracted to the center pivot situation, he finds two opponents in a pushing contest; one is exerting pressure to maintain his position and the other is attempting to move him so that an advantage may be gained.

Since the official did not see the initial action, how can he differentiate between the aggressor and defender of the position? Both are pushing hard. It is obvious that he cannot make a just decision. He can call a double foul, but if one of the players was wholly responsible for the original contact, then the other would be penalized unfairly. The official should see the action at its inception; otherwise, he should not make a decision. This particular type of play is not at all difficult to handle if the official will watch it develop. The players will quickly become aware of the fact that

Don't imagine or suspect—you must see it happen

an official is on the job in this instance, and they will eliminate the problem of their own accord. Here is an instance where the "potential of presence" eliminates illegal play.

The football rules specifically charge the officials with the responsibility of seeing the beginning, as well as the completed act, of clipping. If, when an official first sees the situation, a blocker is lying across the back of the legs of an opponent he shall not call a clipping penalty. The official must see the initial contact.

No criticism of officials is intended in this discussion. It is the duty of the official to see all and to know all. However, there are human limitations. Something may happen right in front of an official and entirely miss his attention because at that moment he was concentrating on another phase of play or he had his vision blocked by players.

Coaches, players, spectators, need to recognize this fact. An official should be commended for his refusal to render a decision when he does not see the total action. He should not be accused of partiality or lack of courage. It is remarkable that officials are able to see as much as they do. These particular situations can be kept at a minimum by techniques that will be discussed in Parts Two and Three.

5. Officials must rule on acts completed—not on anticipation.

It is a common fault among officials to anticipate play to the extent that they make decisions too hastily. In basketball, two players go for a loose ball. Two players rebound the ball and both get their hands on it. A player sees an opportunity to steal the ball from an opponent. The official sees the action. He senses the possibility of a held ball or concludes that a held ball is inevitable. Consequently, he blows his whistle for a jump ball before the conditions for a held ball have been met. He may act to prevent rough play. In either case, he is wrong. His move has been too hasty. As a result, he deprives a clever player of capitalizing on his skill. Here is a situation where it is better to hesitate than to be too quick. Be sure the conditions that justify calling for a held ball are complied with, before making a decision. This is not the time to imagine what might occur and to act on supposition.

Again, a player, moving rapidly, receives the ball, stops, and then lifts his pivot foot. He may do this at the end of the dribble. The official is watching the play intently. The moment the pivot foot is raised from the floor he anticipates a violation of the running

Don't act, if you don't see

rule. As a result, he blows his whistle before the violation occurs. The player shoots or passes and very often a score results. He is penalized for a legal play.

Or, the football referee blows his whistle before the forward progress of the ball is stopped. The ball carrier breaks away for a touchdown. Because of hasty action, a team is deprived of a score. There is no such thing as a correct quick whistle. The play has or has not been completed. No whistle should be blown until the play is completed.

In tennis a lineman judges that a ball will be out and calls the play before the ball hits the surface. Even though his judgment was subsequently correct, he should not announce his decision until the play is completed.

Of course, officials should be alert. They should be anticipatory to the extent that they instantly size up possible situations. They should be poised in readiness to act instantly, but they should make no decision until a violation or a foul has become an accomplished fact.

6. *Except in situations where specific jurisdiction is given by the rules or the manual of officiating to one official, all officials should make decisions on any play which they see anywhere.*

There should be no division of authority. It is true that by reason of many of the mechanics developed for the efficient administration of games, one official will tend to focus his attention on specific phases of play or on definite areas under certain play situations. Because of this fact, one of the officials would be more likely to see the movements of players more closely in a certain area.

These are the areas of special concentration; however, an official should not be oblivious to what the other players are doing. Although particular assignments are laid out for the cooperation of the officials and for the coordination of their work, they should so far as is humanly possible keep the total field of play within their vision. They should make decisions on any situation that comes to their attention and that requires their official action. In many of the rule books, under the section on the duties of officials, statements authorize all the officials to make decisions on all plays that come to their attention. The basketball and football rules are typical examples. The baseball and tennis rules, however, set limitations on this practice. Thus, each official must be conversant with his prerogatives in each sport and conduct himself accordingly.

Don't blow on anticipation

PART TWO

The fundamental principles of officiating which have been presented and developed in Part Two are applied in Part Three to those sports that require a decision on every action that takes place. Baseball, softball, track, swimming, tennis, volleyball, badminton, and handball are included in this section and in this order.

chapter 5

BASEBALL

Every fan thinks that he is an authority on the baseball rules and on the art of baseball officiating. Yet there is probably more misinformation at large about baseball than any other sport. Consequently, more opportunities for argument arise about play situations in baseball.

These arguments no doubt arise because baseball is our national pastime and is a common subject for conversation summer and winter, and because most of the decisions that must be made are surprisingly simple. Balls and strikes, fair and foul balls, safe or out decisions, are for the most part obvious and childlike in their simplicity. Because these are so simple, the erroneous analogy is

Baseball requires a decision on every play

made with respect to all situations, many of which become quite involved.

L_ The rules of baseball are precise and carefully codified. There are, however, many conditional factors upon which correct decisions depend. A sufficient number of problems of this type arise during a game, so that only a very astute individual can qualify as a capable umpire.

The fact that an umpire must make repeat decisions inning after inning requires a consistency of judgment unequaled in the other sports. Few games are played where less than 100 decisions on balls and strikes are made. There are 51 to 54 out decisions in each nine-inning game and at least as many more decisions in which the player may be declared safe. Many fair- and foul-ball decisions are required. Any one of these called incorrectly may be the deciding factor in a ball game. Any evidence of vacillating judgment produces an erratic ball game.

The above points are emphasized in order to demonstrate the necessity for the highest qualities of good officiating in baseball. The umpire must be constantly alert lest he slip up on one tiny bit of his duty. Although his job appears to be a passive one, he is under tremendous pressure every moment the contest is under way. He must make a decision on every single play.

The further fact that the very nature of baseball seems to invite and sanction protest, argument, and disagreement on the part of players, coaches, managers, and captains, does not make the task of the umpire any easier. He is challenged continually. Unless he has great endurance, fortitude, and mental and emotional poise, he is likely to falter.

The comments that follow are applied to games administered by one or two officials. Our amateur games seldom have more than two officials.

Pregame Preparation

The uniform for the baseball official is the only one that has remained comparatively unchanged through the years. His dark-blue outfit with the ample pockets for balls is historic. He is very much in the limelight because he is looked to for every decision.

Consistency is the life blood of the umpire

Consequently, he should be sure to keep his clothes well pressed and his shoes shined. He needs a special protector, a mask, shin guards, and special capped shoes. This is equipment for the umpire-in-chief. Figure 2 shows the umpires in proper dress and with full regalia.

He should without question have an indicator for recording balls and strikes. It is rather easy to lose count of balls and strikes. An intervening play or game interruptions, which require the attention of the umpire, may cause him to forget the ball and strike count. The indicator, therefore, is his only safe protection from embarrassment.

Pregame Duties

1. When two umpires are involved, they should review their plans for cooperation during the game. For example, they must team together on balk movements, on covering bases when more than one runner is on base, and on some fair- or foul-ball situations. One may assist the other upon request in clearing up questionable plays such as whether a ball was trapped or caught on the fly, whether a runner missed a base, whether or not a player dropped a ball in catching it or throwing it.

Some of these problems are specifically covered by the rules, but all should be discussed for the purpose of review and also for the distinct purpose of establishing a harmonious and understanding relationship between the umpires. Each should remember that there is no overruling of judgment of one official by the other, but that either may ask for the opinion of the other on a decision he has made. Certain duties are the sole responsibility of the umpire-in-chief.

2. Probably the most important pregame duty of the umpires is to get a clear understanding before the game starts concerning ground rules. They should also discuss these with both coaches and captains so that there is a mutual understanding. Failure to follow this pattern is likely to invite trouble during the game. After the game starts, the full responsibility rests with the umpires. The ground rules may be perfectly clear to the home team, which makes them, but the visitors and the umpires must have the same interpretation.

Planned pre-game co-operation assures efficient support

3. Before the game, the umpires should survey the field and appurtenances. By doing this, they assure themselves concerning all matters that violate the rules and need special ground rules to cover them.

4. The umpire should get a supply of balls from the home team. As a general rule, the supply of balls for amateur games will not be so generous as in professional games. Often, only two new balls are available. Seldom will there be more than a dozen. As a consequence, the umpire must use greater discretion before throwing balls out of the game than would be the case in a professional game.

5. The umpire-in-chief should secure the starting line-ups from each captain before the game begins. Following receipt of the line-ups and after ground rules discussions, the batteries should be announced. It is customary and courteous to announce the visitors first. The pitcher is announced first and then the catcher.

6. Begin games exactly on the scheduled time.

Position and Duties
on Balls and Strikes

When there are two or more umpires, the umpire-in-chief is always behind the plate, where he calls all balls and strikes. His position is slightly to the side of the catcher, so that he may look over the catcher's shoulder. Most catchers crouch, so that the umpire can maintain a semicrouched position from which he can get a full view of the ball, the plate, and the batter.

If the batter is right-handed, the umpire will usually be able to see better by looking over the left shoulder of the catcher. If the batter is a left-handed batter, the umpire should look over the right shoulder of the catcher. There is no hard and fast rule for this procedure, but experience has demonstrated that better results accrue from these practices. Figure 3 shows the umpire in position to call balls and strikes on a right-handed batter.

Low balls are the most difficult to judge. The umpire should, therefore, get as low as possible on low balls in order to better judge their position with respect to the batter's knees. Inside balls are next in difficulty. The fact that the umpire's position is toward the inside of the plate places him in a strategic position for judging

Neglect ground rules and invite trouble

FIGURE 3. Umpire-in-chief in proper position to call balls and strikes on a right-handed batter. Note that his position is slightly to the left of the catcher so that he can look over the catcher's left shoulder.

inside balls. Batters are more cautious about inside balls. They may dodge a ball that cuts the inside edge or corner of the plate. Because of this fact, the umpire must be particularly alert to judge inside balls correctly. Looking over the inside shoulder of the catcher gives him a direct line from the pitcher to the plate.

Curve balls can be very deceiving. A pitch is a strike if it goes over the plate at the right height. The position of the ball when it hits the catcher's glove is of no consequence whatever.

This latter leads to the admonition that the umpire should announce his judgment on balls and strikes without hesitation. It is never reliable to attempt to retrace the imaginary path of the ball. Neither should the umpire be persuaded by jerking actions or other attempts by the catcher to influence his judgment. It is not bad practice to assume that the pitch was a ball if the catcher by his action has attempted to alter the actual direction of the pitch by his attempts to deceive.

The field umpire should take his position about 20 feet behind first base and on, or just outside, the right-field foul line. Many umpires stand at the back edge of the skinned area.

Diagram 1 (see page 45) shows the position of the two umpires at the start of the game and at any time when the bases are unoccupied.

Remember the low ball bogey

If the game is being officiated by one umpire, he should take his position behind the plate whenever possible. Decisions on balls and strikes are by far the most difficult to make. To be able to make accurate and consistent judgments, it is necessary to be as close as possible to the plate.

The umpire should, therefore, be stationed behind the plate:

1. When no runners are on bases.
2. When the bases are full.
3. When third base only is occupied.
4. When second and third bases are occupied.

On all other occasions it will be necessary for the umpire to take a position behind the pitcher. These occasions would include:

1. Runner on first base.
2. Runners on first and third bases.
3. Runner on second base.
4. Runners on first and second bases.

Under these conditions, the umpire must not only call balls and strikes, but he must be able to make decisions on plays that may occur at first, second, or third base. For this reason, he places himself in a middle position. Certainly, he could not make accurate decisions on pick-off plays at second base or at first base from his position behind the plate.

His position behind the pitcher should be just off the mound. If the pitcher is right-handed, the umpire will have a more uninterrupted view of the flight of the ball if he stands behind the right arm of the pitcher. If the pitcher is left-handed, he should get to the left side.

The foregoing procedure for a single umpire is recommended so that he will be close to the plate as often as is feasible. Here is where the majority and the most difficult of his decisions must be made. In most ball games he will be able to work from behind the plate from two-thirds to three-quarters of the time.

There is, however, a school of thought which feels that when there is only one umpire for a game, he should make all decisions from behind the pitcher. The reasoning for this is that there will be more consistency throughout the game because all decisions are made from the same spot. Further, that any mistakes on close

Work behind the plate as much as possible in a one-umpire game

(a)

(b)

(c)

(d)

(e)

(f)

(g)

FIGURE 4.   Signals commonly used by umpires to convey decisions.

pitches where depth perception is involved would be equal for each team. Thus, the team that was unable to get men on bases would receive the same treatment as the team which, because of base running situations, was forcing the umpire to rule from behind the pitcher.

One must recognize a certain validity in this line of reasoning. Since there is no rule or objective evidence that dictates that either technique be followed, the practice one should adopt becomes a matter of personal preference. The author has tried both procedures on many occasions and feels he can do a much more efficient and accurate job by the method he recommends.

The umpire should keep the edges of the plate clear at all times. When it is necessary for him to work from behind the pitcher, he should be doubly sure that the edges of the plate stand out sharply.

To declare a strike, the umpire swings his right arm in a chopping movement. At the same time he announces, "Strike!" Some dramatics are desirable for the purpose of making the decision crystal clear. Figure 4(a) shows the action of the umpire in announcing a strike. No motion at all denotes a ball. The umpire should, however, call, "Ball!"

Position and Duties
On Fair and Foul Balls

Any time the ball is hit, the umpire-in-chief should move so that he may sight along the foul line in the direction of the ball. In this way, he is able to judge more accurately those hits which fall beyond the base or roll along the foul line before reaching the base.

If the base umpire is on the foul line behind first base, he may assist the umpire-in-chief with difficult decisions on balls that are hit sharply along the right-field foul line. The arm raised horizontally and pointing toward foul territory indicates a foul ball. Pointing toward fair territory or no signal at all indicates a fair ball.

Figure 4(d) shows the umpire-in-chief in a position to rule on balls hit along the right-field foul line. He is indicating a foul ball. For balls hit along the left-field foul line, he should stand so that he can sight along the left-field foul line.

The umpire has six possible situations upon which he may be required to rule in connection with batted balls:

Sight the foul—avoid the howl

1. Balls that settle or are touched by a fielder before reaching first or third base.

2. Balls that when bounding to the outfield may or may not go over first or third base. (The field umpire may assist on this situation.)

3. Balls that hit first or third base.

4. Fly balls that first hit the ground beyond first or third base.

5. Fly balls that are touched by a fielder.

6. Fly balls that are knocked out of the park.

In all cases of balls being touched, the position of the ball at the time it is touched and not the position of the fielder who touches it determines whether it is fair or foul.

Position and Duties of
Field Umpire in Covering Bases

With no one on base, the field umpire is behind first base and on the foul line. When the batsman hits the ball, the field umpire

DIAGRAM 1.   Position of umpires at start of inning or with no one on base.

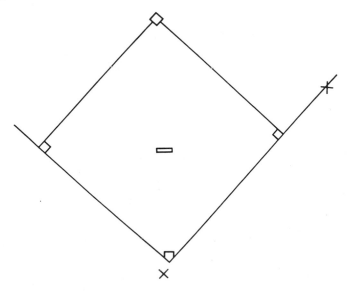

Position of touched ball determines fair or foul

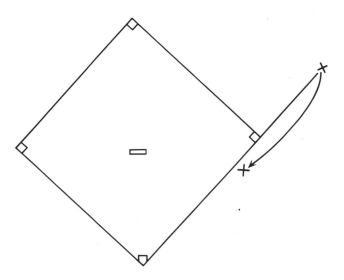

DIAGRAM 2.   Field umpire in position to make a decision on play at first base.

moves to a position where he can see the ball (after it is fielded and thrown) hit the first baseman's glove, see the first baseman's feet with respect to the base, and at the same time have a clear view of the runner and the base.

The field umpire's preferred position for balls hit to the left of the plate and for all balls fielded inside the base lines is in fair territory behind the base line. For balls hit to the right side of the plate and beyond the base line the umpire will usually move into foul territory behind first base. See Diagram 2. These positions will permit him to see whether or not the ball is caught before the runner touches the base, and, at the same time, whether or not the baseman is touching the base after or at the time he catches the ball. If the runner and the ball reach the base at the same time, the runner is, of course, safe. In no case should the umpire be in line with the flight of the ball.

If, in the opinion of the umpire, the runner is out, he should throw his hand above his head with the thumb pointed up. At the same time he should declare the runner out. If the runner is safe, the umpire indicates his decision from a crouched position with arms outstretched in front of him. The palms of the hands face

For play at first—"see the ball, the base, the baseman, the runner"

downward. In making a base decision, the umpire should not turn away from the play until the action is completely finished. The baseman may drop or juggle the ball. The runner may at first be safe and then an instant later be tagged out. If the umpire turns away too quickly, he could miss this kind of action. Figure 4(b) shows the umpire demonstrating the signal to declare a runner out, and Figure 4(c) shows the motion to indicate the runner is safe.

With a runner on first base, the field umpire should take a position behind and to the side of the pitcher and about midway between the pitcher's mound and second base. He should be sure that he does not obstruct the view of any fielder/From this middle position, he is able to cover plays just as accurately at any base. He is also in an advantageous position to judge balk movements.

Diagram 3 shows the position of the field umpire with a runner on first base. If second base, first and second bases, or third base is occupied, the umpire usually stands on the opposite side of the line connecting the pitcher's mound and second base. The umpire must be alert for throws to catch a runner off base. When the ball

DIAGRAM 3. Field umpire behind pitcher with runner on first base. Dotted X shows position when runner is on second base.

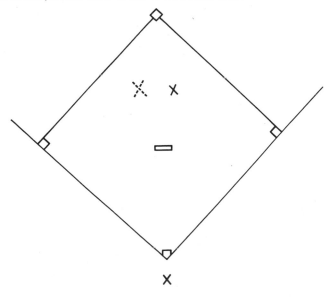

Turn away and rue the play

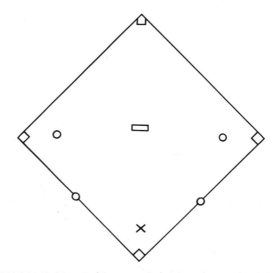

DIAGRAM 3A. Field umpire behind pitcher and infield when bases are filled and infield is drawn in.

DIAGRAM 4. Position of umpire-in-chief on a fly to right field with a runner on third.

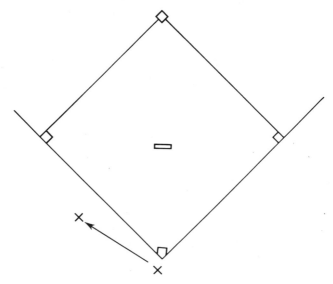

Was the fielder catching or throwing when the fumble occurred?

is hit to the infield, he must follow the movements of the fielder who catches the ball in order to be ready to make the decision at whichever base the ball may be thrown. The umpire should not decide on his own judgment that the play will be at a certain base and then turn his attention to that base. The fielder might decide to throw to another base, with resulting embarrassment to the umpire.

When there is a play at first or second base and at the same time or subsequently a play at third base on another runner, the field umpire should cover the play at first or second base. The umpire-in-chief must assist the field umpire by covering the play at third base. To be ready for such an eventuality, the umpire-in-chief should move along the foul line toward third base. (See Diagram 4.) The umpire-in-chief will also make all decisions on runners at home base. He should remove his mask in readiness for these decisions.

The umpire-in-chief is king at home plate

chapter 6

GUIDES TO
SPECIAL PLAY SITUATIONS:
BASEBALL

Several situations arise during practically every baseball game that create difficult decisions for umpires. These are discussed here for emphasis, with the hope that fewer mistakes will be made in the future in these particular situations. Most of them seem to center around the plate.

Batted Balls Hitting Plate

Pitched balls hit on top and driven almost directly to the ground create difficult problems for the umpire. The ball may hit the plate,

Balls hit directly down may be fair

50

or the ground behind the plate, or in the batter's box, and then roll and settle on fair territory.

If the ball has not hit the person of the batter while he is in the batter's box and has not been touched by the catcher while it is on or over foul territory, it is a fair ball. If the ball has hit the batter while he is in the box (this is the most common occurrence), or, the catcher while it is on or over foul territory, it is a foul ball. The umpire cannot always be certain whether or not the ball has hit the batter. As a consequence, many umpires have adopted the habit of calling every play situation of this kind a foul ball. This is not at all fair to the defensive team.

The umpire should be on the alert for these plays. When it is clear that the ball has rolled fair without touching the batter and without being touched, it should be declared a fair ball. Of course, if there is doubt, it seems fairer to declare a foul ball.

Hitting Batsman

Balls that without any apparent deflection barely graze the uniform of a batter may escape the attention of the umpire. He cannot rule that a batsman is hit unless he witnesses the fact. On the other hand, he must be very alert so that he does not penalize a batter when the ball actually hits him, however slightly.

The umpire must remember, however, that a batter may feign being hit on a close pitch. Dramatics should play no part in the decision. As a matter of fact, the decision should be made so quickly that there is no time for an act by the batter. Likewise, the umpire must remember that the batter is required to attempt to avoid being hit. He should not be awarded a base for deliberately getting hit or refusing to dodge a pitched ball.

Stepping Out of the Batter's Box

Batters attempt to crowd the front of the batter's box for the purpose of hitting curve balls before they break or for meeting slow balls. They take a stand to the rear of the box to gain a little

Batters must avoid a pitched ball

more time for swinging at fast balls. They leave the box to bunt a pitchout on a squeeze play. In following this strategy, it is not at all uncommon for them to have one foot out of the box.

By rule, the batter is out for leaving his box when batting a pitched ball. Umpires have a tendency to be lax in administering this rule. The usual reason for this is that the markings for the box become obliterated after a few innings. They should not, however, permit a batter to gain an unfair advantage by violating a rule.

Interference by the Batter or the Catcher

If the catcher interferes with the bat or the batter and thus prevents him from swinging at a pitched ball, the batter is awarded first base. This violation occurs when the catcher takes a position in his box too close to the batter. In such a position, the catcher's glove touches the bat as he goes after the ball. There is also interference when the catcher leaves his box to catch a pitched ball in an effort to tag a runner on a steal of home or a squeeze play.

The umpire must be quick to catch these happenings. In the case of steals or squeeze plays, he can anticipate the possibility of interference and thus be ready for it. In the case of the catcher touching the bat or the batter, there is usually no warning unless it is noticed that the catcher habitually crowds the plate. The umpire must discriminate between a deliberate attempt by the batter to reach back with his bat and thus interfere with the catcher and bona fide interference by the catcher himself.

Although the batter is entitled to stand in his box on plays at the plate, he may not move to block the attempt of the catcher to make a play on a runner. Certainly he cannot leave his box to block the catcher. Neither may the batter move his bat or body and by so doing interfere with the catcher who is throwing to a base. The batter may, of course, take a legitimate swing at a pitched ball.

Striking at the Ball

What constitutes an actual swing at the ball? According to the rule, the swing is not complete unless it is carried through to the

The catcher or the batter may cause interference

point of the snap of the wrists, which constitutes the last of the sequence of movements in swinging at the ball. This means that a swing may be started and may go through to the final action, but if the batter can check his movement at that point, he has not struck at the ball.

The umpire should rule on the pitch in accordance with whether or not the ball went over the plate at the right height. If the pitch was not a strike, then he should declare a ball. The umpire must continually anticipate this situation so that he does not penalize a quick reacting player who is able to make split-second judgments and regulate his swing accordingly.

Tagging Situations

Four suggestions can be made that will aid umpires materially in rendering decisions on close plays at the bases when runners slide in attempts to avoid being put out.

1. The umpire should observe what part of the runner is touched with the ball. The proper technique by the baseman for tagging is to hold the ball at the level of the base, between the base and runner. If this is done and the runner comes in contact with the ball with that part of his body (foot, leg, or hand) which is farthest advanced toward the base, the decision of the umpire is simple. The runner is out. If, on the other hand, as the runner comes into the base, the fielder reaches toward him and touches him farther back on his leg or body than the advanced portion that has made contact with the base, the probabilities are that the runner is safe. If there is any question in the umpire's mind, he should call the runner safe, because of the faulty technique in attempting to make the put-out.

2. The umpire should be within a few feet of the play. It is not possible to make accurate judgments on close plays from a distance. Tricky movements of runners may prevent the fielder from touching them with the ball. This cannot be detected unless the umpire is right on top of the play. The impact of the runner may cause the fielder to juggle or fumble the ball. Unless the umpire is right at the base with an unobstructed view of the ball throughout the play, the fielder may cleverly recover the ball and cover up his error.

Where did the baseman hold the ball to tag the slide?

3. The umpire should fix his gaze upon the play until the action is completed. The action is completed when the ball has been thrown or the fielder has come away from the play with the ball securely in his possession. This procedure will avoid missing fumbles or cases of oversliding or missing the base. Some umpires have developed the bad habit of immediately turning their backs on, and hastily walking away from a play once they have rendered a decision. Such action invites trouble if one or the other of the above situations occurs subsequently. Figure 4(c) shows the umpire in the proper position to render a decision at a base.

4. At the instant action occurs at a base, umpires should indicate out or safe by their signals. If subsequent actions such as fumbles or missing or oversliding require a new or changed decision, one may follow. It is justified in view of new developments. It in no way reflects upon the first decision of the umpire. He should not hesitate to change his decision under changed circumstances.

Fumbling Ball Before or After a Catch

Questions frequently arise concerning the time when a fumble occurs. The umpire must have a clear view of the action in order to determine whether a fumble occurs as a part of catching the ball or whether the fumble was incidental to taking the ball from the glove preparatory to throwing it.

If the player is seen to hold the ball securely, that play—whatever it may have been—is completed. Any subsequent happenings are related to the next play. They will in no way require a change of decision on the previous play.

Several examples may be cited to illustrate this situation. A fielder catches a fly ball. As he attempts to retrieve the ball from his glove or starts to throw it, he juggles the ball or drops it. The fly was actually caught and that play completed. The fumble occurred as part of the act of throwing the ball, not of catching it.

The first baseman catches the ball to retire a runner. He starts to step from the base to throw to third to catch a runner advancing from second base. In his effort to get the ball into his throwing hand, he drops it.

If the ball is caught, the play is completed

The second baseman receives a throw from the shortstop to force a runner coming to second base. In his haste to complete a double play he drops the ball as he starts his throw to first base.

The catcher catches a foul tip and strides to throw out a runner stealing second. He drops the ball in his attempt to transfer it to his throwing hand. Catchers have been known deliberately to drop the ball when they see that it is impossible to catch the runner at second base.

In all these situations, the fumble was part of the next play and in no way affected the completed one. The team affected adversely will often argue that the ball was never caught. The umpire must, therefore, be sure that he sees these actions in their proper sequence. If he has any doubt concerning the accuracy of his judgment, he may ask for an opinion from his colleagues. These are vitally important decisions to make. But, if the umpire has followed the movements of the fielder throughout, he should have no difficulty differentiating between the completion of one play and the start of the next.

Leaving the Base After a Caught Fly Ball

This situation introduces the need for the exercise of split vision. The umpire must see the ball as it touches the glove of the fielder. At the same time, he must see the start of the base runner from the base. Here is a case where distance from both the fielder and the runner is an advantage. When possible, the umpire should be slightly off the imaginary line that connects the ball with the base. Of course, this is not always possible. But the umpire usually has time to move so that he can approach this position.

For an extreme example, a runner is on third base. A fly ball is hit to right field. The umpire at the plate should move toward third base but as far away from the line as possible. If he can get halfway to third, he will be better able to encompass the ball and the base in his visual field. After the catch he will have plenty of time to return to home plate to cover the play there. Diagram 4 shows this situation.

The umpire must develop a visual sense of timing. He first sees

Sense the rhythm of the play when runner advances on a caught fly

the ball hitting the fielder's glove and then the dash of the runner from the base. So long as this rhythm is not reversed, he may be sure the play is legal.

Touching All Bases

On every hit ball when there is the possibility of base runners advancing more than one base, the umpires must observe whether or not the runners touch all bases. An umpire must condition his routine actions so that he is conscious of this responsibility.

When more than one runner is on base, this job is not a simple one if a long hit is made. The duties of the umpires are divided, however, so total coverage may be handled with facility. The umpire at the plate will watch the runners at third base and home while the field umpire observes first and second bases.

This is an action (leaving the base after a caught fly is another) which the umpires must notice, but on which they do not rule unless a ruling is requested by the team in the field.

Signals

The baseball signals the umpire employs to convey his decision to spectators and players are the fewest in number but the most revealing in all our sports. The seven signals shown on page 43 constitute his complete stock in trade. They are illustrated by actual photographs to portray their use.

Each umpire may develop some mannerisms that constitute a slight variation from the signals represented here. The illustrations, however, show the fundamental pantomimes. Every umpire should learn these and employ them whenever he is required to render a decision. His tool kit for use in carrying out his job is not complete without signals.

Balks

The umpires must always be conscious of the possibility of balk motions by the pitcher when there is a runner on a base. Either

Know when to see all but say nothing

umpire may call a balk so both must observe the movements and position of the pitcher very carefully. Illegal action by the pitcher can deceive the runner, place him at a disadvantage not intended by rule, even cause him to be put out.

The umpires must know all the balk rules and see that they are enforced so the pitcher is not given an unfair advantage. If necessary, the umpires may consult each other on balk observations and rulings.

Know the balk rules—don't be fooled

chapter 7

SOFTBALL

Most of the techniques described for the baseball official apply with equal force to the softball official. The softball rule that does not permit a runner to leave his base until the ball leaves the pitcher's hand precludes the possibility of one umpire successfully handling a softball game.

Also, because of this rule, the field umpire must always face so he can see both the pitcher and the base runner. When more than one runner is on base and there is only one field umpire, he must, of necessity, take a position back of the infield rather than between the infield and the pitcher (see Diagram 5).

Two umpires are necessary

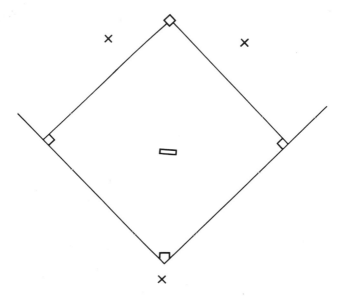

DIAGRAM 5.   Positions of base umpire with a runner on base in a softball game. He must be able to see both the runner and the pitcher.

Because of the rule which restricts the arm movements and the manner of delivery of the ball by the pitcher, the umpires must check the action of the pitcher carefully in order to prevent illegal pitching action.

No other alterations of the techniques of the baseball umpires will be necessary. The reader, therefore, is referred to the section on baseball officiating.

chapter 8

TRACK

Track officiating, unlike all other sports officiating, is diversified and nonprofessional. For the most part, laymen are called upon to assume the responsibilities of officials. Except for the starter and referee (the two jobs are often combined), the track officials do not receive compensation for their services. This situation seems quite incongruous when one realizes that winners are determined and records set by the difference of a tenth of a second or an eighth of an inch.

Inasmuch as 25 to 50 officials are required to conduct a track meet in an efficient manner, one can understand why the officials for a track meet cannot be organized on the same highly profes-

Track officials have been volunteers throughout the years

sional and technical basis that has been attained in the officials' organizations for football, basketball, baseball, hockey, soccer, and wrestling.

Fortunately, through the years a certain prestige has become attached to track officiating. As a result, many prominent and capable persons have maintained an active interest in track. They volunteer their services readily for officiating.

Unfortunately, a few of these continue to express their desire beyond the stage of their dependability as officials. Problems are thereby created. Out of gratitude for past services it would be discourteous to eliminate these people. On the other hand, their unreliability due to the inevitable slowing up processes induced by age makes them useless as officials.

The best that can be done is to add extra officials whose judgments will be accepted and use the others in honorary capacities in recognition of valued services rendered in the past.

Because of the nature of the personnel for track officiating, those responsible for organizing and conducting the meets must allow for the shortcomings and the lack of training and preparation of lay officials. Written instruction should be given to each. These instructions should cover the technique and procedure to be followed in carrying out his duties. The instructions must of necessity be short. They must, nevertheless, be adequate. It has been found that sufficient information for each official can be typewritten on a 3 x 5 card. W. H. McCurdy [1] has worked out instructions along this line for some field events.

The discussions, explanations, and directions that follow have been worked out to include the implementation of this procedure. Since the rules of the National Collegiate Athletic Association [2] are most universally adopted, these are used as the basis for this presentation. It is recognized that some other associations and conferences have their own rules. However, the departure from the NCAA, which is the parent body to most of the others, is not significant enough to justify the space to discuss the differences.

---

[1] W. H. McCurdy, *Unpublished Thesis* (Springfield, Mass.: Springfield College, 1949).

[2] *Official Track and Field Guide* (New York: National Collegiate Athletic Bureau, 1967).

Provide short, concise written instructions

The Officials

The officials for a track meet include:

1. referee
2. starter (assistant starter)
3. clerk of course (assistant clerk of course)
4. scorer
5. announcer (assistant announcers)
6. five timers (one is head timer—one is a substitute)
7. judges of finish (twice as many judges as places to score) and a chief judge of finish
8. head field judge
9. field judges (three for each event—there can be some doubling up)
10. four track inspectors
11. one inspector of implements
12. surveyor (usually the track is measured and certified before the meet)

The foregoing includes a comprehensive list needed to conduct a large meet. Dual meets can be handled with fewer officials. For example, the starter usually acts as referee and head field judge. No assistants are needed for the starter, announcer, or clerk of course. The field judges can double up in some of the field events. Two sets of judges can handle the weight events and two sets can handle the jumping events.

In many meets, officials are requested to conform to a standard dress. There is no official uniform for track, but white trousers and blue coat are customarily worn. In some indoor meets, the officials appear in full formal dress. On some occasions, dark blue trousers and white shirts are worn. Uniform dress presents an attractive appearance on the field and makes identifying the officials easy.

Duties and Instructions to Officials

More space is devoted by track rules to the specific duties of officials than by the rules of other sports. Itemizing the pertinent job for each official is thus a comparatively simple task.

25-50 officials are needed for a meet

THE REFEREE

The referee has general overall supervision of the meet. He is the final authority when any disputes arise. If the rules do not specifically cover the point at issue, it is his responsibility to decide the matter. He reviews the general organization of the meet to make sure that all competitors receive equal opportunities. He checks the plans for each event to see that they are run in accordance with the rules of the meet.

Although the rules designate that the referee shall name the head judges, this has usually been done in advance by the management in charge of the meet as a part of the preliminary preparation.

The referee should be provided with a copy of the rules under which the meet is run. He is expected to be familiar with the rules that govern each event. The referee may not have a single decision to make. He should, however, keep in close touch with the progress of each event and be available for consultation at all times. As previously stated, in many meets the starter, who is the only paid official, is often named as referee. The duties that are commonly his, and which arise most often during the course of a meet, are the following:

> 1. To decide on disqualification for reported violations of track rules such as leaving one's lane, cutting in too soon so as to cause interference, crowding, exchanging baton outside of restraining lines, bad sportsmanship, illegal hurdling.
> 2. To act on the validity of a record after checking watches, wind velocity, heights, distances, verification of legality of implements, surveyor's affidavit, etc.
> 3. To determine questions of procedure when protests or disputes arise.

THE STARTER

The starter is considered the most important track official. His success in getting races started fairly, in not exciting the runners, and in gaining their confidence is a mark of his ability as a starter. He must be consistent. To hold runners unduly long one time, to start fast the next, and so on, upsets the emotional control of the

The referee is the final authority

FIGURE 5. Starter with gun up, ready to start race. Note the recall pistol in his left hand and arm band which is a visual aid to the timers. Some starters wear a brightly colored sleeve or jacket.

runners and ruins the races. Research [3] has shown that the best results are obtained when runners are held approximately two seconds after the command, "Get set!" Of course, all runners must be stationary before the race is permitted to start. If this steadiness is not obtained without undue delay after the order to "Get set," the starter should call all runners off their marks and make a new

---

[3] George Breshnahan and W. W. Tuttle, *Track and Field Athletics* (St. Louis: C. V. Mosby Co. 1956), p. 456.

The starter—the headlineman of the meet

start. If a competitor makes a false start, he should be warned. If he makes a second false start, he should be disqualified. (These are the NCAA rules). A quiet, unhurried but firm voice will do much to calm the jumpy athlete and get all runners away to an even start.

The starter should wear some kind of an identification so he can be located easily by the timers. A brightly colored hat or coat is a typical identification. Recently, a green arm band or sleeve has been recommended so the starter's gun can be seen readily when the gun is up. Figure 5 shows the starter in position to start a race. The gun is up. He is wearing an arm band on his upraised arm. He should stand in front, and to the side, of the runners so they can see him. In a race where all start at once, he should stand at the outside edge of the track. In staggered races, he will find that he can best see all runners if he stands in advance of all runners but on the inside lane. He is sufficiently far away from the runner on the pole so he will have plenty of time to get off the track after firing his gun.

The rules do not specify position for the starter. The foregoing has been found to give the starter the best view from which to judge the steadiness of the contestants. Some starters prefer to be behind and to the side of the contestants so they can sight across their hips. Wherever the starter stands he must be able to see each contestant and he must be clearly seen by the timers. Where the background does not permit the starter to be seen clearly a dark screen may be used.

He should have two guns, one of which is a recall gun. His starting gun should be one that can be cocked for instant firing. A .32-caliber gun is best. A .22-caliber gun does not give off sufficient smoke. If an assistant starter is used, he acts as the recall starter and handles the second gun.

The starter takes charge of a race as soon as the clerk of course has placed the runners for the race and has given them their necessary instructions. Before calling the runners to their marks, he shall determine by means of a whistle, or other signal, the readiness of the timers and judges. The head timer should return the signal when judges and timers are ready. Immediately after all are ready, the starter should get the race under way. He is responsible for starting events promptly.

A steady start is an acquired art

No written instructions are necessary for the starter since he is probably the one professional official in the meet. He should be well acquainted with the rules.

THE CLERK OF COURSE

The most arduous assignment at a track meet, particularly a large one, is that of clerk of course. The games committee may handle all the preliminary arrangements, but usually this committee will delegate these duties to the clerk of course and his assistants.

The clerk of course will find it necessary to spend many hours in his preliminary preparation for a large meet or relay carnival. When the necessary data on entries are not available until the day before the meet, he may find himself working far into the night arranging heats and preparing his records of entries in each race. This information must be available for the coaches and competitors in advance of the meeting. Although the rules hold the competitors responsible for prompt reporting for a race, the clerk must check the entries in each race, assign each competitor to his proper lane, give the necessary instructions covering the race (that is, whether the race is run in lanes or not; starting positions for staggered starts; touch-off points in relay races; position for second, third, and fourth runners; the number of laps; the finish point; number of places in case of heats); make decisions concerning rearrangement of heats and lanes when all competitors do not report or all lanes are not filled; and finally report to the starter that all is in readiness and turn the race over to him.

The clerk must, if humanly possible, maintain the time schedule that has been set up. He may not start events in advance of the time schedule.

The drawings for heats are usually made in advance of the meet by the clerk. He is usually aided in this tedious task by information from the coaches concerning the ability of the competitors.

If semifinals are necessary, the qualifiers of the preliminary heats are assigned to the semifinal heats in advance. For example, if there are to be six preliminary heats and two semifinal races, it can be determined in advance that the qualifiers in the first three preliminary heats shall make up the first semifinal race, and the last three heat qualifiers the second semifinals.

The clerk—the workhorse at a meet

Usually the clerk has the competitors draw for lanes in the semi-finals and finals when they report for the start of the race. A simple device for making such drawings is to use blank cartridges that have the lanes numbered on the end. The clerk should keep a record of the drawings for purposes of reference in case of dispute, errors in judging, or violation of rules.

In meets that have a large field of competitors or in relay meets, the clerk will need assistants. One assistant may be organizing the event that follows the one about to start. In relay races, his assistants conduct the second, third, and fourth runners to their starting places and point out to them the restraining lines. They signal to the starter when all runners are ready.

The following list of duties and instructions may be handed to the clerk of course several days before a meet:

1. Secure list of competitors in each race.
2. Arrange competitors in heats according to record of previous performances (fastest men as heat leaders—runners from same school in different heats).
3. Make record of drawings. (A program and clip board are useful for this purpose.)
4. Check contestants five minutes before each race. Make any rearrangements necessitated by withdrawals and make a record of any changes.
5. Number a blank cartridge for each lane to use in drawing for places in semifinals and finals.
6. Keep a record of placements for finals and semifinals.
7. Instruct runners.
8. Maintain time schedule.
9. Send record of all starters to scorers.

THE SCORER

The scorer should be stationed in a place on the field where he is easily accessible throughout the meet. He needs a table on which he may place his score sheet and file the results of the various events as they are brought to him.

He should prepare a master score sheet to record the point winners of each event, their schools, and their records. Each entry on the score sheet should be carefully checked and the original record kept for auditing if necessary.

If the meet is on time, the clerk is fine

He should make no entry except from the official results delivered to him.

If a scoreboard is kept, he should furnish the information for this board and through assistants see that it is kept up-to-date. His record should be the source of information for the announcer.

The record of the official scorer is the basis for awarding all medals and trophies. He should prepare the award cards for each place after each event. These should be signed by each competitor as he receives his award. The signed card represents a record of the fact that the award has been received.

At the end of the meet, all records should be turned over to the manager of the meet or to the games committee.

The duties of the scorer may be condensed on a 3x5 card for his guidance.

1. Establish headquarters in central place.
2. Prepare master score sheet.
3. Record only from official results signed by the head judge of the event.
4. Record name, school, points of each winner in proper space.
5. Furnish official results to announcer and custodian of public scoreboard.
6. Prepare award cards for each place in each event.
7. File original results for auditing purposes.
8. Deliver all records to manager of meet at conclusion.

ANNOUNCER

The announcer at a track meet (or at any athletic contest) has a single duty. His one and only job is to be informative so those attending the meet can intelligently follow its progress and maintain interest at a high pitch throughout.

To fulfill his role effectively, the announcer must maintain an impersonal attitude toward all teams. His main requisites are a clear, resonant voice and a sense of good taste. It is wise for him to say too little rather than too much. He must not act as a cheerleader for any person or group. He should remember that he is not an entertainer, a comedian, or a clown. The spectators came to see a track meet, not to listen to a vaudeville act nor a dramatic production. It is not his duty to excite or to incite. His facilities are

The scorers accept officially signed results only

not to be used for advertising, as a social calendar, or for general announcements of any kind.

Specifically he should:

1. Give a background of records and performances in previous runnings of the same event.

2. Give the calls for all events.

3. Announce the official results of all events as soon after their completion as possible. (Give names, school, times, heights, distances.)

4. Give the lane positions of runners in each event.

5. In field events, announce the qualifiers, those still remaining in events, and from time to time the height of the bar and who has cleared, and the best distances and who made them.

6. Give a periodic résumé of the scoring of the teams and their standing on the basis of the number of events completed.

7. Assist the marshal when necessary by requesting spectators to help maintain conditions that will help everyone enjoy the meet to the fullest.

8. Give information concerning rest rooms, exits, etc., which are for the convenience of the spectators.

9. Present the winners as they receive their awards.

10. At the close of the meet, give the final scores and standings of the teams.

11. Thank the spectators and bid them good afternoon.

TIMERS

Accurate timing requires good eyesight, quick eye-finger reaction and coordination, and correct technique. It is assumed that reliable stop watches properly synchronized are available. Watches should measure to one-tenth of a second.

In the 100- and 220-yard dashes, the high and low hurdles (and on some tracks, the 440-yard dash and one-half-mile run), which start at the end of the straightaway, it is necessary to be able to see the flash of the starting gun clearly. When the signal is given that all is in readiness, the timers should be alert. It is customary for the head timer to call, "Gun up!" as a command to bring everyone to attention. All must concentrate on the starter. Each must have an unobstructed view of the starter's gun. Figure 6 shows a timer in readiness to start his watch.

Simultaneously with the flash of the gun (light travels faster than

The announcer is not a cheer leader

FIGURE 6. With watch poised and ready the timer watches for the flash of smoke from the starter's gun. Note that the forefinger is on the stem of the watch for quickest reaction.

sound), the timers must start their watches. Two techniques have been developed that produce more accurate timing. First, it has been discovered that the forefinger reacts more quickly than the thumb.[4] Consequently, the forefinger should be used to push the stem of the watch to start and stop it. Second, the stem of the watch should be pressed to the point where all the slack in its movement has been removed. The stems of most watches will move a short distance before activating the hand. If this slack is taken up, there will be less lag between the firing of the gun and the actual start of the watch. These same procedures should be followed when the watch is stopped at the finish of the race.

When the watches are checked out to the timers, they should practice starting, stopping, and reading them. In this way they will familiarize themselves with the characteristics of their watches.

[4] Breshnahan and Tuttle, p. 468.

The forefinger reacts more quickly than the thumb

Such practice will give the timers greater confidence in carrying out their responsibilities and will tend to produce more accurate timing. No two watches operate exactly alike.

The ability to read the watch correctly is also necessary. Almost all watches now used for timing track events are calibrated to one-tenth of a second. One should, however, check the markings on the dial. He should take several practice readings. It is a good practice for the timers to read each other's watches in order to check each other. A small magnifying glass, commonly used for reading, is a desirable and useful aid in making accurate readings.

The synchronization of watches can be checked by simultaneously pressing the stems of two watches. To the extent that the tension in the two stems is the same, the watches will start together. They should be stopped in the same manner. They should be tested over a short period (ten seconds) and over a long period (one or two minutes). If the watches read the same, one can be fairly sure that discrepancies in timing the meet will be due to differences in the individual timers.

After the race has started, the timers should take positions on either side of the track opposite the finish line. They must be able to sight directly across the track along the finish line. The timers may watch the runners until they approach within ten yards of the finish. Then, they should sight along the finish with their watches poised in readiness to stop them. The watch should be stopped the instant any part of the competitor's torso reaches the finish line.

After stopping the watch, each timer should read his own watch and record this reading on the cards provided for the purpose. The card should be handed to the head timer. The hand of the watch should not be snapped back to its starting position until clearance is given by the head timer. The head timer may desire to check all readings in case wide discrepancies arise.

The timers should not announce their readings or compare the time their watches recorded. This is the responsibility of the head timer. Strict adherence to this policy will avoid controversies in races that are run against time or where records may be at stake.

Occasionally it is necessary to recall competitors because of an unfair start. When this happens, the timers must be doubly sure they snap their watches back in readiness for the next start.

The head timer should remind the timers repeatedly to check

Learn about your watch before the race

their watches before the start of a race. He should also review with them all the procedures mentioned above before the meet begins. These precautions will tend to prevent timing problems during the progress of the meet.

Three timers are necessary to establish an official time for each race. For this reason three timers are designated as official and one as a substitute. In case one of the three fails to record the time of the race, the watch of the substitute timer is used as extra insurance. The head timer should also operate a watch. His watch may be used when necessary to supply the third timer. He may also desire to check the time of his watch against that of the other timers.

When the official time for a race is determined, the head timer should record the time on the proper card, sign the card, and send it to the scorer.

One set of instructions should be prepared for each of the timers and one set for the head timer:

Instructions to Head Timer

1. Check out watches from manager.
2. Distribute watches to timers, review timing procedures, suggest practice (see timers' instructions).
3. Appoint official timers and substitute.
4. Assign positions on either side of track.
5. Signal to starter when ready.
6. Collect recorded times, compare, determine official time. (Middle time, if watches are all different—if two watches agree, that is the official time.)
7. Check readings of all watches, if necessary.
8. Record official time and send to scorer.
9. Organize and prepare timers for next race.
10. In case of records, have referee check watches.

Instructions to Timers

1. Check out watch from head timer.
2. Operate several times for practice.
3. Use forefinger to start and stop.
4. Take up slack in stem in readiness to start at "gun-up" signal. Stop with the same technique.
5. Start watch at flash of gun (sight of smoke).
6. Stop watch when torso of first runner reaches finish line.

Record the time—don't discuss it

7. Sight along finish line when runner is within ten yards of finish.

8. Record watch reading on blanks provided for purpose, sign, and hand to head timer.

9. Preserve reading on watch until cleared by head timer.

10. Do not discuss or compare time with anyone.

JUDGES

The judges of the finish have the most delicate job of all the track officials. Tremendous responsibility rests upon their shoulders. It is their job to determine the order of the winners. In races where several competitors are bunched at the finish, mistakes in judgment are likely to be made in spite of the most concentrated and conscientious effort. Instances are not uncommon where winners have been overlooked entirely because the same contestant has been chosen for two places. It is also comparatively easy to overlook runners who are in the lanes closest to the judges. Here is one phase of officiating where closeness to the play is not an asset. As a rule, first place is not difficult to pick; but second, third, and fourth places can create a nightmare for the judges. Above all else, the judges must not be excitable individuals. They must be keen, discriminating, and dependable. Men with track experience are preferable.

Through experience, some techniques have been developed that have proven helpful. For purposes of double checking, two judges are recommended for each place. One judge is stationed on one side of the track and one on the other.

A judge can be more discriminating in his judgments and see the relative positions of runners more clearly if he is some distance away from the track and elevated above it. As a consequence, platforms built at graduated heights like stairsteps and placed as much as twenty feet from the edge of the track are now available at most tracks.

Judges should watch the runners as they approach the finish line (see Figure 7). But when the runners are about ten yards away, the judges should sight across the track along the finish line. Figure 8 shows the judge intently sighting along the finish line in readiness to pick winners. The first contestant whose torso reaches the finish line is the winner. The judges who are to pick second, third, and fourth places must carefully and quickly count the runners who

Judging is delicate work—experience is essential

FIGURE 7.   Judge watching the approach of a runner.

FIGURE 8.   Judge's attention has moved with the runner. He is now sighting along the finish yarn to pick the winner of the race.

cross this line in order to select the place for which they are responsible. As the runner who fits the place the judge is picking reaches the line, he should follow this runner down the track in order to identify him. He is identified by a number on his back, or, in dual or triangular meets, by the color of his jersey, which represents his school.

Follow the runners as they approach the finish

Each judge should write down on a card the number or school of the winner of the place he is picking and hand this card to the head judge. He should do this without consulting the other officials or anyone else. The head judge will then record the results and send them to the scorer.

When conflicts in judging arise, the head judge should draw the judges apart from contestants, coaches, other officials, and spectators for consultation. By this means, it is usually possible to straighten out any irregularities without confusion. The rules provide that if a runner is picked for two places the decision of the judges picking higher scoring places takes precedence.

If errors in judgment cannot be solved, the matter must be referred to the referee. If, perchance, official pictures were taken of the finish, these can be used to settle the matter.

The head judge should always appoint judges to pick one more place than the number to score.

Instructions for Head Judge

1. Assign place each judge is to pick, including one more than the number to score. Two judges for each place.
2. Review procedures to be followed (see *Instructions for Judges*).
3. Tabulate results turned in by judges and send to scorer.
4. In case of discrepancies, assemble judges apart from others to resolve.

Instructions for Judges

1. Judges picking same place get on the opposite sides of track.
2. Watch race until runners approach within ten yards of finish line, then sight across track along line.
3. When any part of torso reaches line, runner has finished.
4. A fallen runner must be completely across line.
5. Write on finish card the winner's number or name of school for place you are to pick.
6. Sign and hand card to head judge.
7. Do not consult or discuss decision with anyone.

TRACK INSPECTORS

There should be at least four track inspectors. One of them shall be chief inspector. The chief inspector should place the inspectors

Privacy is golden when conflicts arise

where they can most effectively perform their duties for each race. In large meets a drawing of the track showing the location of each inspector for each race is usually provided. For races around curves, they are stationed at the start and finish of the curves, so they can see the passing zones. In hurdle races, they should be spread equally along the hurdle route. In relay races, inspectors must be able to see the restraining lines for exchanging batons. Their job is to report any violation of the rules to the referee. The inspectors have no authority. They are observers, but they must know the rules that control the contestants on the track. Former track competitors are most desirable as inspectors. They usually have better judgment as to what constitutes a violation.

The following rules are of particular importance:

1. In races run in lanes, each competitor must finish in the same lane in which he started.
2. In hurdle races, hurdlers may not run around a hurdle or advance or trail a leg around the side of a hurdle.
3. A runner may not impede the progress of a competitor by jostling, obstructing, or cutting across his path. There may not be any contact in such maneuvers.
4. A competitor may not leave his lane and gain an advantage thereby nor leave the track and return later to continue the race.
5. In relay races, runners must exchange batons within the restraining lines.

As a rule, there are not many violations of the track rules. When violations occur, they usually involve jostling or passing illegally. The fact that few violations occur does not minimize the importance of the duties of the inspectors. The potential of their presence may act as a deterrent in a heated race. They may find it expedient to remind runners as they pass that they must not cut across too soon or jostle.

Instructions to Inspectors

1. Report to referee for direction and placement.
2. Review rules on passing a runner, staying in lanes, jostling, and hurdling.
3. Report violations immediately to referee by giving a full description of what happened. Inspectors have no authority to make decisions.
4. Caution runners to prevent fouls.

Inspectors report—they do not decide

chapter 9

FIELD EVENTS

CHIEF FIELD JUDGE

In large meets, the field events are supervised by a chief field judge. He assists the referee. He has a fourfold job.

1. Through the inspector of implements, he checks all implements to be used in the meet to see that they conform to the standards specified in the rules.

2. He sees that the proper relationship is maintained between the field events and the track events. Time schedules must be maintained. Those who compete in both track and field events must be handled so no unnecessary delays in running off events are permitted.

Implements must be checked

77

3. He supervises the administration of all field events to the extent that they are conducted according to rule. He is available to rule on disputes or other problems that may be referred to him. He must know the rules under which the meet is being conducted.

4. He shall check and approve the scorecards for each field event and then turn the results over to the scorer.

In small meets, there is not usually a separate official for this job. The referee assumes these duties.

The field events may consist of as many as nine events. These divide themselves into the continuous type of field events—the high jump and pole vault—and the limited trial field events such as the shot, discus, and broad jump. In general, the duties of the officials in each can be classed under four headings. These should be included when a list of instructions is prepared for the judges.

1. *Determining the order of competition.* In all field events the order of competition shall be determined by lot. In dual meets, the contestants are often alternated. The visitors are permitted to choose whether they shall be first or second in the order. Occasionally in large meets the contestants in continuous type events may be divided into flights of as many as ten in a flight. One flight jumps in order, until all have successfully cleared the bar or been eliminated. Then the next flight starts.

In the limited trial events, the common practice is to perform in pairs or groups. Each pair takes two trials in order. Then the next pair or group follows. This procedure is continued until all have competed, then the second round of trials is started.

If the field of competitors is large (40 or more), the pairs may be grouped into flights. Each flight completes all of its trials before the next flight starts.

The general practice in pairing and in arranging the sequence is to pair contestants of comparable ability and to place the pairs in the reverse order of their ability. The pairs with best performances compete last.

In the finals or semifinals of all limited-trial field events, the competition is in reverse order of the best performances in the preliminary rounds.

2. *Measuring the results of performance.* In the continuous field events—high jump and pole vault—the height of the bar is measured

The order of competition may be determined by agreement

at the conclusion of the event or at the height at which a record is broken. If a record is broken, the height of the bar must be measured before the bar is moved. All measurements are made from the ground vertically to the upper side of the bar at its lowest point.

In the limited-trial events, two practices are followed by necessity. In the shot, 35-pound weight, and the broad jump, measurements must be made and recorded after each trial. If performances were marked to be measured at the conclusion of the trials, some of the marks would be lost or distorted by subsequent performances that alighted in the same area. In the other events, markers may be used to indicate the best distance of each contestant until all trials are completed. Then, measurements are taken and recorded to determine the qualifiers or the winners.

The distances in the broad jump and javelin are measured at right angles to the scratch line to the nearest break in the ground. The distances in the events in a circle are measured along an extended diameter of the circle. (See pages 80-84 for detailed instructions.)

3. *Judging the legality of performance.* Each event has a list of those acts that constitute a foul. They are listed below under the specific instructions on the duties of the officials in each event. In general, they constitute touching the ground or advancing beyond the scratch line, or restraining line, for that event.

4. *Recording and reporting the results of the event.* At the completion of an event, the results must be recorded. Then the records must be studied to determine the winners of the various places. When the winners have been indicated, the chief judge of the event signs the reports and delivers them to the scorer. The assistant judges return all implements and tapes to the proper custodian.

Instructions for Field Events

There are, in addition, some duties that are peculiar to a particular event. These are listed below under the special instructions to the officials for the event.

If the mark can be lost, measure it

The High Jump

1. Report to chief judge.

2. Secure entries and record cards from scorer.

3. Call roll and arrange for draw by lot if order is not already established. Call jumps in order of drawings.

4. If starting height has not been determined by the games committee, start bar at height to fit class of competition, but at as great a height as is reasonably possible. (The better jumpers may pass the lower heights.)

5. Raise the bar by one- to two-inch increments. It is customary to determine the height at which to start the bar and the increment at each change before the event begins. Remember that the best performances are not attained by prolonging the event.

6. Give each jumper three trials at each height. Trials must be taken in order. A record must be kept of each jumper's performances at each height. (See Form I for sample record sheet.)

7. A trial consists of clearing the bar with all parts of the body, knocking the bar off the standards, passing under the bar or the line of the bar extended, or leaving the ground in an attempt.

8. Jumpers must take off from one foot to make a fair jump.

9. Continue event until all have failed to clear the bar or all but one are eliminated.

10. Measure the greatest height cleared (see Diagram 6).

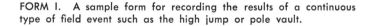

FORM I.   A sample form for recording the results of a continuous type of field event such as the high jump or pole vault.

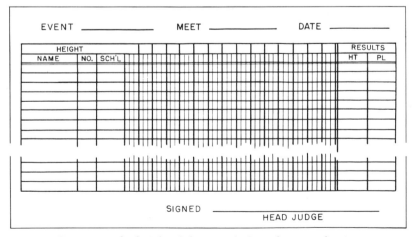

Determine the height of the raise before the event begins

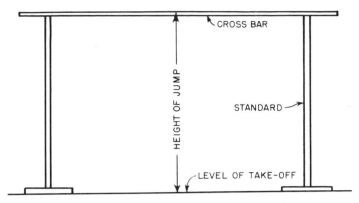

DIAGRAM 6. The correct point of measurement for the high jump.
The pole vault is measured in the same manner.

11. Check records to designate place winners. In case of ties, the points are divided equally between the contestants concerned, unless other provisions or rules are announced in advance.

12. Sign report and return records and tape to scorer's table.

13. Special arrangements may be made for those competing in other events at the same time.

The Pole Vault

With the following exceptions, the officials should follow the same procedure for conducting the pole vault as listed for the high jump:

1. The bar may be raised as much as six inches for the first or second raises. Thereafter, three- to four-inch increments should be used.

2. A trial consists of displacing the bar, passing under it, crossing the line of the bar extended, carrying any part of the competitor's pole beyond the line of the bar extended, or leaving the ground in an attempted vault.

3. The top hand may not be moved up nor the lower hand moved above the top hand.

The Broad Jump

Instructions 1, 2, and 3 for the high jump apply. In large meets, the drawings by pairs and by flights will undoubtedly be made in

Measure a record when it is made

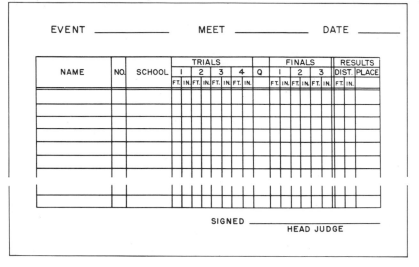

EVENT _____ MEET _____ DATE _____

NAME	NO.	SCHOOL	TRIALS									FINALS						Q	RESULTS	

FORM II. A sample form for recording the results of a limited trial field event such as the broad jump, shot put, discus, or javelin.

advance. Form II shows a sample chart for recording the results of limited-trial field events.

4. Give each jumper three jumps or trials in the preliminaries and three in the finals.

If the candidates are competing in pairs or groups, then each pair or group shall take two jumps or trials before the next competes.

5. A trial occurs when a contestant's shoe extends over the scratch line when taking off for a jump or if he runs across the scratch line or scratch line extended.

6. Measure each jump at right angles to take-off board and from front edge of board or board extended to nearest point on ground that is touched by the jumper (see Diagram 7).

DIAGRAM 7. Method of measuring distance in the broad jump.

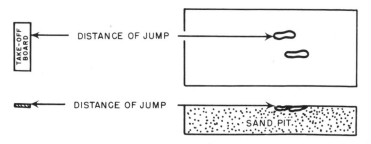

Use a chart to record the mark

7. Use knife-edge or flat blade to mark nearest point of jump.

8. Have zero end of tape at jumping pit.

9. Chief judge calls order, records distances, and calls fouls. Other two judges mark point of jump and measure distance.

10. Judge at pit keeps sand at same level as take-off before each jump.

11. Judge at take-off keeps ground in front of scratch line smooth and at same level as take-off.

12. Determine qualifiers and place winners, sign results, and deliver to scorer. One more than places awarded qualify for the finals.

The Shot Put

Procedures 1, 2, 3, 4, 7, 8, 9, and 12 of the broad jump apply to the shot-put. Numbers 5 and 6 are as follows:

5. A foul occurs when the foot touches the top of the toe board or the circle or when the contestant steps outside the circle before the put is marked. A foul counts as a trial but is not measured. The shot must land within the prescribed sector.

6. Measure each put from the nearest edge of mark made by put to the nearest point on the inside edge of the circle. This point

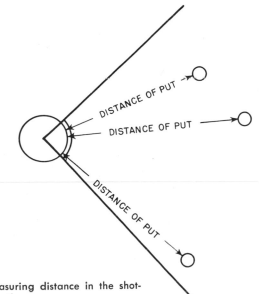

DIAGRAM 8.   Method of measuring distance in the shot-put. The discus is measured in the same manner.

Measure the shortest distance

may be found by moving the tape through an arc along the inside edge of the circle until the shortest distance is found (see Diagram 8). The zero end of the tape should be held at the mark of the put. The other end extends through the circle and should coincide with the diameter of the circle. The exact point on the edge of the circle may be determined by moving the tape slowly back and forth through an arc. The zero end is used as the center of rotation. The shortest distance from the mark of the put to the inside edge of the circumference of the circle is the correct distance to record.

The Discus Throw

The shot-put and discus are conducted in exactly the same manner with two minor exceptions:

1. Throws to be legal must fall within a 90-degree sector, which is marked on the ground. Figure 9 shows the chief judge of the discus watching the feet of the contestant in order to determine the legality of the throw.

2. The best throw of each competitor is marked by means of metal or wooden pins and measured at the end of preliminary and final throws.

The Javelin Throw

The distance for the javelin throw is measured the same as for the broad jump.

The point of the javelin must strike the ground first to constitute a legal throw. The javelin must be held at the grip.

The thrower must not touch the scratch line, scratch line extended, or the ground beyond the line until the throw is marked. Figure 10 shows the judge watching thrower until he regains his balance after a throw.

If perchance the implement should break while in flight, the trial does not count and a substitute trial should be awarded.

Aside from the above, the javelin event is conducted the same as the other implement events.

The radius extended is the distance intended

FIGURE 9. To detect any foot faults by the discus thrower, the head judge must have his eyes focused on the feet of the contestant and upon the ring.

FIGURE 10. The judge of the javelin throw checks the thrower's position relative to the scratch line until he regains his balance.

The discus must park in a 90° arc

The Hammer Throw

The hammer and discus events are conducted in the same manner. It is not illegal for the head of the hammer to hit the ground during the swing. The contestant may not, however, stop his throw and start anew.

INSPECTOR OF IMPLEMENTS

The inspector of implements works under the supervision of the head field judge. It is his job to check all implements against the specifications in the rules. He needs a standard steel tape and scale.

The following standards must be maintained in the various implements:

> *Shot*—College, 16 pounds minimum; high school, 12 pounds minimum.
>
> *Hammer*—College, 16 pounds minimum; high school, 12 pounds minimum: maximum length, for college and high school, 48⅛₆ inches.
>
> *Discus*—Weight, 4 pounds, 6.548 ounces minimum. (High schools use the modified discus, weight 3 pounds, 9 ounces.)
>
> *Javelin*—Length 8 feet 6⅜ inches minimum; 8 feet 10¼ inches maximum; weight, 1 pound 12¼ ounces minimum; grip, 43.31 inches to 35.43 inches from point.
>
> *35-Pound Weight*—Over-all length, 16 inches maximum; weight, 35 pounds minimum.

When implements are approved, they should be stamped with an appropriate mark. Judges will then permit the use of approved implements only. In many meets, the implements are furnished by the games committee, and no others are permitted.

SURVEYOR

Before the beginning of each season, the track should be measured by an engineer to make sure that all distances from start to finish are correct. An affidavit attesting the results of his work should be filed for use in case of records. Likewise, all take-offs, circles, scratch lines, and the level of the track and broad-jumping pit should be carefully checked.

Professional attest assures that the track is the best

An anemometer should be available on the day of the meet to determine wind velocity and the direction of the wind.

The surveyor can be used to inspect the implements in the absence of an inspector for this purpose.

chapter 10

SWIMMING AND
DIVING

The concept that a swimming and diving official can be any person who is interested but untrained as an official is no longer tenable. A growing need exists for local, county, and district organizations of swimming and diving officials. Such organizations could establish certification standards and officiating technique standards, serve as the accrediting body, and conduct training clinics. Interest in competitive swimming and diving on the part of the spectator, contestant, and administrator is growing constantly. To maintain this growth in interest, adequately trained and accredited officials must be readily available, or the dignity and prestige of competitive

Organize and instruct officials before the start

swimming and diving will not attain the high position it rightfully deserves in the physical education program. Each prospective official should become thoroughly acquainted with the written rules as published in the *Official NCAA Swimming Guide*.

Number of Officials

One of the first questions confronting both the swimming coach as he prepares for a dual meet in his pool and the planning committee for a championship meet is: How many officials are needed to conduct the meet efficiently?

Eleven officials are needed to conduct properly an interscholastic or intercollegiate dual meet. Of course, when competent officials are available in excess of the following assignments, they should be utilized to the fullest extent.

1. One official serves as the meet referee, starter, diving referee, and inspector of strokes, lanes, and turns at the end of the pool opposite to the starting end.

2. Three officials serve as the judges of finish and judges of diving. Two of these judges serve as take-off judges and one is inspector of lanes and turns at the starting end of the pool. One of these officials is also appointed head judge of finish.

3. One official serves as announcer and scorer.

4. One official serves as clerk of course.

5. Two officials serve as computers of the diving scores. The referee always makes a final check.

6. Three officials serve as timers. The possibility of record-breaking performances should be anticipated and a fourth timer secured to serve as an alternate in case one of the three regular watches fails to function properly. One of the three regular timers should be appointed head timer.

The number of officials needed to conduct a championship meet depends upon such factors as: 1) number of lanes, 2) use of time or place as the method of qualifying the finalist, and 3) changes of assignments for timers from trials to finals.

A championship meet conducted in a six-lane pool requires the following officials:

At least 11 officials are needed

1. One official serves as meet referee.
2. One official serves as starter.
3. One official serves as head judge of finish.
4. Twelve to eighteen officials serve as judges of finish.
5. One official serves as referee of diving.
6. Five officials serve as judges of diving.
7. One official serves as secretary of diving.
8. Two officials serve as computers of diving.
9. One official serves as head timer.
10. Eighteen to twenty-four officials serve as timers. One of each group of three or four uses a split-timer to record the split times for that lane. One of each group of timers is appointed head timer for that group.
11. One official serves as the announcer.
12. One official serves as clerk of course. He should have several assistants.
13. Six to twelve officials serve as inspectors of lanes and turns.
14. Six officials serve as take-off judges.

When the finalists are determined on the basis of time, each performer must be timed by at least three timers during the trials. Therefore, 18 to 24 timers are needed depending on the use of alternate timers. This same procedure may be followed for the finals, or the number of timers may be reduced by using four timers to time only the first place winner and one split-timer to take splits in each lane.

DUTIES OF REFEREE

1. The referee shall have full jurisdiction over the meet and shall see that all rules are enforced. In other than championship meets, he shall decide all questions arising on the conduct of the meet, the final settlement of which is not otherwise covered by the rules, and he shall have discretionary power to set aside the application of a rule when there is apparent unfairness.

2. The referee shall prohibit the use of any bells, sirens, horns, or other artificial noisemakers during the meet.

3. The referee shall be given a list of the officials and shall assign each to his particular duty, being certain that each understands his responsibility as indicated by the rules. He shall have authority to change any assignments of duty.

4. The referee shall see that the results of each event are an-

Be sure the swimmers are motionless before the start

nounced as quickly as possible at the completion of the event, and that the next event starts promptly thereafter. In case of stalling delay, he shall order the event to start without waiting further for any contestants who have not reported and shall impose the penalties according to the rules.

5. After the conclusion of the last event of the meet the referee shall audit carefully the scorers' tabulation of results of each swimming and diving event and if found correct shall sign such tabulation, thus establishing the official score. After this has been done no changes or corrections may be made even though an error appears.[1]

DUTIES OF STARTER

1. The starter shall have control over the contestants after they have been assigned to him by the referee and until a fair start has been achieved. He may elect to start the events from a position on the pool deck about 20 feet from the starting mark or from a point about three feet in front of the starting marks.

2. Forward Start. In all swimming races with the exception of the backstroke, each contestant shall stand erect with both feet on the starting mark in readiness to assume a starting position. Upon the command, "Take your mark," he shall assume any desired starting position provided he holds a steady balance for an appreciable length of time. When the starter sees that the contestants are completely motionless, he starts the race with the "pistol shot."

3. Backstroke Start. In the backstroke start, each contestant shall line up facing the starting mark with both hands grasping the starting grips and with both feet in contact with the end of the pool. Upon the command, "Take your mark," he shall assume any desired starting position that does not remove him completely from the water, or his hands from the starting grips, or his feet from contact with the end of the pool. When the starter sees that the contestants are completely motionless, he starts the race with the "pistol shot."

4. False Starts. 1) All contestants leaving their marks before

---

[1] Vic Gustafson, ed., *Official Swimming Guide* (New York: The National Collegiate Athletic Bureau, 1966), p. 14.

Starter, be calm

the pistol is discharged shall be charged with a false start unless the starter verbally relieves one or more of these contestants of the responsibility for the false start. 2) When the pistol is discharged and one or more contestants has obtained an unfair 'advantage, all contestants shall be recalled at once by a second pistol shot. The starter shall then indicate the contestant or contestants, if any, to be charged with a false start. 3) A contestant who unnecessarily delays in assuming a completely motionless starting position after the command, "Take your mark," should be charged with a false start. 4) At the starter's discretion, he may order the contestants to "stand up" any time prior to the discharge of the pistol. 5) Any contestant charged with two false starts shall be disqualified and may not swim the event.

In interscholastic competition the starter shall discharge the pistol when the leading swimmer has two lengths plus five yards to swim in the 200- and 400-yard freestyle events only.

In intercollegiate competition the starter shall discharge the pistol when the leading swimmer has two lengths plus five yards in the 500- and 1640-yard freestyle events only.

When the starter is serving as both referee and starter, he shall attract the attention of the judges and timers by saying, "Judges and timers, ready," and receive a signal of readiness from the head judge and head timer before proceeding with the start. In a championship meet, the starter shall receive a signal from the referee indicating that the judges and timers are ready.

In the case of a false start by competitor or starter, the starter shall recall the competitors by several rapid pistol shots. A recall rope lowered into the water at the 30-foot mark by two officials will recall the competitors if pistol shots are not heard.

DUTIES OF LANE JUDGES
AND TIMERS IN CHAMPIONSHIPS

Although the following procedure is specified for championship meets, it is strongly recommended for dual meets. The combined duties of lane judges and lane timers shall be to determine the placement and official times of the contestants in the assigned lanes. Two lane-place judges and three timers shall be assigned to each

If two watches agree, that time is official

lane. The judges for each lane shall be placed on opposite sides of the pool at the finish line. The three timers for each lane shall be placed directly over their assigned lane at the finish. The alternate timer only shall take split times. Cards shall be provided for each lane as follows: Lane 1, blue; lane 2, red; lane 3, white; lane 4, orange; lane 5, green; and lane 6, yellow. Timer's and judge's cards shall be the same color for each respective lane. Each judge determines independently where the contestant in his lane finishes in the race and records it on the card provided for that purpose. Judges must not record a tie. Each judge must record the highest place his lane contestant actually may have attained. For example, if a lane judge determines that the contestant in his lane has finished in a tie with another contestant for first place, he shall record a first place for his lane; the same procedure applies to similar situations involving other place positions. The cards are delivered to the scoring table where the appropriate ballot value is recorded on the basis of one point for first place selection, two points for second, three points for third, and so forth.

The time of each watch is recorded on the timer's card and the official time is established. This card is delivered to the scoring table where it is evaluated by the chief recorders in comparison with the other official lane times and marked with the appropriate ballot value on the basis of one point for the fastest time or times; two points for second fastest; three points for third fastest, and so forth. Equal ballot values are recorded for identical times. For example, if A, B, and C have identical official times of 22.1 in a heat or final of the 50-yard freestyle, and D, E, and F have identical official times of 22.2, then, A, B, and C shall each receive a ballot value of one for fastest time; D, E, and F shall each receive a ballot value of two for second fastest time.

The chief recorders determine the finish order of all contestants in any heat or final event by adding the numerical value of the three ballots for each lane. The lane (contestant) having the lowest numerical total shall be declared the winner, the second lowest shall be second, and so forth. If two or more total ballot values are equal, the result is a tie. After this procedure, the official time for each contestant shall be recorded.[2]

---

[2] Gustafson, p. 15.

Your judgment could decide a record

DUTIES OF JUDGES IN DUAL MEETS

If the ballot system or automatic timing and/or judging device is not used, the following procedure shall be used for dual meets. The judges of the finish shall be designated as first-, second-, and third-place judges and shall determine the order in which the contestants finish. The minimum number shall be two judges for first place and one for each of the other places.

The chief finish judge shall check the individual decisions of the judges indicated independently in writing on cards supplied for that purpose, before announcement of the final result of the event is made. If there is disagreement among the judges, the precedence in decision shall follow numerical order. For example: If first- and second-place judges both select contestant A, the decision of the first-place judge is final. The same procedure shall apply in selection of other places.

Although the fastest swimmers are usually placed in the center lanes, the judges should avoid the mistake of overlooking the finish of swimmers in the outside lanes during a close finish. Judges should not confer with each other until they have submitted their judgments in writing to the chief judge. Judges should be on the alert at all times for an underwater finish touch by a swimmer. This touch is not so easily seen as an above-the-surface touch but the possibility should be recognized.

DUTIES OF TIMERS IN DUAL MEETS

If the ballot system or automatic timing and/or judging device is not used, the following procedure shall be used for dual meets. The chief timer shall instruct each timer to start his watch instantly on the flash of the starter's pistol and stop his watch simultaneously with the finish of the winner of first place. Only three timers shall act officially. Alternates shall be named in a definite order and called upon in said order if circumstances require. The chief timer shall read all watches and shall determine and record the official time for the race.

If two or more of the official watches agree, their time shall be the official time. If all three disagree, the middle time shall be the official time. If times from only two official watches are available for any lane or place, the average of the two watches to the nearest and slowest tenth of a second shall be the official time.

The host institution is responsible for securing sufficient watches for dual or championship meets and having them examined for accuracy by an expert. When a watch is assigned to a timer, he should acquaint himself thoroughly with it by starting, stopping, and snapping it back several times. Judgment errors will be avoided if the timer knows the watch he is using.

DUTIES OF DIVING REFEREE

The diving referee shall manage the competition and enforce all regulations. He shall carefully check the list of dives submitted by each diver to avoid mistakes in degrees of difficulty, terminology, repetition of dives, use of nonlisted dives, and signature of the diver.

Just prior to the start of the diving competition, the diving referee calls the diving judges together to explain any rule changes, to provide them with scorecards, and to assign them to their positions for judging. When the diving board is in the center of the pool and sunlight is not reflected from the surface of the water, the judges should be placed on opposite sides of the pool. When the diving board is not in the center of the pool, however, the diving judges may be placed along one side of the pool, opposite the end of the diving board, with the sun at their backs. All diving judges should have a clear view of the diving.

During dual meets, the diving referee usually serves as a diving judge and may appoint the clerk of course or announcer to blow the whistle following each dive and to read off the scores flashed by the diving judges. During championship meets, he should not serve as a diving judge, but he should blow the whistle following each dive and read off the diving scores so they can be recorded by the diving secretary. During the diving competition, he should be constantly alert to any infractions of the rules and be ready to instruct the diving judges and diving secretary regarding the nature of the ruling.

DUTIES OF DIVING JUDGES

For a championship contest there shall be not more than five judges, diving referee, and a diving secretary. In dual competition one diving referee and three judges are sufficient.

Judges must have a clear view of the dive

The technique of judging diving cannot be mastered quickly. To become a competent diving judge, one must know the mechanics of diving, see the best divers perform, frequently observe diving, have access to slow-motion pictures, and be intensely interested in this aspect of swimming competition.

There are several methods used by expert diving judges to evaluate diving. When these methods are based on the principles of diving, the slight difference in the awards will be insignificant. When diving judging is based on an inaccurate interpretation of body movement and the physical principles involved, however, a wide divergence of opinion is the rule rather than the exception.

The following standards will serve as a basis for judging diving:

1. Approach: The approach shall be smooth, erect, forceful, and confident. No penalty should be incurred because of individual mannerism.

The running approach includes the starting position, the steps preceding the hurdle, the hurdle, and the landing on the board in preparation for the take-off.

The term "run" is used in connection with any dive preceded by three steps and a hurdle, and should not be construed to mean a "run" in the true sense of the word.

2. Take-off: The take-off shall be forceful.

The take-off includes the angle of lean, the coordinated action of arms and legs from the time the board is fully depressed until the diver's feet leave the board.

3. Elevation: The elevation or height shall be sufficient to permit proper execution of the dive.

Elevation is the result of a properly executed take-off and signifies the distance or height of the diver above the board or the water.

4. Execution: The execution shall be graceful and controlled.

The execution is the performance of the dive from the time the diver leaves the board until his body disappears beneath the surface.

5. Drop: For all dives, excluding the plain dives, there shall be a marked "breakout" followed by a definite drop with the body aligned for entry.

The drop is the distance from where the diver completes his dive to the surface of the water.

To judge diving is technical—the judge should be professional

6. Entry: The entry shall be clean-cut and as nearly perpendicular as possible.

The entry is the vertical or nearly vertical flight of the body (with the body straight and toes pointed) into and beneath the surface of the water.

Judging a dive may be thought of as a comparison of the actual dive performed with a mental impression of what constitutes a ten-point dive. The preceding six basic parts of a dive should help the diving judge achieve a well-rounded concept of each dive. As a dive is performed, the diving judge should compare it with his impression of what the dive would look like if it were a ten-point dive. As the dive fails to achieve this high standard, it should be penalized according to the amount of difference that exists.

Points shall be awarded from 0-10, according to the options of the judges and the following table. A one-half point scale may be used.[3]

	Points
Very good	9—9.5—10
Good	7—7.5—8—8.5
Satisfactory	5—5.5—6—6.5
Deficient	3—3.5—4—4.5
Unsatisfactory	1—1.5—2—2.5

In the event of a contestant making a balk or false start on the springboard and not completing a dive that has been started, the diving referee, upon completion of the second attempt, shall instruct the secretary to reduce the final total award by one-third. If the second attempt to obtain a balance or take-off is unsuccessful, it shall be considered as a "failed" dive. No further attempt shall be permitted.

DUTIES OF DIVING SECRETARY

The diving secretary records the individual awards on the score sheet as they are called out by the diving referee. When five judges are used, he cancels the highest and lowest awards or any two

---

[3] Gustafson, p. 24.

There are six parts of a dive to judge

when the five awards are identical and adds the three remaining awards. When three judges are used, as in dual-meet competition, no cancellation of awards is made. He announces the sum and degree of difficulty to the two computers who quickly complete the scores, with the use of diving computers, and check with each other for error in their calculations. He then records this number on the score sheet and announces it to the spectators, who may wish to keep a progressive score. Following this announcement, he adds the score to the previous sum total and passes the score sheet to the computers for checking. When the competition is finished he collaborates with the diving referee, lists the order of the competitors, adds his signature with that of the diving referee, and passes the final results to the announcer for announcement.

DUTIES OF ANNOUNCER

The announcer should be supplied with complete information before and immediately following each event. This information should include the name of each contestant, the school or club he represents, the order in which each contestant finished, first-place time for final events or the time for each contestant for trial events, and all records and previous holders and dates in case a new record is established. His announcements should be carefully and clearly presented. They should not distract from the actual competition in progress.

DUTIES OF CLERK OF COURSE

The clerk of course shall be provided with the names and lane assignments of all contestants in each event and shall make certain they are in the proper lanes and ready for the start. He must know the scope of his job and carry out his responsibilities effectively or the progress of the meet will be seriously hampered.

DUTIES OF STROKE INSPECTORS
AND TURN JUDGES

Within the limits of responsibility assigned to him, each stroke inspector and turn judge shall report to the referee any violations.

Carefully check the divers' scores

Infractions of rules must be reported with full particulars to the referee immediately after the finish of the event. These officials should station themselves directly above the end of the pool when inspecting turns and push-offs and should observe the different strokes from the rear, front, side, and above, before making the final decision. Whenever possible, there should be one inspector for every two lanes at each end of the pool. Disqualifications should be based on what is actually seen, not on what is imagined. Refraction errors are possible when a contestant is observed from the side only.

DUTIES OF TAKE-OFF JUDGES

In all relays there should be a take-off judge assigned to each lane for the purpose of judging whether the second, third, and fourth contestants are still in contact with the starting mark when the preceding teammate touches the end of the pool. He should station himself in such a position that he can see the end of the pool and have his little finger in light contact with the little toe of the contestant. He should lean forward over the edge of the pool in order to see the incoming swimmer's finish touch. Eyes should be fixed on the contact point at the end of the lane. The take-off judge sees the incoming swimmer touch and feels the starting swimmer leave. When the contact of the finger and toe is broken simultaneously with the finish touch, the relay take-off is legal. Of course, the starting swimmer may leave after the finish touch is made, but if the starting swimmer breaks the finger contact (leaves the mark) before the finish touch is made, the relay take-off is illegal, and the judge must report the infraction to the referee for disqualification of the relay team.

The take-off judge does not signal, tap, slap, or use any other method to inform the swimmer that the touch has been made. He simply uses the hand-eye method of determining the legality of the take-off. He should resist the tendency to duck back to avoid being splashed by the incoming swimmer.

DUTIES OF SCORER

The scorer shall keep an accurate record of the results of each event and of the cumulative point score of the meet.

Announcing should be direct and informative

chapter 11

TENNIS

Tennis may be characterized as the sport with the fewest players and the most officials. One singles match, which involves two players, requires 13 officials if a full coterie is used. In a dual meet where six singles matches are underway at the same time, 73 officials would be necessary if all places were filled. Only 12 players would be participating.

It is clear that the problem of furnishing a sufficient number of competent officials for a dual match between two schools or for a tournament becomes practically insurmountable. Except in very few instances it is impossible to obtain the number of officials re-

No officials are better than poor officials

quired by rule to conduct a match. Even if they were available, they would have to volunteer their services. If they demanded remuneration, the cost would be prohibitive, except probably in the large national and international tournaments.

It is much more desirable to do without officials than to secure untrained and incompetent ones. Wrong decisions of any type in tennis do more to annoy the players and, many times, to decide the outcome of a match than erroneous decisions in any other sport. It must be remembered that the decision of an official that is based on judgment is final. He may not be overruled on a question of judgment.

The problem of officials may be the reason for the high ethical standards and good sportsmanship that has developed in tennis competition. The contestants are forced to officiate their own games. Each player makes the decision on the balls on his side of the net. As a consequence, a spirit of fairness pervades practically all play. In case of doubt, a player almost invariably rules against himself.

On the surface, this practice may seem to be the ideal solution to a difficult problem. Experience has shown, however, that the practice of self-officiating is not satisfactory at all and in many instances decidedly unfair. For instance, in the case of foot faults, it is impossible for a player to be sure that he has or has not violated the rules. In a crucial stage of a match, the pressure of circumstances requires that he rule against himself on a decision that is questionable to him but which may have been actually in his favor.

For these reasons efforts should be made to train, develop, and provide officials for all tournaments and league and conference matches. While it is recognized that a full quota of officials may be impossible to attain, a fairly satisfactory partial solution can be worked out. There is tremendous social interest in tennis, and students and followers of the game are eager to assist in its administration. If the leadership and the stimulus for training officials are furnished, surprisingly favorable results may be attained. The discussion of the officials and their duties that follows is directed toward supplying this need. The United States Lawn Tennis Association [1] has done much to encourage an interest in tennis officiating.

---

[1] *Rules of Lawn Tennis* (New York: United States Lawn Tennis Association, 1966).

It is difficult to self-officiate foot faults

The Officials

The officials for tennis consist of a referee, two umpires, and ten linesmen.

It may be of interest to point out that the rules of tennis do not list the officials required for a match, nor do they, except in one instance (Rule 28), refer to the officials and their duties in any way. These instructions are found only in the umpire's manual.

THE REFEREE

The referee is the final authority on appeals that involve questions of law. He has the general overall supervision of a match or tournament. He must be available at all times when play is in progress.

In general, it may be said that his authority covers those factors incident to the play, such as assigning officials; changing or removing officials; assigning courts; starting, stopping, postponing, defaulting, and delaying matches; and excusing players from competition for a definite period, as his judgment based on the prevailing conditions may indicate.

Only in cases of appeal or referral on points of rules does he enter into the decisions that govern the actual play.

THE UMPIRE

The umpire is the principal official of a match. An umpire should be provided for each contest, even though it is not possible to enlist the services of any other official. To a limited extent, he can cover the assignments usually assigned to the ten linesmen. With an umpire in charge, considerable responsibility is removed from the shoulders of the contestants and greater fairness can be administered to both on most of the play situations that require decisions.

The umpire should have a seat on a platform which is at least five feet high. The platform should be centered on the line of the net extended and several feet away from the net post. Figure 11 shows such a platform, with an umpire seated and ready for duty.

The duties of the umpire in chronological order follow.

Wrong decisions annoy contestants

FIGURE 11. Umpire in um-
pire's chair, ready for duty.

Preliminary Duties

Like the officials in other sports the umpire in tennis has the usual routine pregame duties. He must:

1. Measure height of net at posts and at center and observe the net's condition and placement.
2. Check facilities for other officials.
3. Check necessary supplies of balls at the umpire's platform.
4. Secure scorecard and pencil.
5. Learn correct pronunciation of names of contestants.
6. Supervise the toss for the choice of court and service.
7. Prepare scorecard for first set.
8. Check and instruct other officials.
9. Start match promptly at scheduled time. Three minute warm-up is sufficient.
10. Determine readiness of other officials and announce match.

The umpire is the principal official

Duties during Match

1. Announce each player as he serves for the first time.
2. Record each point and then announce the score.
3. Announce all decisions that affect the play (for example, "out," "let," "fault," "not up").
4. Repeat any decisions made by other officials.
5. Change balls when necessary. The decision to replace the balls is the sole responsibility of the umpire.
6. Announce game, set, and match scores.
7. If no other officials are available, assume their duties.
8. Control disturbances by gallery.
9. Suspend play as circumstances require and make such other decisions as the proper conduct of the match may indicate.

Concluding Duties

1. Announce the final score and winner.
2. Record final score and winner.
3. Sign scorecard and file with proper officials.

NET UMPIRE

The net umpire is in a sense an assistant to the umpire. In this capacity, he should keep a duplicate score. In addition, he is responsible for calling "let," "fault," or "through." When the ball goes under or through the net and when requested by the umpire, he calls, "not up." His position is on the court level and near a net post.

There is usually insufficient personnel, so net umpires are not available. As a result, the umpire assumes the duties of the net umpire.

THE LINESMAN

If a full complement of officials is at hand, there are ten linesmen for each court. They are stationed in accordance with the positions shown in Diagram 9. The positions of the linesmen are designated by the number inside the square. Assignments are usually made by number. By superimposing the diagram on the court, one may locate without difficulty the position to which he has been assigned.

The linesmen should sit in chairs, which are placed as far from

The umpire announces the match, controls the crowd

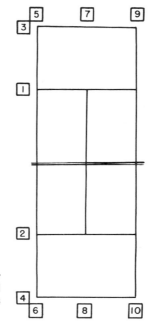

DIAGRAM 9.   Position of linesmen for a tennis match. Linesmen 5, 6, 9, and 10 also judge the sideline in a doubles match.

the boundaries of the courts as possible, in order to avoid interference with the players. The chairs should be of a dark color, preferably green, and the uniforms of the linesmen should be of dark color.

If all positions are not attended, the linesmen should be assigned to cover those stations which are most difficult for the umpire to see. These would be the base lines and the side and service lines farthest from the umpire.

The primary job of the linesman is to call "outs" on the lines assigned to him. He does not make decisions on any other lines. Neither does he make any comment if a ball is in play. The base linesmen who are stationed at positions 3 and 4 (Diagram 9) have the additional responsibility of calling foot faults. Figure 12 [2] is reproduced to show the five types of foot faults which may be committed. Figure 12 also shows the legal position for serving. See the two pictures in the bottom of the figure.

---

[2] *Umpire's Manual and Rules of Lawn Tennis* (New York: United States Lawn Tennis Association, 1948).

Linesmen dress dark, sit quietly

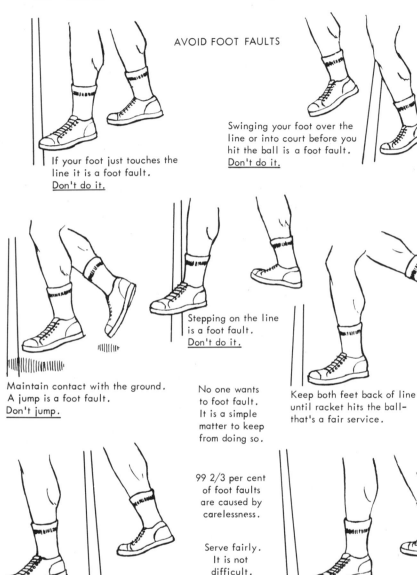

AVOID FOOT FAULTS

If your foot just touches the line it is a foot fault. <u>Don't do it.</u>

Swinging your foot over the line or into court before you hit the ball is a foot fault. <u>Don't do it.</u>

Stepping on the line is a foot fault. <u>Don't do it.</u>

Maintain contact with the ground. A jump is a foot fault. <u>Don't jump.</u>

No one wants to foot fault. It is a simple matter to keep from doing so.

Keep both feet back of line until racket hits the ball— that's a fair service.

99 2/3 per cent of foot faults are caused by carelessness.

Serve fairly. It is not difficult.

Stepping into the court is a foot fault. <u>Don't do it.</u>

Keep a little back of the line— like this—and avoid trouble.

FIGURE 12. The four top figures show types of foot faults. The bottom two are legal positions for serving.

Focus on court ahead of the ball

The following guides, if followed by linesmen, will aid in raising the efficiency of their work:

1. Be constantly on the alert and concentrate on the job at hand. Most decisions are not difficult. However, if one permits oneself to be distracted or if one relaxes one's vigilance for a moment, that is likely to be the moment when a close call escapes one.

2. Anticipate decisions but do not make an announcement until the ball hits the surface.

3. Watch the ball. If the direction of the ball is such that it may, in the judgment of a linesman, fall in the area for which he is responsible, the linesman should quickly focus his gaze on about the spot where he thinks the ball may hit. When the eyes are moving rapidly from one spot to another, one's vision is not accurate. For this reason, it is important that the focus be on the surface in advance of the ball in order to make reliable judgments.

4. The linesman should announce his decisions in a loud, clear voice. He announces a decision only when the ball is "out" or there is a "fault." No decision is ever announced when the ball is in play.

5. The linesman must not move about and must be quiet while play is in progress. Movements such as retrieving balls and smoking, and disturbances by talking are very disrupting to the players.

6. If, after making a decision, a linesman discovers that he is wrong, he should not hesitate to correct his mistake.

7. The linesman should wear dark clothes. White shirt or trousers create a bad background for the ball when it is between the linesman and the player who is facing him.

Announcing Techniques

A specific form and etiquette has been developed for announcing. It is important for the umpire to learn the announcing procedures and to follow them strictly. The established practices will serve the spectators best. The dignity and refinement peculiar to tennis will be maintained.

In the first place, all announcements should be timed so as to secure the greatest audience. The umpire should pause until any applause or confusion has subsided and then make his announce-

No decision is announced on ball in play

ment in a clear, strong, unhurried voice. The manner in which announcements are made can add much to the enjoyment of the match.

At the beginning of play, the umpire makes the following statement: "This match is between Mr. Doe and Mr. Roe. Mr. Doe is serving." If the contest is between schools or if it is a tournament between schools, the name of the school the player represents should also be given. It is important to get the correct pronunciation of each name. Most people are annoyed when their names are mispronounced. It is also customary to ask, "Linesmen, ready?" and then, when all is in readiness, to declare, "Play!"

The score of the game is announced after each point. The score of the server is always announced first. Thus, if the server wins the first point, the announcement is, "15-love." If he wins the second point and then loses the third, the announcements are in order: "30-love"; "30-15"; and so on until the game is finished. If there is a deuce game, the point after deuce is always announced in the following manner: "Advantage, Mr. Roe." No other terminology is acceptable.

At the end of the game, the winner is announced thus: "Game, Mr. Doe" or just "Game, Doe" omitting the formal titles. At the completion of each game, the games score should always be given, for example: "Game, Mr. Roe. Games are 3 to 2, first set; Mr. Roe leads."

If a game also determines the winner of a set, the announcement should be: "Game and first set, Mr. Doe, 6 to 4." After the first set, the set score is announced after every 3 or 4 games. As an example: "Games are 3 to 1; Mr. Roe leads, third set. Sets are 2 to 0; Mr. Doe leads."

At the conclusion of a match, the umpire says: "Game, set, and match, Mr. Roe; score, 6-4, 8-6, 3-6, 0-6, 14-12." The games won by the winner of the match are always announced first.

If, during the progress of a match, the umpire should make an error in announcing a score or a decision, he should correct the error immediately after it is discovered.

If it becomes necessary to ask the spectators to avoid the possibility of disconcerting the players, the umpire's statement should be a dignified, courteous appeal. Such an approach will not fail to gain the cooperation of the people in the stands. Applause during

There is etiquette and art to announcing

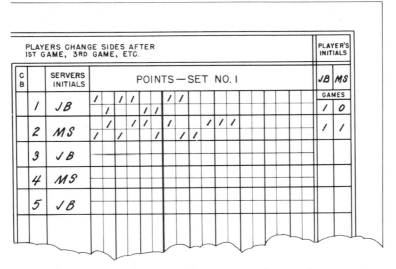

C B	SERVERS INITIALS	POINTS — SET NO. I	JB	MS
			GAMES	
1	JB	/ / / / / / /	/	0
2	MS	/ / / / / / / / / / / / /	/	/
3	JB			
4	MS			
5	JB			

PLAYERS CHANGE SIDES AFTER IST GAME, 3RD GAME, ETC.

PLAYER'S INITIALS

FORM III. A sample scorecard for tennis, showing the order in which the points were scored in the first two games of set number 1.

a rally and before a point is won, excessive mass movement, etc., can cause considerable annoyance to the players. When it persists, the umpire should speak up.

Scoring

Regulation scorecards are available for all matches. If special ones are not provided, printed forms will be found at the bottom of the boxes that contain a dozen balls.

A sample of such a scorecard is reproduced in Form III to illustrate the form and the method of keeping a score. In the upper left-hand corner of the card is space for the initials of the players. These initials head the columns in which a progressive game score is kept. To illustrate: J. B. won the first game, which is shown in column bearing his initials. The score of the opponent at this stage was "love" and is shown by the zero. M. S. won the second game. The next score in the column is thus shown as "1–1," and so on. It is wise for the umpire also to write out the names, so he will have a ready reference.

Prepare the score card in advance

In the left-hand column, the numbers refer to the game. The initials in the next column designate the player who serves each game. The service is alternated so, after the toss when the player who is to serve first is determined, the umpire should insert the initials of that player for the first game. He should then alternate the initials of the servers for each game for the first set. This should be done before play starts to prevent error in the record. For each succeeding set, the server's initials for each game should be inserted after the proper game before the set begins.

The tally marks in the squares on the body of the card indicate the winner of each point. The tallies in the top row of squares represent the scores for the server, and the tallies in the lower row of squares record the points scored for his opponent. Note that the order in which the points were scored is shown by the progressive position of the tally along the row. For example, in the first game, the order of scoring was as follows: J. B. was the server; he scored first, 15–love; 15–all; 30–15; 40–15; 40–30; deuce; advantage J. B.; game J. B.

This is a simple method for keeping a complete record that will avoid the possibility of mistakes. Umpires should record a score before announcing it, to reduce errors.

The score card should be signed at the bottom, when the match is completed. If, later, a question about a score should arise, it can be referred to the signing umpire.

Record the score before announcing it

chapter 12

VOLLEYBALL

Officiating volleyball demands the same qualifications and high standards of performance which prevail in any other sport: intense love of the game, many and varied experiences in officiating, thorough training, a basic philosophy of sport and officiating, the realization that as an official one is there to expedite the fullest enjoyment of the game by players and spectators under the rules, and a thorough knowledge of the game and its rules.[1]

---

[1] Marshall L. Walters, *Official Guide and Rule Book* (Published annually by the USVBA Printer, Box 109, Berne, Indiana, 46711).

Volleyball—a truly amateur sport in letter and spirit

Certification

The basic development of an official should begin in the class matches of school, college, YMCA, or club. The future official should experience serving as player, linesman, umpire, scorer, timer, and referee. Under the guidance and supervision of an experienced official one may then move up to inter-agency matches. Eventually one should seek a rating from the regional chairman of the United States Volleyball Association (USVBA) by officiating in regional tournaments.[2] The DGWS, Division of Girls' and Women's Sports, also operates a system of certification of officials for their organization.[3] The trend in the United States is for girls' and women's volleyball to follow the national USVBA rules and the game as played around the world, rather than maintain a separate set of rules.

The applicant for certification must pass a written test on the rules and conduct of matches. He is also rated during actual officiating of two or more matches by three or more certified officials. Certified rating is maintained by officiating at least every three years in regional or national tournaments, and being recertified by the Officials' Certification Committee. A listing of the certification committee members appears in the *Annual Guide*.

A · Team of Officials

The coordination of the team of officials is as important to a match as is the team work of the players. Necessary tournament officials are: referee, umpire, scorer, timer, linesmen.

Good officials need as much training and practice as good players. Practice sessions are a necessity. During these sessions one should analyze one's own performance, attitudes, and efficiency. *After* the matches one may want to seek suggestions from those players and coaches who show mature judgment and who are students of the game.

---

[2] Names and addresses appear in the *USVBA Guide and Rule Book*.

[3] DGWS, American Association for Health, Physical Education and Recreation, 1201 Sixteenth St., N.W., Washington, D.C. 20036.

Competent officials are developed by officiating

Clinics are another method of furthering the training of officials. These may be of only one-session duration or may run for several sessions. The clinic should make use of lectures, question and answer periods, discussions of problem situations, audio-visual aids, and actual participation and analysis. The clinic will be more meaningful if two or more good teams are in competition. If the level of play is poor, the officials tend to be lax. As a result, the experience has little value.

Clinics can be set up by colleges, schools, YMCA's, and others, but they should be planned under the direction of persons with experience in this area. Leads in procuring trained personnel can be found by contacting a USVBA Regional Representative.

It is not easy to become an official. In addition to deep interest in the game, knowledge of the rules, and good officiating mechanics, there is one paramount qualification: The person must have the personality qualifications. The kind of person who is a spotlight seeker, who takes the game away from the players, who takes an arrogant attitude, who is officious rather than an official, should be eliminated or eliminate himself from the beginning.

l.   THE LINESMEN

The linesmen may be looked upon as insignificant, but this is not true, any more than the foul line judge in a big league baseball game is insignificant. Linesmen must be alert; they must not become absorbed as a spectator and fail to note *exactly* where the ball hits the floor. In many cases championships have hung on the decision of the linesmen.

In informal matches two linesmen may be sufficient. These officials should be placed at opposite corners of the court. In tournament matches four linesmen should be used, one to be placed at the end of each of the four side-lines in order for the official to sight straight down the line.

The linesmen should stand, not sit. If seated the official may be a hazard to the players, but if standing the linesman can retreat from a ball being played.

The linesmen calling the back lines are also responsible for spotting a foot fault in the serve; that is, one who steps *on* or *over* the end line *before* the ball is hit on the serve. When a foot fault occurs

A line ball is in play

Ball in

FIGURE 13.   Linesman's signal indicating ball is in play.

Ball out

FIGURE 14.   Linesman's signal indicating ball is out of bounds.

the linesman should step into the court immediately with both arms upraised to get the attention of the umpire and referee and indicate by pointing to his foot, that a foot fault has taken place. The linesman does not ordinarily use a whistle.

The linesmen working the sidelines have the duty of watching balls that cross the net in the vicinity of the net sideline tapes, which are on the net, parallel with the sideline. Any ball crossing the net over, or inside these tapes is good. The ball must be completely outside the tape to be out.

A ball striking inside the court, or any part of the ball hitting the line is good. The linesman should indicate *immediately,* as soon as the ball hits the floor, whether or not the ball is good or out. The signal used is the same one used by the base umpire in baseball: both hands with palms down toward the floor, as shown in Figure 13, if the ball is good, the thumbs thrown back over the shoulders if the ball is out, as shown in Figure 14.

Touching the service line is a service foot fault

A ball is out if: 1) it hits outside the line, 2) it touches any part of a player who has any part of his body touching the area outside the line (if a player *thinks* a ball will go out, but it has not struck the floor as yet, and the player is inside the court, the ball is ruled good), and 3) the ball hits an object or apparatus outside the court.

2. THE TIMER

In tournaments with many entries, games are run on a time basis, as well as on the basis of 15 points. In time games the timer is one of the most important factors in the game. This person must be especially alert at all times.

Ordinarily an electronically controlled clock which shows minutes and seconds is used. A time game is eight minutes of actual ball-in-play time. The timer starts the clock at the exact moment the ball is contacted in the serve, and stops the clock at the moment the ball hits the floor or an out-of-bounds object, or the referee or umpire blows his whistle indicating a dead ball for a violation, error, or foul. In close matches, seconds can be all important, and therefore the timer must not allow the clock to start before the ball is in play or to keep running when it is dead.

Lacking an electric clock, the timer may use a sports timer on which he keeps running time and use an auxiliary watch or clock for time-outs. When such a system is used the timer should have some method of flipping over the timetable a sign device that shows the number of minutes remaining.

If the game has not been won by 15 points and the end of the 8 minutes is approaching, the timer should not sound the buzzer or noise device if the ball is in play and the 8 minutes expire. Such noise will distract the players and cause serious arguments. When the 8 minutes expire and the ball is in play, the timer waits until the ball is dead before notifying teams and officials by the sound system that time has run out.

3. THE SCORER

The score on the score sheet of the match scorer is the *official* score. The score appearing on scoreboards and other score sheets are for the benefit of players and spectators, but they are not *the*

The scorer keeps the order of the serve

official score. The scorer, therefore, must be alert at all times to the current play, to the officials, and to the records he is putting on his score sheet. The scorer should also check the public score device after each point or side out, in order to have this scoreboard match his official score sheet. An assistant to the scorer is an asset, as this assistant can call plays, be alert for substitutions, and act as a double check on procedures.

There should be at least one large scoreboard visible to both players and spectators. When the score device is on one side of the court, another should be placed so the score can be seen by spectators and officials from either side.

The scorer is seated at a desk or table opposite the referee and at a safe distance off the court. He should get the captains to observe his flip of the coin for choice of serve or court. The captains should then submit their lineups with the player numbers entered in the exact order in which they will serve.

When a substitute enters the game the scorer needs only his number, e.g., "Number 7 for Number 4." The scorer crosses out Number 7 and enters 4. The scorer must also be alert to the fact that Number 7 can only re-enter the game in the same relative position (see Substitution Rule).

The scorer must know positively at all times who served the ball and whether a point or a side out can be recorded. He must keep

FORM IV. A sample score sheet which merely shows the running score of a game.

VOLLEYBALL SCORE SHEET

PLACE _____ COURT _____ EVENT _____

DATE _____ TIME _____ MATCH NO. _____

REFEREE _____ UMPIRE _____ LINESMAN _____

WINNER _____ SCORE _____

FIRST GAME

TEAMS	1	2	3	4	5	6	7	8	9	10	11	12	13	14	15	16	17	18	FINAL
L.A.	X	X	X	X	X	X	X	X	X	X									10
CHIC.	X	X	X	X	X	X	X	X	X	X	X	X	X	X	X				15

The umpire calls center line and net contact fouls

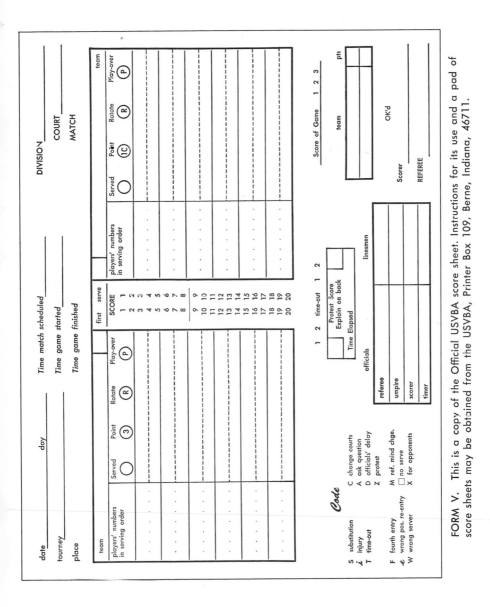

FORM V. This is a copy of the Official USVBA score sheet. Instructions for its use and a pad of score sheets may be obtained from the USVBA, Printer Box 109, Berne, Indiana, 46711.

The referee should look and act his part

a record of which player served and be alert that the players serve in the right order. The scorer must immediately correct any mistake in serving order and report it to the referee. He must keep an accurate record of the number of time outs in each game, and he must record points and side outs. The scorer should also record the date, place, time, tournament, teams playing, match number, court number, line-ups, and officials' names.

Instructions for use of the above form, and a pad of score sheets may be obtained from the USVBA Printer, Box 109, Berne, Indiana, 46711.

4   THE UMPIRE

The umpire takes a position on the floor, opposite the referee. His place in the game has been increasing in importance recently, and it is a rather safe prediction that volleyball will soon use the umpire as a second referee. Thus, one referee would be on the platform, with head above the net, and the second referee-umpire would be on the floor.

The uniform of the umpire matches that of the referee. The umpire is the official through which captains and coaches may ask for time out, ask for substitution, and request information on score or amount of time remaining.

The umpire takes a position outside the side of the court of the receiving team and makes decisions in regard to player position of the receiving team. After the serve the umpire calls plays relating to players crossing the center line. The umpire should learn from the referee to what degree the referee wishes the umpire to assist on calls involving ball handling.

5   THE REFEREE

The referee is the chief official, and should look and act the part. Organizations vary in their standards for the dress of the referee; even in class games the referee should have some type of neat, clean, distinguishing outfit. The United States Volleyball Association has a recommended uniform for both men and women (Details are found in the USVBA Guide). The referee's signaling device is ordinarily a whistle, but he may use a horn, buzzer, or other sound system. It is best if it is of a different tone than that of other officials.

Check with umpire before play starts

Prematch Procedures

The referee should be introduced by the tournament committee to the captains and coaches, or introduce himself to them. He should see that the flip of the coin in the presence of both captains is done well in advance of game time. He should determine game time and then notify both captains of the amount of warm-up time they have before the match begins. If there are any special ground rules he should be sure the players are aware of them. He should make it clear to the players and coaches how he will signal his calls, and how substitutions are to be made.

The referee should check the game ball for proper inflation and roundness. The net height should be checked for accuracy with a measuring stick. He should check the net tapes on the sidelines to be sure they line up with the side line. He should also check his team of officials. The linesmen should understand clearly how the referee will look to them for calls on close balls. He should be sure linesmen know how to indicate calls, and which lines they are responsible for, both floor lines and net tapes.

The referee should have a clear agreement with the umpire as to the decisions and calls he will expect the umpire to make and which the umpire is not to make. He should make sure the timer has tested his devices and knows the step by step method of timing. The referee also confers with the scorer and makes certain the scorer understands the procedures.

Position

The referee must be in a position at the end of the net with head and shoulders above the net. It is not possible to see over-the-net infractions from a floor position, nor from a balcony position far above the net.

Starting Play

Before the serve is made at the start of a game, after a time out, and after a substitution the referee should ask each captain if his team is ready for play to start. He should have instructed the captains to respond affirmatively by raising an arm when asked if "ready." The referee, after checking both captains, points toward

Have a plan to check the serve

FIGURE 15. Referee's signal to stop play. Hands are raised with a palm facing each court.

the server and sweeps the arm toward the opposite court, and with a short blast on the whistle calls "Play!"

The referee should establish some method of remembering which team has served. Some officials hold the whistle in the hand on the side of the serving team. Others shift the whistle to the side of the mouth of the serving team and keep the whistle there in order to make instantaneous calls. Some place the foot forward toward the side that serves and shift feet when the serve shifts. Many place a towel over the guy wire on the side of the serving team and shift it as the serve changes. Some system needs to become a habit.

After "play" has been declared, if it becomes necessary to stop the game before the ball is served, or for an emergency, the referee should give two short, sharp whistle blasts and hold up both hands with the palms open (see Figure 15).

The referee's head must be above the net

Ball in Play

Once the ball is in play the referee must keep his eye on the ball, with the peripheral vision ahead of the play. Both this direct concentration and the "field of play" vision are equally important and are attributes that are vitally necessary to a referee.

A referee must train to be able to keep the attention focused on the game every second and yet be physically relaxed. Otherwise, the official becomes fatigued quickly and in long matches the visual acuity will be impaired. To be at maximum efficiency no referee should work more than two matches in succession.

Net Play

When the play involves the ball being near the net the referee needs to crouch with his face level with the top of the net, one eye closed and the other sighting down the top tape of the net. There is no other method that can make the hair-line decisions necessary in over-the-net calls. On the instant that the offending player's hand or fingers go over the net the referee gives a blast on the whistle, gives the signal indicated in Figure 16, points to the offending player and calls out, "Number 6 over."

In cases where players of both teams are over the net, resulting in a double foul, the referee gives a whistle signal, makes the visual signal shown in Figure 17, and indicates the players who are over. It is most important not to anticipate over-the-net. Do not make the call *until* it occurs. When it does happen, do not hesitate with

FIGURE 16. Referee indicating that a net violation has been committed by a player to his right.

Then point to offender

Be technical on over-the-net violations

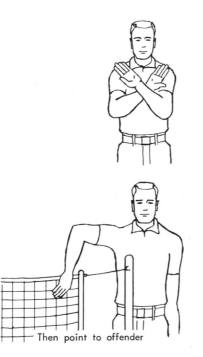

FIGURE 17. Referee's signal to indicate a net violation by each team.

Then point to offender

FIGURE 18. Referee's signal to indicate that a player has touched the net.

the whistle. If inadvertently the whistle is sounded ahead of the foul and no over-the-net actually took place, stop play, bring in both captains, honestly admit the error, and ask for a replay. Never attempt to "even up the calls." Better one error than many.

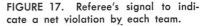 Touching the Net

Touching the net at any time the ball is in play is a violation. The referee and the umpire must be quick to recognize this call. Not many sports have the high code of ethics that volleyball enjoys. All top players are accustomed to calling their own net contacts, and the referee is honor bound to accept their call. The signal given by the referee is shown in Figure 18.

In order to determine if the served ball hits or "ticks" the net the referee cannot always trust his sight. Therefore, before each serve he should place one hand on the top cable of the net until the ball passes over the net. Even a slight contact can be felt by the referee.

A man's word is honored in volleyball

8 Playing the Ball

The greatest divergence of opinion and the widest interpretation between officials comes on the call of whether a ball is hit or whether it has been pushed or lifted. The rules state that the ball must be clearly and visually hit or batted. Some officials supply a narrow, ultra-strict application of this rule, and some even call the contact play from the sound.

The laws of physics tell us that any object when changing direction comes to rest a measurable amount of time. But the human eye cannot gauge such close measurements. The referee must learn to watch very carefully all ball contact by the players. Only by practicing and studying the work of certified referees can the prospective referee form accurate judgments that are valid and that conform to the modern game.

It is well for the referee to make a habit of complete concentration on the play. He may work out for himself such a technique as saying to himself, "a hit, hit, hit. . . . hit, hit, carry . . ." Whistle! Officials in all sports vary in their accuracy of calls. The factor players should expect is *consistency,* otherwise the player becomes confused.

a. A ball played underhand is not automatically a shove or carry. If the hand or fingers do not follow the ball in flight it is not a carry. If the ball rebounds from the hands with no lift visible it is played within the rules. If the fingers and/or wrists flex and follow the ball the referee should call a foul. The referee signal for such a call is shown in Figure 19.

FIGURE 19. Referee's signal to indicate the ball has been carried.

One, two, three, over

Close fingers twice

FIGURE 20. Referee's signal to indicate that a player has pushed or shoved the ball and has not batted it.

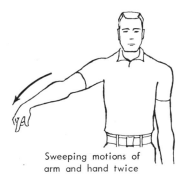

Sweeping motions of arm and hand twice

FIGURE 21. Referee's signal to indicate the spiker has thrown the ball and not batted it.

FIGURE 22. Referee's signal to indicate a player has hit the ball twice before it has been hit by another player.

If the ball comes to the player at chest height or higher the player makes the play overhand. The same principle holds in making calls, in that it must be hit or batted. If the fingers or hands follow and push or shove the ball, it is a foul. This call is shown in Figure 20.

The official must decide if the ball was batted or pushed

FIGURE 23. Referee's signal to indicate 4 hits by a team before batting ball across net.

If the ball is misplayed or the player makes an error with the ball skipping past the hands, it is not necessarily a foul. A held or pushed ball may occur not only on a pass play, but it is rather common for it to occur on a set-up, and some referees have a tendency to allow this violation of the rules to get by. On the spike or attack the ball must be hit, not pushed or thrown. The referee will indicate a pushing or throwing violation as shown in Figure 21. This violation takes place in almost all instances when both hands are used to propel the ball downward into the court of the opposition.

When a ball is hit twice in succession by the same player before it has been touched by a teammate, it is a double hit. This call is indicated in Figure 22. The ball may have only three distinct contacts before it is returned over the net. The referee is responsible for keeping count of the contacts. If a fourth contact takes place, he indicates the violation as shown in Figure 23.

Point or Side-out

When a point is scored the referee should call, "Point" and raise his arm with forefinger pointed upward on the side of the team that scored the point as shown in Figure 24. He should keep his arm upraised until he is sure that both teams recognize the call and that the scorer has seen the call and recorded the point on the scoreboard.

If the play results in a side-out and no point is to be scored, the referee should extend the arm at a point lower than the hips, to-

Never even up the calls

Then point to team requesting

FIGURE 24. Referee's signal to indicate a point has been scored.

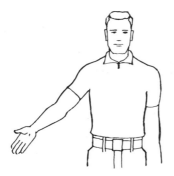

FIGURE 25. Referee's signal to indicate side out—no score.

ward the team that is to receive the ball for the serve. This call is shown in Figure 25. Some referees also rotate the arm in a circular fashion indicating the team must rotate.

Other Calls

When a time-out is asked for by the manager, captain, or coach, the referee should indicate such. The request may also be made to the scorer or umpire who then signals the referee. The referee indicates this time-out as shown in Figure 26. If time is called because of injury, or is needed by any of the officials, the referee points to himself. If called by a team he points to that team.

The umpire ordinarily makes the call for over-the-center line. Whether the umpire or the referee makes the call the referee should give the signal shown in Figure 27, point to the offending player, and call out, "Number 12 over the line."

When a team indicates they are making a substitution at the time

Better one error than many

FIGURE 26. Referee's signal for time-out.

For official's time out then point to self

FIGURE 27. Referee's signal to indicate a player has touched the opposite court across the line of the net.

Then point to offender

FIGURE 28. Referee's signal to indicate a substitution.

Then point to team

the ball is dead, the new player must take the place of the player being removed at once with no warm up or stalling. The referee uses the signal shown in Figure 28. If too much time is used he charges the team with a time-out. Otherwise no time-out is charged.

When players are out of position on the serve, the referee stops

Underhand hit not automatically a carry

FIGURE 29. Referee's signal to indicate players are out of position on the serve.

FIGURE 30. Referee's signal for a technical foul.

FIGURE 31. Referee's signal to call attention to good sportsmanship by a player.

play and makes a call with a signal as shown in Figure 29. He and the umpire indicate to the captain of the offending team the players who were out of position.

If any infraction of the rules calls for a technical foul the referee gives the signal shown in Figure 30. It is good practice for the

Don't be a whistle tooter

referee to give one warning to the players or the bench occupants before making such a call.

As previously pointed out, the sportsmanship in volleyball is of the highest order. Therefore, when a player indicates he has touched a ball even though no official detected it, or when he calls net contact when no official noticed the touch, the referee gives the signal shown in Figure 31, directing his motion toward the player or players.

Use of the Whistle

Nothing is as disturbing to players and spectators as the "whistle tooter," that official who blows long and loud for every small detail. A good referee uses the whistle when necessary to indicate an infraction, foul or violation, or to stop play. A short blast is sufficient. It is not necessary to toot a whistle when a ball has sailed into the balcony, or when a ball has been driven by a spiker into the opponent's court. Underuse of the whistle is also disturbing. Those present should know the instant play starts and ends. And they need to know the instant it occurs, not some time later.

Attitude

Officials need to maintain a pleasant, courteous attitude toward all players and spectators, but this must be blended with firmness and fairness. The best officiated match is that in which players, coaches, and spectators are hardly aware that the official is part of the contest. It is not out of place for the referee to compliment players or teams on excellent play, after the match, or to thank them for their sportsmanship and cooperation. As much importance should be placed on the study of human nature as on becoming a master of the rules. Volleyball has remained an amateur sport as has no other. The officials are one of the main keys in helping it to remain amateur in spirit and attitude!

Be pleasant and courteous

chapter 13

BADMINTON

The job of officiating a badminton match is in many respects similar to that of handling a tennis match. Although the action is fast, the shuttle, because of its construction, moves fairly slowly and tends to float or sail. It does not bounce like the tennis ball. Consequently, it is much easier to make decisions on the shuttle than it is on the tennis ball.

Fewer officials, particularly linesmen, are needed for a badminton game. An umpire and eight linesmen conduct the match. This is two linesmen less than for tennis. Actually, four can handle the match effectively. The umpire can make the short-service line deci-

Badminton is similar to tennis—but is simpler

sions easily because this line is only six and one-half feet from the
net. This eliminates two linesmen. The four linesmen who cover
the side boundary lines can also rule on play at the back boundary
line and the long service line in doubles matches. This eliminates
two more linesmen. There may be a referee. This official is customarily present in a tournament but may not be appointed for other
matches.

Umpire

The umpire should be on an elevated platform as in tennis. He
is the head official of a match. In the absence of a referee, he is the
court of final appeal on any point in dispute.

It is his duty to appoint linesmen at his discretion. Although the
umpire's decision is final, he should uphold the decision of a linesman. The umpire shall call "fault" or "let" when either occurs, without an appeal from the players.

For the positions of the officials on the court, the reader is referred to Diagram 10. The officials who are indicated by an "X"
with a square around it are the linesmen who may be eliminated.

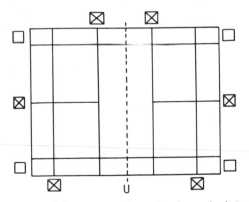

DIAGRAM 10.   Position of linesman and umpire for a badminton
match. The linesmen indicated by the boxes marked X may be
eliminated if space is limited without jeopardizing the effectiveness
of the officiating.

The umpire should uphold the decision of a linesman

Helpful Guides to Efficient Officiating

1. Check the height of the net.
2. Place and instruct linesmen.
3. If the rules of the match permit, have three or four correctly-weighted shuttles ready for play.
4. Do not change shuttles without good reason.

1. Watch to see that the shuttle when struck is below the server's waist. Linesmen, who are on the floor, are in a better position to judge this point. This duty should be delegated to a linesman.
2. Watch for a "let."
3. Watch that the player on the "out" side does not leave his court before the service is delivered.
4. Watch for scoop or throw shots; they are illegal.

1. Always watch the shuttle.
2. The player who strikes a shuttle before it passes the net loses the point.
3. Touching the net or supports with the racket, person, or clothes before the shuttle is dead costs the point.
4. Keep track of the number of hands in. It is easy to make mistakes on this point unless great care is exercised. It may be advisable to keep a written record of this point. See Form VI for a suggested method. As a player finishes his serve, an "X" is drawn through his initials. This indicates that the next player in order is the next to serve. The initials of the players are in rotation.
5. When a score at which setting is permissible is reached, the player who first attained this score should be asked if he wishes to set.
6. See that the players change sides at the proper score in the third game.

Number of hands in—be alert at this point

BADMINTON SCORE CARD

~~SINGLES~~
DOUBLES   MATCH — BILL J. / FRED M. — VS — JOHN D. / TED S. — DATE 10/10

HAND IN	B.J.	J.D.	T.S.	B.J.	F.M.	F.M.					
PLAYERS											

B.J. – F.M.	X	X	3	4	5	6	7	8	9	10	11	12	13	14	15	16	17	18	19	20
J.D. – T.S.	1	2	3	4	5	6	7	8	9	10	11	12	13	14	15	16	17	18	19	20
	21	22	23	24	25															
	21	22	23	24	25															

FORM VI. Umpire's score card for keeping a record of Hand In and of continuous score in a badminton game.

General

1. Officials should not be influenced by the players or spectators in making their decisions. Promptness in making decisions will avoid this.

2. An official should not make a decision if he is unable to do so. The opinion of the players may be accepted if they agree. Otherwise, the official must call a "let."

3. Decisions should be given promptly, but they should not be anticipated.

4. The score should be announced at the end of each rally. This should be done in a clear, loud voice that can be heard by both the players and spectators.

5. A linesman's decision on all points relative to the line over which he has jurisdiction is absolutely final.

6. The umpire should keep a written record of the score. A sample score card is shown in Form VI.

7. At the conclusion of a match, the score should be filed with the proper authority.

Scoops are illegal

8. The reader is referred to the chapter on tennis for further suggestions in the techniques of officiating a badminton match. Much of the procedure recommended for tennis is applicable to badminton. The reader must, of course, make the necessary adaptations in accordance with the rules and nomenclature for badminton.

Always watch the shuttle

chapter 14

HANDBALL

It is believed that handball is one of man's oldest games. Archeologists have discovered evidence of games played with a ball, the hand, and a wall from the times of early Egypt. From this simple type of competition many other games have developed.

Because of this development of the basic sport it is natural that several types of handball now exist. There is the one-wall, softball type of game of Celtic origin, still played in the Lackawanna Valley of Pennsylvania by the Welch and the Irish. There is the one-wall, hardball type of game played mainly in the Northeast. There is also a three-wall game, which seems closely related to the games of Fronton and Jai Lai.

Two basic sets of rules exist—decide which to use

Since officiating in any of these types of handball is similar, most of the guiding principles will apply to all. The official should, of course, be a student of the rules under which the tournament or matches are being conducted. In the four-wall game there are two basic sets of rules, the main variance being in the court dimensions. The most popular set of rules is that used by the YMCA and many clubs.[1] The Amateur Athletic Union also publishes a set of four-wall rules and one-wall rules.[2]

In the game of handball, singles or doubles, only two officials are used: a referee and a scorer. For official matches and tournaments these two persons should have been trained as players and as officials of informal competition. They should have observed experienced officials and called tournament matches under the watchful eyes of more experienced officials.

The Scorer

The scorer records the scoring as announced by the referee: points made, hand-outs, service. He should also announce the score after the completion of a point or hand-out so players and spectators know the standings. He should give the server's score first. If the player serving is leading he would announce "18–11." If the player behind was serving his call would be "11–18." Some scorers have the habit of saying "18 serving 11," or "11 serving 18."

The scorer needs to use some type of official score sheet. On it should be recorded date, place, match or tournament, players' names, court number, time, final score, and winners. The scorer and referee should sign the sheet after the match.

The Referee

The referee is the judge and jury for all decisions during play. He should know the rules thoroughly and be intimately conversant with all shades of interpretations on close decisions.

---

[1] *Official Unified Handball Rules,* Champion Glove Manufacturing Company, 2200 East Ovid, Des Moines, Iowa.

[2] *Official Handball Rules,* Amateur Athletic Union, 233 Broadway, New York, N. Y., 10007.

The server's score is announced first

HANDBALL SCORE CARD

PLACE _____ COURT NO. _____ DATE _____ TIME _____

EVENT _____ MATCH NO. _____

WINNER _____ SCORES _____

PLAYERS	1	2	3	4	5	6	7	8	9	10	11	12	13	14	15	16	17	18	19	20	21	22	23	24	25	26	FINAL
JONES	x	x	x	x	x	x	x	x	x	x	x	x	x	x	x	x	x	x	x	x							21
DAVIS	x	x	x	x	x	x	x	x	x																		9

JONES	X		X1X2X	X		X3X		X4X		X5X6X 7X		X8X9X	X10X11X
DAVIS	X1X		X2X		X		X3X		X		X4X		X5X	X

X12X13X 14X	X15X16X	X17X		X18X19X	X20X21					21
X6X		X		X7X8X	X9X					9

FORM VII. A sample scorecard showing two methods of keeping
score. The record at the top merely shows the score at a particular
stage of the game. That at the bottom gives a complete record of the
order in which scores were made together with a serving record of
each player. The latter is preferred.

For reasons not yet determined, handball seems to draw more
arguments from the players than most sports. Therefore, the referee
should know his rules well and have a pleasant personality, yet he
should make decisions fairly and immediately. His decisions are
final, and it is best that he let the players know his firmness and
thus to terminate any arguments about his decisions from the
beginning.

The referee should introduce the players to each other, to himself, and to the scorer and then flip a coin to determine who shall
serve first in the first and third games. He should make it clear to
the players how much time they have for warm-up and warn them
when only three minutes remain before the game begins. He should
test the match balls for rebound and be certain that all shirts,
towels, or other matter are out of the court before the match starts.

Just before the first game the referee introduces the players to
the spectators. He should then ask players if they are ready, and

In case of doubt call for a replay

call "play." It is important that he have a system of remembering who serves. He may hold in the right hand the server's card with name then shift to the left hand when the player loses the serve. Or he may have a card with the players' names on opposite sides and turn the card over as the serve shifts.

The referee should make sure to call foot faults from the start. Many players have a bad habit of foot faulting, and unless called from the beginning useless bickering will result.

The most debatable point in handball is the call on "hinders" or interference with opponent's play, or of "avoidable hinders." No rule of thumb can be used in these calls; only experience can teach a referee the difference. A player may move and commit an intentional interference, or he may move and make an unintentional interference. The same possibilities are present if a man does not move. A player is entitled to a fair chance to see the ball and to play the ball. Any movement or failure to move out of the way by an opponent can cause a "hinder."

The referee should not wait for a player to protest he could not play or see the ball, for it is the referee who must make this call. The referee must be fast and decisive on these calls, not being antagonistic in voice or attitude, but letting it be known he is calling these plays and the contestants are making these plays.

A favorite procedure with some players is to stall for time. They may do this to work a psychological advantage or in a long match they may do this to get a rest. Such tricks as wiping with a towel, getting a drink, wiping off the ball, bouncing the ball more than three times on the serve, are a few samples of stalling. A player is allowed ten seconds to make the serve, but he must also allow his opponent to be in position and to get set for the serve. To avoid the wet-ball stall, the referee should keep extra balls handy and throw in a dry ball when he judges the ball being played to be wet.

Not more than two minutes is allowed between the first and second games of a match, and the players may not leave the court without approval of the referee. Between the second and third games the maximum rest period is ten minutes, but in this period the players may leave the court without permission.

Another call for the referee to make is a "short." If a serve is illegal for any of the six reasons under the rules, the referee immediately calls "short." If this is on the first serve and the opponent

Avoid the wet-ball stall

does not play it, the call remains a "short." If the opponent chooses to play it, then the serve is deemed good and play continues. If the second serve is also a "short" or illegal serve, then it cannot be played and a hand-out results.

Before the match starts the referee should make plain to the contestants that in case of double hinders or infractions, or where he decides he acted too quickly and made a bad call, he has the right to ask for a replay. In four-wall handball the position of the referee is generally in the balcony. In the Celtic outdoor, one-wall game he stands outside the court and outside one side line but must "float" up and down the line as the positions of the players change.

The referee in handball is the key to the atmosphere that permeates the match. The right kind of practice for the referee will increase competence, but practice does not necessarily make perfect if the practice is faulty!

PART THREE

The officiating techniques discussed in this section of the book include those for football, basketball, soccer, wrestling, hockey, lacrosse, and skiing. These are the sports that, for the most part, require in their administration the discriminating judgment of the official. They are the sports in which the decisions depend upon the effect created.

The rules in these sports permit the official to exercise discretion. Because of this fact, considerable space is devoted to the development of guides to specific play situations. This is by way of implementing the philosophy expressed in Part One and of providing bases for uniformity in officiating.

chapter 15

FOOTBALL

Any directions which are given in the football rule book for the guidance of the officials in carrying out their duties will be found in the back of the rule book [1] under the heading, "The Officials— Jurisdiction and Duties." With these as a pattern, and from years of experience in the administration of contests, a rather definite plan of operation has been developed. This plan will be presented in the order in which the officials perform their duties. Since games are conducted by both four and five officials, their duties and methods of working are presented under both conditions. The commis-

---

[1] *Official Football Rules* (New York: National Collegiate Athletic Bureau, 1967).

sioners of college conferences have worked out a manual of football officiating,[2] which is now rather universally adopted. The treatment here follows the outline of this manual in some respects, but goes beyond this manual by attempting to give a background upon which to develop the art of football officiating. In addition, specific play situations are discussed. The procedure here is intended to assist the novice as well as the seasoned official. As a general guide, the following seven hints are given at the outset. Detailed development follows.

Officials

1. The referee is the commander-in-chief who has general control of the game.

2. All officials have concurrent jurisdiction and responsibility for the enforcement of the rules.

3. The field judge (or back judge in a five-official game) is responsible for the time.

4. The umpire's primary responsibilities are to observe the action of the linesmen during each scrimmage.

5. The head linesman is primarily responsible for ruling on play involving the neutral zone. He should always know the down and check with the referee on this point when necessary.

6. Signal to indicate a foul does not stop the play.

7. The sound of any official's whistle causes a live ball to become dead. The referee, however, blows his whistle to declare a dead ball in most situations.

These points are listed here to emphasize the primary jobs of each official and thus to give a bird's-eye view of the total coordinated job of officiating a game. In doing this, there is no intention of minimizing the importance of other duties, which are discussed subsequently.

B. PREGAME DUTIES

The officials have four specific duties to perform before the game actually begins.

---

[2] *Manual of Football Officiating*, National Association of Football Commissioners, Eastern College Athletic Conference, Biltmore Hotel, New York.

Don't neglect pregame duties

1. The first of these duties might be classed as partly social. It consists of getting acquainted, of reviewing duties, of discussing methods of cooperation on the field, of checking personal equipment (such as horns, guns, watches, pencils, record cards, and signal devices).

The referee should take the leadership in this meeting. If he desires any special arrangements, here is the place to instruct his fellow officials. In this way clashes of personalities on the field can be avoided and full harmonious cooperation secured.

2. The officials have duties with respect to equipment and facilities. The referee must inspect the ball and then turn it over to the field judge. He must also inspect the field to see that it is properly laid out and marked. Many times, through oversight or error, mistakes that may create embarrassing problems have been discovered. For example, on one occasion an end zone was found to be 15 yards long on one side. On another occasion, when a severe storm had hit in the morning before a game, the lines were entirely obliterated. Special corner markings had to be set up by the officials, and chains were strung on both sides of the field so that the officials might sight across to get bearings. Fields that are not marked off in five-yard distances make certain phases of officiating difficult.

As a result of spilled lime or poor marking, the goal line sometimes is irregular—too broad in some places and indistinct in others. Close goal-line decisions—and there are many of them—can be made very difficult unless situations of this kind are observed and corrected before game time.

The surroundings should also be checked for obstructions and hazards. The yard line markers may be constructed of hard, sharp materials and may be placed too close to the side lines. Any serious conditions should be corrected before the game begins. For this reason, the referee should make his inspection 15 to 30 minutes before game time.

The umpire is required by rule to inspect the equipment of players to see that it is legal according to the rules. He must also inspect the taping and bandaging of players to make sure that nothing is worn that might be dangerous to an opponent. The head linesman should secure the chain that is to be used and check its length and condition. The field judge should check the timing de-

Check the field, check the chain, check the timepiece

vices if an electric field timer, which is operated from the side lines, is to be used.

3. The head linesman will need three assistants. He should select an assistant linesman who will hold the down marker at the side lines and two chainmen who will hold each end of the chain. Sometimes, it is possible to have a neutral assistant linesman, but usually both the assistant linesmen and one of the chainmen are associated with the home team. The other chainman will be assigned from the visiting team.

The instructions to these assistants are most important. It must be emphasized to them that they must not make any moves whatever unless directed to do so by the head linesman. To act otherwise could cause great confusion.

For example, if the chainmen were to move the chains and the assistant the stake, after a punt, before being directed to do so, and a penalty should occur that would require that the ball be brought back and played over, it is evident what problems would arise.

Specific instructions for the assistant linesmen are:

a. The assistant should place his stake on the side line at the forward point of the ball as directed by the head linesman.

b. He should turn his stake to indicate the proper down.

c. He should never move the stake nor change the down until directed to do so by the head linesman.

The chainmen should:

a. Be placed so that the chainman associated with the home team is holding the end of the chain that is toward the goal defended by his team. The other chainman will, of course, hold the opposite end. In this way the head linesman will have no worries about the chain being held taut at all times. The head linesman will always direct the placing of that end of the chain on the side line which is nearer the forward point of the ball at the beginning of each new series of downs.

b. Be cautioned never to move the chains until directed to do so.

c. When play comes close to the side line, in order to prevent injury, the chainman nearer the point where the play may go out-of-bounds should move his stake away from the side line. If the other end is held in place, the position of the chain will not be lost.

An officiating sin—to move the chain without orders

The field judge, when time is to be kept with an electric timer, must check with those who are to operate the clock:

a. To make sure they know when to start the clock. (The clock starts only when the ball is put in play after time is out, except by order of referee.)

b. To demonstrate the signals for time-out. The clock is stopped only upon signal from the referee. (The signal is always repeated by other officials.)

c. To advise concerning notification when four minutes remain in each half.

d. In cases where the field judge keeps time on the field, he should cooperate with the scoreboard operators. They will need regular information on time remaining to play in each period. He should also keep the referee informed concerning the time remaining to play, as the end of the second and fourth periods approaches.

Diagram 11 illustrates the arrangements of the chainmen and assistant linesmen.

4. The last pregame duty of the officials is to meet with the captains in the center of the field for making the toss. The umpire and head linesman upon completion of their specific duties shall go to the linesman's side and remain seated until three minutes before game time. The referee and field judge shall occupy the bench opposite the linesmen. Each pair shall escort the captain or captains on his side to the center of the field.

The following duties are performed:

a. Everyone should be introduced. The officials should determine the playing position of each captain.

b. Any special instructions should be given, special arrangements explained, any questions answered, and requested interpretations given.

DIAGRAM 11. Positions for the chainmen and linesman for a scrimmage play. ⊠ indicates down marker.

The time-out signal is most important

c. The referee makes the toss after designating the visiting team captain to call it. The winner is indicated by placing a hand on his shoulder. The proper signal should be given to indicate the choice: a kicking movement of the leg for choice to kick, a catching movement to signal the choice to receive, a point to goal to indicate the choice of goal.

The choices left to the loser should be explained, and the selection made should be properly signaled. Each official should make a written record of the winner of the toss and his choice.

The game is then ready to be started.

The Kickoff

The positions of the officials at the kickoff are shown in Diagram 12. The positions indicated permit the officials to surround the play and at the same time to cooperate in covering all possible play situations that may occur at the kickoff. The positions of the officials on the field are determined by the position taken by the head linesman. He has previously placed his assistants and so must take a position on the same side of the field with them.

The head linesman will take a position on the receiving team's 20-yard line and not more than five yards inside the side line. He must be sure that he does not obstruct the view or interfere with any member of the receiving team.

The referee will take a similar position on the opposite side of the field from the head linesman.

These two officials will cover the runback of the kickoff and all play immediately converging on the ball carrier. They will make decisions on out-of-bounds plays on their side of the field.

The umpire takes a position on the side line on the same side of the field as the head linesman and between the restraining lines of the receiving team. The chief responsibility of the umpire on the kickoff is to see that the receiving team does not violate the rules pertaining to the restraining line for the receiving team. After the kick, unless it is a short one, he observes the blocking of players as they move toward the ball carrier.

The field judge is responsible for the ball and for the enforce-

At kick-off, the position of the head linesman sets the others

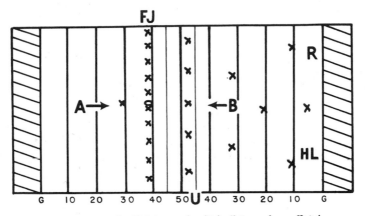

DIAGRAM 12.   Positions of officials at the kickoff in a four-official game.

ment of the rules pertaining to the restraining line for the kicking team. The field judge stands by the ball until everything is in readiness for the kick. He then goes to the end of the restraining line for the kicking team and on the opposite side of the field from the head linesman. After the kick, his duties become the same as those of the umpire. In case of a short kick, he or the umpire observes the play immediately surrounding the ball.

The field judge should help the referee to get the ready signal from the captain of the kicking team. The attention of the other captain should be secured by the official who is nearest to him. The head linesman, umpire, and field judge should indicate their readiness to the referee by an upraised hand.

When the captains, the officials, and the timekeepers (when the time is kept on the side lines) have indicated their readiness, the referee who has had his arm raised above his head as a signal for readiness to play, drops his arm and sounds his whistle for play to begin.

When the ball becomes dead following the kickoff or at any other time during the game, the referee shall blow his whistle. If an official other than the referee is administering the play of the ball carrier, he shall indicate a dead ball by blowing his whistle. The referee will, of course, look to the official who has whistled the ball dead for guidance in any decisions incident thereto. This same

The officials surround the play

procedure shall apply on all kick plays at any time during the game and on all kicks following a safety.

As play starts, the officials should be on the alert for any rule violations. The usual situations for which decisions may be required on the kickoff are the following:

1. Restraining-line violations.
2. Kicks out-of-bounds.
3. Kicks into end zone.
4. Fouls with ball in possession of neither team.
5. Clipping and illegal use of hands.
6. Fumbles and legal possession.
7. Out-of-bounds play.
8. Dead ball.

Scrimmage Play

On all scrimmage plays, the referee takes a position behind the offensive team. He should take a position behind the deepest backfield man and toward the nearer side line. If the ball is in the center of the field, and he has discovered that a team is running most of its plays to the right, then the preferable position would be on the left side of the deep back. The referee must always be able to see the ball and, if possible, all backfield men, in order to be able to rule on the legality of the start of a play. He must always be able to see the ball throughout the scrimmage. The referee must be able to see the movement of the backs in relation to the snap of the ball. This is his primary job on all scrimmage plays.

The head linesman stays on the same side of the field as his assistants. He should take a position from ten to fifteen yards from the nearer end of the line of scrimmage, so that he can see clearly all players on the lines of scrimmage. He must always be outside any flanker back, in order to determine legality of position for passes. His primary job is to administer the rules that govern the encroachment upon the neutral zone, before the ball has been put in play. The head linesman assists the referee in determining the forward point of the ball on his side.

The umpire assumes a position behind the defensive team. He probably will not be closer than five yards to the line of scrimmage

Any official's whistle stops the play

nor more than ten yards away. It is his primary duty to observe the blocking and the use of the hands of both the offense and defense on the line of scrimmage in particular, and of the linebackers. The impossibility of sharply focusing attention on approximately 15 players at one time requires the umpire to change his focus of attention on practically every play. Consequently, he will be ranging somewhere between the defensive ends. He must be careful that he does not obstruct the view of defensive linebackers nor interfere with movement during forward-pass plays. An effective umpire will not be concerned with the ball. Rather, he will be concentrating on all other players but the ball carrier. The players should find him looking at their blocking maneuvers. The potential of presence created by such a situation will do much to discourage illegal blocking. An umpire who is able to keep a game free from illegal play by such tactics deserves a very high rating. It is much more to the credit of an umpire to be knocked down during a scrimmage play because he is not watching the ball than it is to be constantly, showing the referee where to place the ball at the end of a scrimmage. This latter is the duty of the referee.

The field judge stations himself on the side of the field opposite from the head linesman and the same distance from the end of the line as indicated for the head linesman. He watches for off side play and other fouls on his side of the field. Both the field judge and the head linesman must be ready to cover passes and kicks down the field. They can often anticipate such play situations and thus be on the move after the ball is snapped.

The decisions of the head linesman must also be reasonable and realistic. To be hypertechnical is the greatest weakness of head linesmen. In carrying out their duties they should exercise the discretion allowed them by the rules. In this respect the same caution should be given to the umpire. It has been said that few plays in football have been completely free from illegal blocking. Nor is this fact particularly important. It is important, however, to see that a player is not unfairly affected by an illegal act. In such instances, the experience and good judgment of the official must be relied upon.

From scrimmage, the common situations requiring official attention and, frequently, action are the following:

1. *Shift or motion plays.* These are the primary responsibility

The referee must always see the ball

of the referee, as already noted. However, the head linesman and the field judge can assist in determining forward motion on spread plays or flankers where it is difficult for the referee to keep all backs and the ball in his field of vision. It is important that the referee be alert to prevent illegal shifts. This requires a careful analysis of the rules, which is not a part of this text. The referee must be sure that the offensive team does not get an advantage by a premature start or an illegal shift.

2. *Off side play or encroachment on the neutral zone.* The head linesman and the field judge are actually the only officials who are in a position to make a decision on this play. They must use discretion in administering the rules on this phase of the game.

Inexperienced players quite often fail to get up to the line of scrimmage on offense. In most cases, this violation is of greater detriment to the team committing it than to the opponent. The officials should bear this in mind and thus be realistic in their judgments.

Likewise, a finger or a swinging hand slightly ahead of the near point of the ball probably makes little difference in the play. A word of caution from the officials is usually sufficient to correct an error of which the player is not conscious.

The situations from which a real advantage is gained are those which involve actual movement or change on offense just before the ball is put in play. These are the violations which require action on the part of the officials so opponents will not be placed at a disadvantage.

3. *Blocking maneuvers of all kinds.* These involve the blocking that occurs in the line to displace linemen or to prevent them from getting to the ball carrier. They include the attempts of the offense to screen out the secondary defense in order to provide a breakaway for a ball carrier in case he gets beyond the line of scrimmage, and are particularly concerned with the hand, arm, and body tactics of the personal interferers for the ball carrier.

Here again the insignificant and inconsequential violations, which invariably and unavoidably occur during a play, do not constitute cause for action on the part of the official. As in other instances already mentioned, he must use discretion. His judgments must be conditioned by the possible effect such violations may have upon the play.

Umpire—observe the block—leave the ball to the referee

The acts of holding, locking a leg with the upper arm, extending the arms full length from the body in order to reach an opponent, use of the hands and forearms as a flail in driving an opponent back or striking him in the face or under the chin, slipping and grabbing the foot of the opponent in close line play so that he cannot lift it from the ground in stepping or retreating, are the types of fouls for which officials must be alert to take immediate action.

All four officials will be in position to make decisions on plays that involve the illegal use of the arms, hands, and body. The umpire is in the best position to watch the close line-play and the secondary defense. In addition, the head linesman and field judge will assist in watching the players on the end of the line nearer to them. The referee is in the best position to observe the action of the ball carrier, players immediately ahead of the ball carrier, and particularly the personal interferers for the ball carrier. The other officials can best cover the down-field blocking and any other action that may come to their attention from their positions where they can get an over-all view of the play.

4. *Delay of the game.* After the ball is ready for play, the offensive team has 25 seconds in which to get the ball in play. It is the referee's duty to enforce this requirement. He must be particularly conscious of this situation toward the end of a game. The team in possession of the ball is attempting to protect a lead by consuming as much time as possible on each play. It is expected, however, that the game will be kept moving with as little delay as possible throughout all periods.

Diagram 13 shows the position of the officials on a scrimmage play.

Runs From Scrimmage

The positions shown in Diagram 13 are the starting positions for running and pass plays from scrimmage. When the ball is snapped, the referee is the only official who moves with the play. He should watch the play carefully and follow closely enough to see the ball at all times and be able to catch the forward progress of the ball when the play is finished. He must not, however, be so close that

Don't be hypertechnical

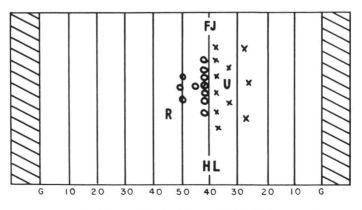

DIAGRAM 13.   Positions of officials for a scrimmage play.

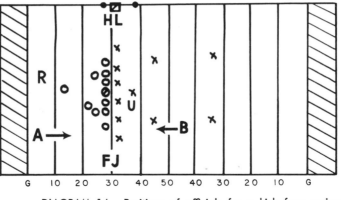

DIAGRAM 14.   Positions of officials for a kick from scrimmage.

he would interfere with a backward pass or a fumble. It is better for the referee to keep somewhat to the rear and to the side of the ball carrier, when he declares the ball dead. It is not a bad habit to inform the players that he sees the ball and has marked the forward point of progress. This practice tends to eliminate continued charging on the part of both teams. It also gives the players confidence in the referee. They feel that he is right on top of every play and will permit no unfair advantage.

Are you prone to call an illegal shift?

The referee, of all the officials, must be in top physical condition. He does more running than any player, because he is following the ball on every running play by either team.

1. He observes the forward point of the ball. The field judge or linesman may assist him by placing the foot foward to indicate the forward point.

When the ball is dead, the referee follows a set routine:

2. He looks toward the linesmen's chains to determine the distance to be gained for a first down. This is done before he rotates the ball into position for the next play.

3. He checks with the head linesman to determine the down.

4. He then places the ball in position for the next play. If it was in the outer third of the field, he moves it to the inbound line.

5. He declares the down and distance and drops his arm to indicate readiness for the next play.

The head linesman must focus on the two lines until the ball is put into play. When this duty is finished, he follows the play. When the ball is dead, he places a foot in line with the forward point of the ball so the referee can determine the yardage to be gained for a first down. He next signals the down to the referee.

When the head linesman has checked to see that no penalty has been called, he motions the assistant linesman to place the down marker in line with the forward progress of the ball. After a first down has been declared by the referee, he motions the chainmen to move up with the chains and personally locates the point of the ball for placing the yardage chain.

The umpire does not move during the scrimmage, except as necessary to keep out of the way of the ball carrier, blockers, and tacklers. If the ball is declared dead in the side zone and near to the side line or even out-of-bounds, he goes to the in-bound line to assist the referee. The referee will toss the ball to the umpire who will place it on the in-bound line as directed by the referee. This type of cooperation tends to eliminate unnecessary delay in getting the ball ready for play.

The field judge must focus on the two lines until the ball is put into play. When this duty is finished he follows the play. He assists the referee in determining the forward point of the ball.

If you are out of condition—don't referee

Forward-Pass Play

The foregoing discussion applies to all running plays and, in general, to all other scrimmage situations. The officials must, however, be prepared to handle forward-pass plays as well.

At times it is possible for the officials to anticipate passes because of the conditions incident to the score, the time remaining to play, the down, and the yards to go. Occasionally, the officials are aware of the strategy of the teams with respect to the use of the pass. In any event, they must never be caught unaware.

In anticipation of a pass, the referee should note the numbers of the backfield men. He should check to see whether or not all are eligible to receive passes. (A player in a position to take a hand-to-hand snap is not eligible to receive a forward pass.) If a pass develops, the referee should stay with the passer. It is his duty to watch the blocking for the passer and to observe the tactics of the defensive players after the pass has been made.

If the passer runs forward before passing, he must know whether or not the pass was made from behind the line of scrimmage. He should have a general view of the total play. If the pass is completed and the subsequent play is covered by a fellow official, that official blows his whistle to declare the ball dead when the play is completed.

The referee will receive a report from the other officials which will indicate whether or not the play was legal from their standpoint. If there is a backward pass before the forward pass, the referee must be sure that the first pass is not forward. If the pass was incomplete, the referee goes to the spot from which the ball was put in play; the other officials will retrieve the ball and relay it as quickly as possible to the referee.

The head linesman should note who is on the end of the line near him. If there is a flanking back the head linesman should look to see if the back is at least one yard back of the line. The head linesman, as the pass develops, covers the play down the field on his side of the field. The umpire covers the play in the center area, and the field judge has responsibilities on his side of the field similar to those of the head linesman.

If the pass is incomplete, the official nearest to the ball retrieves it quickly. If it was a long pass, the other officials get in a line

Did the illegal block affect the play?

between the ball and the referee in order to relay the ball to the referee without delay.

The particular situations that attend a forward pass, and the officials' responsibilities are:

1. Pass from behind the line of scrimmage.
2. Blocking for the passer.
3. Continuing to block or tackle the passer after the pass has been thrown.
(These are all the duties of the referee.)
4. Interference of all kinds beyond the line of scrimmage.
5. Check of eligibility of receiver at time ball is touched.
(These are the responsibility of all the officials.)
6. Ineligible players crossing the line of scrimmage.
(This is the particular job of the umpire.)
7. Holding of eligible pass receivers to prevent them from getting down the field.

Kicks From Scrimmage

When the ball is kicked from scrimmage special situations occur, in addition to the general scrimmage points already mentioned. Officials must give attention to these special situations:

1. *Illegal play against kicker.* The referee should stand back and to the side of the kicker. If a team is known to quick-kick, the referee should be alert to this possibility. He stays with the kicker after the kick to see that there is no foul play committed against him.

2. *Out-of-bounds kick.* The referee watches the flight of the ball in cases where it seems evident that it will go out-of-bounds before hitting the ground in the field of play. If it does go out, the field judge signals time-out, marks the spot where it crosses the side line on his side of the field, as directed by the referee, and then retrieves the ball. If the ball goes out-of-bounds on the opposite side of the field, the head linesman performs the duties indicated for the field judge.

If the ball first hits the ground in the field of play and then goes out-of-bounds, the field judge assumes the responsibility for mark-

Don't let the game drag

ing the spot where the ball crossed the side line on his side of the field, and the head linesman marks the spot on his side of the field.

3. *Conditions surrounding the ball when violations occur.* In the case of kicks from scrimmage, the official must note whether or not the ball has been touched or is in the possession of a player when a foul occurs. This fact determines the point from which the penalty will be assessed.

4. *The freedom of movement of the receiver.* The receiver has the right of way while the ball is in the air. Enforcing this rule is the particular responsibility of the field judge.

When a kick is expected, the field judge and head linesman drop back after the snap of the ball in order to cover the runback of the kick or in case the ball goes out-of-bounds. They blow their whistles to indicate a dead ball when the play is completed. In cases where possession of the ball is at issue, they furnish this information to the referee. The other officials hold their regular positions as in other scrimmage plays before the kick. (See Diagram 15.)

The umpire holds his position but turns to watch the blocking and particularly the clipping by the receiving team. The referee assists in such observations. As soon as the ball is dead, all officials hurry to assume their regular positions for a new scrimmage by the opposite team.

The chainmen and the assistant linesmen should be cautioned not to move their stakes to the new location of the ball until ordered to do so by the head linesman. When the stakes are moved after a kick, the head linesman should mark the spot on the side line where the rear stake should be placed. In this way, there will be very little delay in positioning the stakes for the next series of downs.

Position and Duties If Out-of-Bounds

If the ball goes out-of-bounds on a running play from scrimmage, the referee should mark the spot. He is the one official who is following the ball carrier. If however, the play gets away from him, then the head linesman should be ready to assist on his side of the field, and the field judge on his side of the field.

Head linesman—check the down with the referee

If the ball is carried out-of-bounds after a completed forward pass, whichever official is covering the play (field judge or head linesman) will mark the spot and signal to the referee with the time-out signal. On page 157, the methods of handling out-of-bounds situations on kicks from scrimmage are discussed.

When the ball carrier goes out-of-bounds during a runback of a punt, the field judge or head linesman is the responsible official.

In all cases of out-of-bounds, the official who has marked the spot holds that point until the ball is accurately placed for the next scrimmage. The referee always goes to the in-bound line in order to place the ball. Of the other two officials, whichever is nearer to the ball secures it and passes it to the referee.

A question concerning the down is determined from the spot where the ball crossed the side line, before the official who has marked the spot leaves it.

Goal-Line Play

When the ball is within the defensive team's five-yard line, all the officials must be particularly alert and cooperative in connection with close goal-line plays.

The total area to cover is, of course, reduced because of the proximity of the goal line. The play is completely surrounded with the head linesman and field judge within five to ten yards of the ends of the line, the umpire in the center behind the defensive line and within five yards of the line, and the referee in his usual position. The referee is even more alert to see the ball at all times. Diagram 15 shows this arrangement.

By such a formation of the officials, valuable assistance can be given to the referee on the vital goal-line play. In situations where there may be a question in the referee's mind as to whether or not the ball was carried over the goal line before the carrier was thrown back, he can look to the official nearest the play for advice.

If the play went through the center, the umpire can by a pre-arranged unobtrusive signal convey his judgment to the referee. It should be remembered, however, that the principal duty of the umpire, as on all scrimmage plays, is to watch the blocking in the

Know the eligible receivers

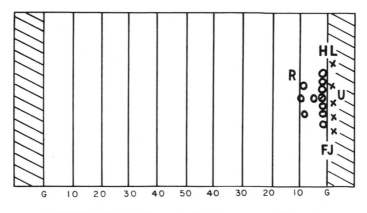

DIAGRAM 15.   Positions of officials on a goal-line play.

line. This is equally true, if not more important, on the goal line. Likewise, the field judge, if the play hit toward his side, or the head linesman if the ball carrier plunged over his side, indicates his observations. The head linesman and field judge by reason of their positions are better able to judge the forward point of the ball. They can sight along the goal line.

The appropriate signal may be a nod of the head or a movement of the body, hand, or foot. Placing the foot to indicate the point of forward advance of the ball is a simple and effective signal.

Since the referee has sole authority for the score and since it is impossible for the other officials to know what the judgment of the referee may be on a goal-line play, they should not use the official signal of arms raised above the head to indicate their opinion. This is the duty of the referee only.

It should be emphasized that there should be little or no lag in announcing the decision on a touchdown play. Consequently, the transfer of information to the referee must be instantaneous.

Try for Point

There should be no delay between the scoring of a touchdown and the try for point.

On a try for point, the officials assume the same positions as for

Be ready for the typical situations

the goal-line play. The importance attached to the attempt for the extra point after a touchdown requires this close supervision of all movements. The referee should stand directly behind the kicker so he can follow the flight of the ball and rule accurately on the success or failure of the try.

The position of the field judge varies in some sections of the country. An earlier practice of placing the field judge behind the goal posts, so he can determine whether the ball goes over or under the crossbar, is still carried out to a limited extent. However, it is now felt that the referee is sufficiently close to be able to make this decision without the assistance of the field judge.

Immediately after the kick, the field judge should secure the ball and place it on the 40-yard line of the kicking team for the next kickoff. The referee will immediately determine the choice of the captain of the team scored upon.

Try for Field Goal

A try for a field goal takes place from scrimmage or occasionally from a free kick after a fair catch. The position of some of the officials is different in each situation.

On both a scrimmage and a free kick, the field judge drops back to the goal posts so he can see whether or not the ball goes over the crossbar. The distance of some kicks from the goal is over thirty yards, so the assistance of the field judge is needed in making this decision.

The referee takes a position behind the kicker and directly in a line from the ball to the goal posts, so he can follow the flight of the ball. Upon completion of the kick he should quickly check with his fellow officials and immediately render his decision on the kick. The arms extended above the head indicate a goal. Hands and arms crisscrossing in a horizontal plane in front of the body signal no goal.

The umpire and head linesman assume their regular positions as on all scrimmage plays when the kick is from a scrimmage. If the try is on a free kick, the umpire stations himself on the side line at the end of the restraining line for the defensive team and on the opposite side of the field from the head linesman. The head lines-

Anticipate the possibilities on a foul after a kick

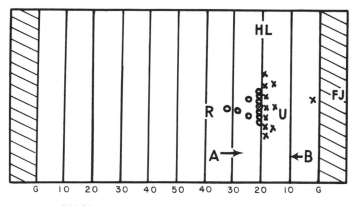

DIAGRAM 16.   Positions of officials during a try for field goal.

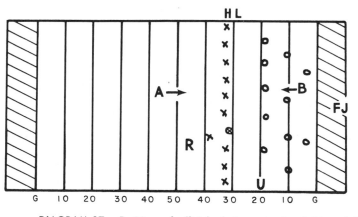

DIAGRAM 17.   Positions of officials during a try for field goal from a free kick.

man takes his position on the side line at the end of the restraining line for the kicking team. (See diagrams 16 and 17.)

It is the duty of the umpire and head linesman to see that the teams do not cross their respective restraining lines before the ball is kicked.

If the kick does not score a goal, the duties of the officials become the same as on a kick from scrimmage. It must be remembered, however, that after a free kick, either team may legally recover the ball.

Out-of-bounds—the umpire places the ball

Time-Out

Because of the rules pertaining to substitutions, it is important that all officials signal clearly so both coaches know when time is out. The time-out signal is indicated by crisscrossing the hands while the arms are extended above the head. In all cases where time-out is taken as a result of an incomplete pass, out-of-bounds play, a foul, a touchdown, touchback, safety, or field goal, the officials proceed with their duties and to their required positions speedily to make ready for the start of the next play. These situations have been described previously.

If a time-out is taken at the request of a captain or because of injury to a player, or for the referee:

1. The linesman immediately goes to the ball and remains near it until the referee takes over after the 30-second warning.

2. If time-out is taken for a team, the referee will indicate the team by extending both arms horizontally in the direction of the team for which time is taken.

If he takes time-out on his own authority, he so indicates by tapping his chest with both hands. After the above procedure, the referee is then free to confer with captains, to discuss points of play with the other officials, or to give any assistance or comment that may be necessary. Although a team is allowed two minutes for a charged time-out, the referee should get the game underway as soon as possible if the teams are ready before the expiration of two minutes. Before play is resumed after a time-out of any kind, it is necessary for the referee to ascertain from the captains if they are ready. Delay can be prevented in this function if the referee pre-arranges with the captains that unless they voice themselves to the contrary he will assume they are ready if he hears nothing from them after his question, "Are you ready?"

3. In order that the signal for play can be given at the end of the two minutes, the field judge should give a fifteen-second warning with his whistle. This will get trainers, attendants, and others off the field within the two-minute limit. In addition, the field judge should go to the defensive team to give any assistance necessary. He should watch the bench for this team so that any requests to come on the field can be recognized instantly.

On the goal line, the field judge is stationed on the line of scrimmage

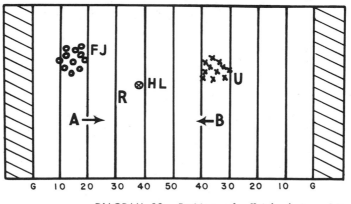

DIAGRAM 18.   Positions of officials during a time-out.

4. The umpire should station himself near the defensive team and watch the bench of this team for any requests coming from the side lines.

Upon the expiration of the time-out period, the officials should quickly assume their respective positions for play. When the referee whistles and signals for play to begin he should begin his 25-second count. If this procedure is not followed, there will be an inevitable dragging out of time-out periods. There is a tendency for football games to extend unnecessarily long. The officials should use every means possible to keep the game moving along. Two hours and thirty minutes is too much time for playing a game. Yet most of our games, which are played in fifteen-minute quarters, last this long or longer. Diagram 18 shows officials in a typical time-out situation.

Between Quarters

At the end of the first and third quarters, one minute is allowed for the teams to change goals and for the officials to transfer the ball to the same relative spot at the opposite end of the field.

1. The referee immediately locates the position of the ball with respect to its distance from the in-bound line and a yard line. He should record this information together with the down and distance

Only the referee declares a score

to be gained for a first down. He then transfers the ball to the same relative spot on the opposite side and end of the field. He checks the down and distance with the head linesman.

As soon as the ball is in place and the head linesman has changed the chain, play should be resumed. This is not a time-out period for the teams.

2. The head linesman should check the down and distance with the referee immediately at the expiration of time. He should next go to the side line and mark a spot either with a metal snap or with his hand on the chain that corresponds to a yard line between the stakes. He should then pick up the chain and have his chain-men reverse the stakes and move to the opposite end of the field. He should place the mark on the chain on the corresponding yard line at that end of the field and then have the chainmen set their stakes after pulling the chain tight in each direction from the yard line on which the chain is held.

When the tasks of the referee and head linesman are finished and they have rechecked the location of the ball, the down, and the distance, the game is ready to continue.

3. The umpire accompanies the defensive team to the opposite end of the field, sees that it complies with all rules, and recognizes any requests from the bench of this team.

4. The field judge administers to the offensive team in like man-

DIAGRAM 19.   Procedures and positions of officials between quarters.

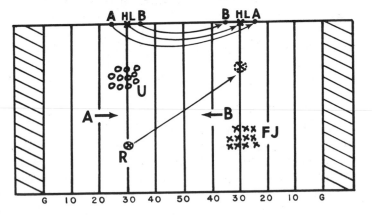

Back-judge—did the ball clear the bar on the try for field goal?

ner. He also keeps a record of the length of the time-out, so play will not be delayed longer than one minute.

Diagram 19 illustrates the method of changing ball and chain between quarters.

Measuring Position of Ball

At the end of every play the referee must be conscious of the approximate distance to be gained for a first down. He should glance toward the chain stakes to check when the decision is a close one. In case of doubt or upon request of a captain in a close situation, he should first call time-out and then signal the head linesman to bring the chain in for a measurement.

The proper procedure for the officials in making a measurement follows:

1. The referee holds the ball in its original position on the ground when it was declared dead. If it was out-of-bounds, he holds the spot on the side line until a decision is reached. If the ball is in the side line zone when declared dead, it is left there until the measurement is made.

The referee stays over the ball while the measurement is made and makes his decision with respect to the position of the forward point of ball and forward edge of the chain stake. If a first down has been gained, he immediately signals accordingly.

2. The head linesman on doubtful first-down situations should go to the side line and place his foot at the point he judges to be in line with the forward point of the ball. If a measurement is decided upon, he should first tighten the chain from the rear stake, because this is the stake he personally sets at the beginning of each series of downs. Next, he grasps the chain or fastens a snap at a point on the middle of the yard line that is farther from the ball. The farther line is used because in making the measurement with the longer part of the chain, greater accuracy can be attained. By using the longer portion of the chain to measure with, it is possible to establish a more nearly perpendicular direction from the yard line to the ball. Then, by using the point of the chain that is on the yard line as a center, the other end of the chain can be swung

Handle a missed try for field goal from a scrimmage the same as a punt

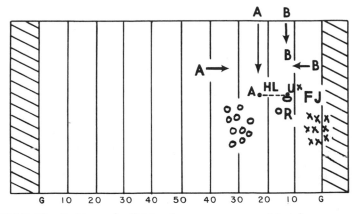

DIAGRAM 20.   Positions of officials when a measurement is taken.

through an arc to determine the farthest distance toward the goal from the center of rotation.

After securing the point on the chain from which the measurement is to be made, he, with his two chainmen, moves quickly with the chain to the position of the ball. The assistant linesman remains at the side line with his stake at the forward point of the ball.

3. When the chain has been brought to the ball, the umpire holds the stake that is next to the ball. The umpire and head linesman then make the measurement under the supervision of the referee.

After the measurement, the umpire returns the chain stake to the chainmen. If a first down has been declared, the head linesman releases the chain. The chainmen hurry back to the side line and set the chain stakes in position for the next series of downs, as directed by the head linesman.

If the offensive team has failed to earn a first down, the head linesman holds his mark on the chain and returns with his chainmen to reset the chain stakes carefully into their former position. He checks the down with the referee and signals when all is in readiness to resume play.

4. The field judge is the emergency official. He stands in a position such that he may acknowledge any requests from either player's bench. He should permit no delay greater than necessary to make the measurement.

Diagram 20 shows the method of measurement.

All officials signal time-out

Between Halves

The following procedure should be followed during the 15-minute intermission between halves:

1. The field judge immediately starts his watch when the ball is dead after the expiration of playing time, in order to time the intermission.

2. The field judge secures the ball from the referee.

3. The head linesman directs his assistants to take the chain to the opposite side of the field in readiness for the second half.

4. The officials immediately go to their dressing room for conference.

5. The officials should use the time during the intermission to review any phases of their work which may be helpful to a better administration of the game during the second half. Sometimes questions, problems, and controversies arise during the first half, which should be discussed and clarified during the intermission.

All such discussions should be carried on in privacy.

6. As the teams return to the field, the referee meets the captains in the center of the field to obtain their second-half options.

7. The field judge waits at the center of the 50-yard line with the ball for instructions by means of signals to indicate the direction of the kickoff.

8. The head linesman reorganizes his assistants in readiness for the kickoff.

9. When all is ready, the officials assume their proper positions for the kickoff, as previously described.

After the Game

1. The referee should obtain possession of the ball at the end of the game and deliver it to the home management or dispose of it in accordance with any instructions that may have been given to him.

2. The head linesman should thank his assistants and see that the chain and stakes are returned to the proper persons.

Get the ball in play promptly after time-out

3. The officials should be wary of making any comments to the press or public concerning the game.

4. The officials should go immediately to their dressing room.

1. Offside (infraction of scrimmage or free kick formation)

2. Illegal Procedure, Position, or Substitution

3. Illegal Motion

4. Illegal Shift

5. Illegal Return

6. Delay of Game

7. Personal Foul

8. Clipping

9. Roughing the Kicker

FIGURES 32, 33, 34. The official football signals used to indicate actions taken by officials.

Between quarters—referee—head linesman—double check the ball, down, distance

10.

Unsportsmanlike

11.

Illegal use of Hands
and Arms

12.

Intentional
Grounding

13.

Illegally Passing
or Handing Ball
Forward

14.

Forward Pass or
Kick Catching
Interference

15.

Ineligible Receiver
Down Field on Pass

16.

Ball Illegally Touched,
Kicked, or Batted

17.

Incomplete Forward Pass,
Penalty Declined, No
Play, or No Score

18.

Crawling, Helping the
Runner, or Interlocked
Interference

Don't rotate the ball until after the measure

19. Ball Dead: If Hand is Moved from Side to Side: Touchback

20. Touchdown or Field Goal

21. Safety

22. Time - Out

23. First Down

24. Ball Ready – for – Play

25. Start the Clock

Measure from the farther yard line

Signals

The signals reproduced on the preceding pages represent the common code used by officials throughout the United States. It is the duty of every official to know these signals perfectly. He should be able to give them instantly.

Signals are the only means by which the action of the officials on the field can be relayed to the public address system and the spectators.

It is not enough to know the signals. The official must have a sense of timing and a flair for the dramatic, so everyone can clearly receive his message. When it is necessary to signal a foul, a first down, a score, etc., the official should pause momentarily before signaling. This pause draws the attention of everyone. Then, in clear, staccato fashion, the official should act out his decision. Both before and after a penalty has been assessed, the official should signal the foul for which the penalty was given. (See Figures 32, 33 and 34 for a list of the approved signals.)

Careful attention to the art of giving signals will add much toward a satisfactory reception by the spectators of the work of an official.

Use the intermission for review

chapter 1 6

FOOTBALL: GUIDES TO PLAY SITUATIONS

When a foul occurs, the officials have well-defined duties to perform. These are partly covered by the section on "The Officials" at the end of the rule book. There are, however, procedures not covered by rule. In addition, an analysis of Rule 10 suggests certain axioms that can be used by officials to guide them in the difficult job of applying the rules that relate to penalties. These procedures and guides are presented and discussed below:

1. The referee does not blow his whistle until the ball is dead.
2. The official who detects a foul drops his marker immediately.
3. All officials follow the play until the ball is dead. (The penalty may be declined.)

When the game ends—leave—don't talk

4. The official who has announced by dropping his marker that a foul has occurred must be sure to get the number of the offender, to mark the spot of the foul, and to notice whether or not the ball is in possession of either team. In the case of a kick from scrimmage, he must know whether or not the ball has been touched at the time the foul occurred.

5. The field judge stops the watch immediately upon signal from the referee.

6. All officials signal time out.

7. The head linesman makes sure that the chainmen or the assistant linesman does not move the stakes.

8. The official who calls the foul reports the foul and the player, and indicates to the referee the spot of the foul and the penalty.

9. The referee explains the foul to the captain of the offended team and states the alternatives.

10. After the captain makes his decision, the referee signals the foul, and if the penalty has been declined he so indicates by crisscrossing his hands and arms in a horizontal plane in front of his body.

11. If the penalty is accepted, he locates the spot from which the penalty will be assessed. He then notes a similar spot near the proper yard line where the ball should be placed after the penalty is assessed. He never steps off the distance penalty.

12. The referee checks the down and distance with the head linesman and resumes play immediately.

Enforcement of Penalties

In the enforcement of all penalties, three factors are involved:

1. *The spot from which the penalty shall be assessed.* The penalty section for the violation of rules states the spot from which the penalty shall be assessed. An analysis of this part of the rules indicates that the spot from which most penalties are assessed can be indicated under two general headings:

a. All personal (contact) fouls are penalized from the spot of the foul, except fouls against the passer or kicker, pass interference by the passing team (these fouls are penalized from the spot of

There is orderly organization to handling a foul—learn it

the preceding down), pass interference by the defense behind its own goal line (ball placed on the one-yard line), and a foul after the ball has been kicked from scrimmage and has crossed the neutral zone, but before the ball has been touched by anyone. This foul is penalized from the spot of the preceding down.

b. All technical fouls, noncontact fouls, are penalized from the spot where the ball is put in play (except hurdling, illegally touching a kicked ball, illegal forward pass). Whether the penalty is from the spot of the previous play or the succeeding play depends on the time at which the foul was committed. If the ball was in play, then the penalty is from where the ball was put in play; if the ball was dead, then the penalty is enforced from the spot from which the ball would next be put in play had no foul occurred.

2. *The penalty for fouls.* In general, the fouls with which officials are most often concerned carry a penalty of five or fifteen yards. There are a very few that involve loss of the ball. Illegally touching the ball is the most frequent. Three handy axioms for determining the yardage involved in a penalty follow:

a. Most personal fouls carry a penalty of 15 yards. Exceptions: interference with an opponent after the ball is ready for play.

b. The technical fouls that are commonly committed carry a five-yard penalty. Exceptions: ineligible player touching pass beyond line of scrimmage, hurdling, unsportsmanlike conduct, misconduct by persons other than players, intermission rules, not ready to play. It will be noted that the exceptions listed above seldom if ever occur.

c. When the ball is not in possession of either team, the penalty is the loss of the ball. The one exception is the case of a foul after the ball has been kicked from scrimmage and before it has been touched by any player. This foul carries a 15-yard penalty from where the ball was put in play.

3. *The down following a penalty:*

a. After the assessment of a penalty for a foul, the down and the point to be gained before the foul occurred remain the same unless the ball after the penalty is beyond the point to be gained for a first down. The exceptions to the above statement occur when the ball is awarded to the offended team as a result of the foul, and cases of pass interference by the offensive team. In the latter case, the play counts as a down.

Explain the options

Guides to an Understanding
of Some Rules

It is the duty of every official to know the rules thoroughly and to know the intent and purpose of each one. It is not, however, the purpose of this text to discuss the rules in detail.

There are a few guides and some analyses, which have been developed after more than twenty years' experience in teaching classes in officiating, that may prove helpful. Many feel that the football rules are the most difficult of all our rules to master. Although they do appear somewhat complicated because of the many different situations and fouls that arise during the progress of a game, those rules with which the officials are actively engaged are not too numerous. There is a consistency in the present code, which greatly simplifies the job of learning and interpretation.

A few suggestions have been given to aid the official in knowing what to do in the enforcement of penalties. The reader may find the following syntheses of additional value for building a comprehensive working pattern for some of the more vexing practical problems.

FUMBLES

The decisions that must be made in connection with fumbles can be clarified by four simple statements, which bring together all the situations that puzzle many officials.

1. Any fumbled ball that is recovered before touching the ground by the team which did not fumble the ball may be advanced. This applies to a fumble of a kicked ball as well as a ball fumbled on a running or forward or lateral pass play.

2. Any fumbled ball that touches the ground and then is recovered by the team which did not make the fumble is dead at the spot of recovery.

3. Any fumbled ball that is recovered by the team which fumbled the ball may be advanced until declared dead by the referee.

4. A ball that is fumbled and then goes out-of-bounds belongs to the team which fumbled the ball.

If one will take these simple statements and apply them to any situation involving possession by the kicking team, he can hand

Enforcement involves—the spot, the penalty, the down

down accurate decisions. He should not let himself become confused by conditional clauses or by the introduction of numerous and complicated incidents.

For example, Team A kicks off. The ball is touched in the field of play, rolls across the goal line, is recovered by Team B, run out to the 20-yard line, lateraled to a teammate who runs to the 50-yard line where he is tackled and then laterals to another teammate. This pass is fumbled, hits the ground and is picked up by a player of Team A who runs for a touchdown.

Much of the foregoing is superfluous. The fact that the ball was fumbled, hit the ground, and then was recovered by the team which did not fumble the ball precludes the possibility of any subsequent play. The ball was dead at the spot of recovery. Had it been recovered before hitting the ground, then the run and touchdown would have been legal.

TOUCHBACK, SAFETY, TOUCHDOWN

Misunderstanding often exists concerning what constitutes a touchback, a safety, and a touchdown, and what play may be made on a ball that crosses the goal line. Mistakes are made because officials permit extraneous circumstances to divert their thinking. If three questions are asked and answered correctly every time the ball crosses the goal line, and no attention is paid to any other factor, no doubts would ever arise concerning a touchdown, safety, or touchback. These questions are:

1. Which team caused the ball to go across the goal line?
2. Is the attacking team eligible legally to recover the ball?
3. Who gained possession of the ball in the end zone?

If the attacking team caused the ball to cross the goal line and is eligible to recover the ball and does recover it, it is a touchdown. If the attacking team does not recover the ball behind the goal line, then, under no circumstances can it score a touchdown. If the attacking team is not eligible to recover the ball, it is not possible to score a touchdown even though the ball is recovered over the goal line by this team. If the ball is caused to go over the goal line by the defending team and is legally recovered by the attacking team, it is a touchdown.

Who fumbled? Who recovered? Did the ball touch the ground?

A safety can be scored only if the defending team causes the ball to cross the goal line and it is declared dead in the end zone in possession of the defending team or rolls out-of-bounds behind the goal line. It should be remembered that a punt by the defending team, which is blocked and rolls over the goal line and is declared dead in possession of the defending team, is considered to be caused to cross the goal line by the defending team. A safety may be scored as a result of a foul—that is, illegally batting or kicking a free ball in a team's own end zone.

A ball caused to cross the goal line by the attacking team and declared dead in possession of the defending team, regardless of attempts to run it out, is a touchback. A touchback may be scored as a result of a penalty—that is, illegally batting or kicking a free ball in an opponent's end zone.

A punt or place kick by the attacking team which is not touched by the defending team and which crosses the goal line becomes a touchback unless the receiving team advances the ball into the field of play.

These statements should help officials to avoid mistakes on play situations involving touchdowns, touchbacks, or safeties.

As a further aid to officials, a specific rule should always be taken as qualifying and refining a general rule. The general rule states the principle. A specific rule places limitations on a particular play and goes beyond the general rule. This is analogous to federal in contrast to state laws. The state laws may not violate the federal law, but may go beyond it, and in so doing take precedence.

The application of these principles can be illustrated in the case of interference by the defense on a forward pass. In general, the penalty is loss of the ball at the spot of the foul. But in the specific case of interference behind the goal line of the defending team, the penalty is a first down on the one-yard line.

Likewise, a kick that goes out-of-bounds before being recovered goes to the receiving team. But in the case of a first kickoff, the ball may be brought back and kicked again.

The penalty for fouls committed when neither team has possession of the ball is loss of the ball at the spot of the foul. However, in the case of a foul after a kick from scrimmage and before the ball has been touched by any player, the penalty is 15 yards from where the ball was put in play.

Answer three questions to solve touchdown, safety, touchback problems

𝔐 BASKETBALL

The position and movement of basketball officials on the court in order best to observe and administer each type of play, and to cooperate with and supplement each other, is known as court mechanics. It is the modus operandi for the official. To a very limited extent, the rules direct the actions and procedures of the officials. However, for the most part, their pattern of action has been developed through a process of trial and error as a result of actual officiating experience.

There are slight differences in the plans of operation adopted by different organizations. In general, however, the plan is quite uniform, so officials from all groups and from all parts of the country can come together and officiate in harmony.

There is only one manual—but two editions with a few variations

The National Federations of State High School Athletic Associations [1] and The Collegiate Commissioners Association [2] each publish a basketball officials' manual. The International Association of Approved Basketball Officials [3] has produced a set of slides that depict the procedures for officials for various situations during the progress of a game. All of these efforts have contributed to the standardization of officiating practices.

The following is a presentation of the more widely accepted court mechanics. The few variations that exist at present will be pointed out. An explanation of, and the reason for, the position and movement of each official for each court situation will be given. This should be of great help to the inexperienced official. If will direct his attention to the important points on which he should focus his attention in each situation. While he is going through the stages of gaining experience and developing his judgment, he can at least look like a good official by being in the right place at the right time. He can be looking in the right direction, even though in the early stages of his experience he may not be able to see clearly or judge correctly.

Only the plan for the double officiating system will be discussed in detail. Practically no organized game today is conducted with one official. The elimination of the center jump and the advent of the fast break have created the necessity for two officials. It is not physically possible for one official to handle a game effectively under present conditions. For this reason, to present the technique of the single official would be of historical value only. Some consideration is currently being given to three-man officiating so a brief presentation will be given for those who may be interested.

Pregame Duties

The pregame activities of the official can be divided conveniently into four categories:

[1] National Federation of State High School Athletic Associations, *Basketball Officials Manual*, Chicago, 1967.

[2] Collegiate Commissioners Association, *Basketball Officials Manual*, Kansas City, Mo., 1967.

[3] International Association of Approved Basketball Officials, Mechanics of Officiating (slides), Hagerstown, Md., 1967.

Be in the right place even though you don't see

a) 1. Pregame conference of officials.
b · 2. Checking equipment and court.
c · 3. Instructing timers and scorers.
d · 4. Meeting with coaches and captains.

2. PREGAME CONFERENCE

- The conference of the officials in the dressing room before the game can be the means of smooth and cooperative action on the court during the game. This is especially true if the two officials who are assigned to work the game have seldom or never worked together. There are sufficient variations and personal idiosyncrasies in court procedures to necessitate a discussion for the purpose of a common understanding before the officials go onto the court. It is also true that some officials are sensitive or jealous of their prerogatives and resent what they term interference or encroachment upon their duties by the other official. Enumeration of several of these points will tend to clarify the issue. A discussion of the different techniques will be presented later on in their proper sequence.

1. What method of switching will be used?
2. Who will toss held balls at the free-throw line?
3. How will out-of-bounds play be covered?
   a. Will both make out-of-bounds decisions anywhere?
   b. Will each have authority in certain areas, except when help is asked of another official?
   c. How can another official cooperate without delay or confusion when asked?
   d. What signal system between officials will be used?
4. Is each official to call violations and fouls wherever or whenever he sees them?

These are pertinent and sometimes touchy questions, which must be resolved before the officials leave the dressing room. Harmony in working the game is dependent upon a common understanding. To neglect to work out a uniform pattern of action may mean a poorly officiated game.

Other matters also lend themselves to a dressing-room discussion. The referee may have some specific assignments for the umpire. These should be given at this time. For example, he may desire that the umpire work with the scorers and timers before the game while he is checking other matters. He may also have a specific plan

Did you confer with your colleague before the game?

for the umpire to follow with the scorers and timers in checking decisions with them during the progress of the game.

Occasionally peculiar and puzzling play situations arise during the season. Interpretations have not always been clarified. The dressing room conference affords an opportunity to discuss these, so the officials will not be opposing each other on the court if the same situation should occur. In addition, the dressing room provides a meeting place for a general rules discussion. The best way to develop a thorough knowledge of the rules and uniformity of interpretation is through continued discussion of the moot points.

Many teams, because of the style of play they employ, present special problems. It is also true that rivalries between teams create conditions that make some games more difficult to officiate than others. Some coaches and some players are more serious problems than others. Audiences in certain localities are more unruly than in others.

If the game at hand presents any of these special situations and they are known to the officials, a plan of approach can be adopted in advance. Such advance preparation may be the means of handling cases satisfactorily and with ease, whereas failure to anticipate and be ready may produce embarrassing moments and may mar contests. A couple of situations, which represent actual experiences, may demonstrate the wisdom of forethought. The identities of those involved are not revealed for obvious reasons.

A certain team that did considerable barnstorming was known always to test the officials in the opening minutes of the game. In the first place, because they carried limited personnel, a request was made to set aside the disqualification rule for too many personal fouls. Next, the players would determine by their court tactics just how technical and how free the officials were, and how much courage they possessed. They would hold, they would block, they would charge, in a clever fashion. If caught, they would evince great surprise and attempt a bit of official baiting—typical professional tactics. If the officials could be intimidated, then this team would run the game as it pleased and proceed to make life miserable for both the officials and the opponents. If forced to do so, however, the players, who were finished performers, would play by the code.

This team had played in a certain locality the previous year and had gotten away with "murder." The following year, when they came for a return engagement, officials refused to work the game. Finally, two competent men were secured. They knew of the reputation of this particular team. Without prejudice they proceeded to keep the game in check from the very beginning. After several attempts by the players of the team to dominate the scene, a time out was called. In the huddle, the following remark was overheard: "Cut out the funny stuff. These officials are going to run this game. They can't be bluffed."

Thereafter, the game went along smoothly and without further incident. The barnstorming team won handily because it was far superior. But it was forced to play according to the rules, because the officials before the game had determined to keep the game under control. The fact that there had been pregame planning to meet this particular situation made it possible to handle a difficult situation with ease.

On another occasion, two officials dared to enforce the rules for unsportsmanlike conduct on a particularly unruly coach. This coach had been browbeating officials for years from the side lines during the progress of the game. His actions caused the crowd to follow a similar pattern. The worst sportsmanship imaginable was displayed by both the coach and the spectators.

The two officials in their pregame planning determined that for such tactics to persist was unfair to the opponent and a disgrace to the game. They also decided that they as officials were at fault for permitting such practices to continue in brazen violation of the rules. Together, they determined that if the usual display occurred during this particular game, they would first warn the coach, then penalize him if their friendly appeal was not heeded.

They had occasion to put their plans into practice. A foul was called on the coach several times. Their courage not only controlled a very bad situation but focused public attention on it, with the result that much improvement was effected.

3 , CHECKING EQUIPMENT AND COURT FACILITIES

Checking equipment and the court is a requirement that must be carried out by specific stipulation of the rules. These requirements

Can you be intimidated?

include an inspection of the ball, the baskets, the backboards, and the markings and clearances on the court.

The rules give the manufacturer specifications for the ball. The official may or may not check these specifications with precision. He should, however, note the bounce and observe the general roundness. All schools should provide the official with the proper facilities for testing the bounce of the ball. A slight difference in pressure can cause the bounce of the molded ball to vary outside the limitations of the rule. Usually two balls are furnished. The official will choose the one he thinks most nearly meets the specifications. It is wise to ask about the ball at the very beginning because there have been many instances when the home team has inadvertently forgotten the ball.

The court markings must be observed carefully. There are often many markings on a gym floor. Those that are to govern the boundaries for the game must be pointed out to the opponents. The home team is familiar with them, but the opponents can easily be confused. If there are two 10-second lines, these should be identified.

The court markings most often neglected are those used for the dispersion of players along the free-throw lanes. These markings save much confusion and delay. If they are absent, it is wise to mark them out in chalk. No provision in the rules has been more helpful to the players and officials.

The method used to hang and support the backboard must be studied. Can the ball hit on the edges, particularly the top of the backboard, without hitting a support? Are there wire supports or bracings which the ball may hit on shots or rebounds? Can the backboard be moved out of line when players run against the supports? Are the backboards protected from the spectators? These questions are of importance to the officials. No game should be started before these items are checked. Unsatisfactory conditions should be corrected, or provisions should be made by ground rules to cover any exigencies that may arise.

The basket itself should be checked. Several times every season, a basket breaks before or during a game. The nets are neglected and game time approaches with the condition of the nets unacceptable. They are not properly fastened, cords are broken, or they are too long or will not release the ball. The latter condition will inter-

Did you check the ball—the court—the basket and backboard?

fere with fast-breaking offenses and should be corrected before play begins.

The clearance beyond the boundary lines is important. If it is less than three feet, then restraining lines must be established for the control of play from out-of-bounds. Inadequate clearance necessitates a check on the restraining line markings on the court. If these are not present, the players must be cautioned to keep ample distance from the player who has the ball out-of-bounds. If the lines are marked, the players must be notified whether or not they are to be used.

In general, the court and surroundings should be surveyed carefully for any obstructions or hazards that might interfere with the game or be dangerous to players. Nonstandard conditions should be corrected or precautions taken to protect the players and to insure playing conditions as normal as possible.

All of the above factors can be checked in less time than it takes to read about them here. They are, however, important. No official should neglect to go through this routine before each game. Considerable emphasis has been given to these details because officials are wont to be lax about them. It is hoped thereby to stimulate a more serious regard for these factors for the purpose of handling them before trouble comes, rather than after it occurs.

The most important piece of personal equipment to the official is his whistle. Without it he is impotent on the court. He should be sure that he has his whistle. Even better, it is wise to carry two whistles. A whistle with a rubber grip for the teeth is highly recommended.

Most officials carry their whistles between the teeth. This is a most dangerous practice. Even with the rubber grip, the danger of being hit on the mouth with the ball, or by an elbow or shoulder from a player when the official is observing play at close range or is tossing a ball for a jump, is too great. One accident may result in broken teeth or badly cut lips. (The author learned this fact the hard way.) Also, one may blow the whistle inadvertently while running with it between the teeth.

Because of the possibility of injury, the whistle should be carried in the hand. As one anticipates the need for blowing it, the whistle can be raised close to the mouth in readiness for immediate use.

Carry the whistle in your hand for safety

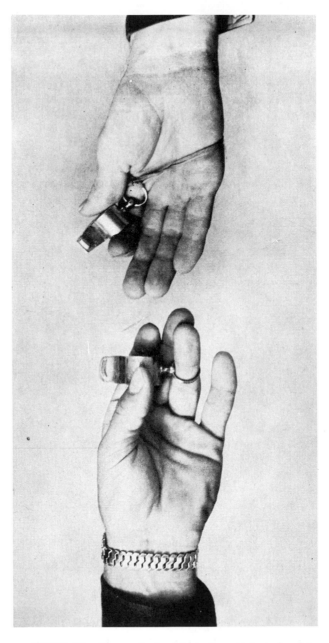

FIGURE 35. Two methods of fastening whistle to hand by a rubber band or ring for ready use. Some officials do not like to carry the whistle in the mouth.

Did you instruct the scorers?

In order that there be no danger of dropping the whistle, two methods of carrying it are in practice. It can be carried on a string hanging around the neck, or a finger or hand device can be used. A metal ring large enough to slip over the ring finger can be inserted through the hole in the end of the whistle. This will prevent the official from dropping his whistle. It can be carried in the hand with the snout lying between the thumb and forefinger so that it can be put to instant use.

Another device for carrying the whistle is to fasten it to a heavy rubber band, by feeding one end of the band through the ring and then drawing one end of the band through the other. The hand may now be placed through the rubber band with the whistle next to the palm. The snout of the whistle again protrudes between the thumb and forefinger. Figure 35 shows various ways of carrying the whistle.

Those two devices are handy, inexpensive, homemade methods for carrying the whistle. Also, one may purchase whistles with either leather hand straps or metal finger straps attached.

4. Scorers and Timers

The rules stipulate that each game shall have six officials. The referee and umpire are usually the only two who are given any consideration. Even the referee and umpire tend to overlook the importance of their four assistants—the two scorers and two timers. It should be realized that either the scorers or timers may decide the outcome of ball games and that their decisions in specific instances become the official ones. For example, in controversies over the score or personal fouls, the record of the official book is final, unless the referee has information that permits him to rule otherwise. Likewise, at the end of the game or period, if the timer's signal is not heard, the testimony of the timers determines whether a score shall count or a foul shall be charged, unless the referee has information that would alter the situation.

The responsibility of the scorers and timers is so great that the referee and umpire must be certain to set up the closest understanding and cooperation with them. Many schools use faculty men or interested citizens to act in the capacities of scorer and timer.

Do scorers know their duties on substitutions?

Others use student managers or other students with the idea that it is a part of the educational pattern. In some places the scorer and timer are employed officials. Preferably the scorers and timers should be mature adults.

Whoever the scorers and timers may be, the referee and umpire should never take them for granted. They should be made to realize that they are not spectators, but that they are an important part of a game and that they must see to it that the game is run smoothly and efficiently.

The following routine checks should be made before every game:

5 .   TO THE SCORERS

1. Designate the official scorer and official score book.
2. Advise nonofficial scorer regarding checking every entry made in the official book.
3. Order immediate action in case of any discrepancy in the record.
4. Caution to make no entry if in doubt, but to ask for an official decision.
5. Arrange for plan of designating player who commits a foul.
6. Instruct concerning time to send substitute into game.
7. Check signal devices for announcing substitutes or calling officials.

The rules provide that the home scorer shall be designated as the official scorer, unless the referee rules otherwise. Except in places where an official scorer is provided, such as in the sports arenas in large cities, the home scorer is practically always designated as the official scorer. Sometimes, however, where an electric timing device is recognized as the official timepiece, which must be operated by the home management, the referee may appoint the visiting score-keeper as official. This divides the responsibilities between the representatives of the two teams.

The nonofficial scorer should check each entry with the official book at the time it is made. For example, each time a player scores a point, the scorers should announce to each other the name of the player scoring and then check on his total scores. Following this the total running score for the game should be changed and the total score for each team repeated. If an electric scoreboard is being operated, this score should also be checked. At the end of a half,

Scoring is accounting—do the books balance?

the sum of the individual scores can be checked against the total running score, which has been kept.

When a personal foul is committed, the name of the player who committed the foul should be repeated. A "P," with the proper numeral indicating the number of personal fouls charged against him, should be entered in the proper column opposite his name. Many of the present scorebooks have numbered spaces so that as fouls are committed, these spaces can be crossed out. The total number of fouls against this player should be repeated by the scorers, so they have a check on this important record. The bonus rule necessitates a differentiation between fouls committed in each half. Different colored marks can be used for this purpose or an "X" can be used one half and the space for the foul blacked out the second half.

As the rules suggest, when a player is awarded a free throw, a circle should be entered in the record opposite his name. If the throw is successful, an "X" should be marked inside the circle. If it is missed, the circle is left blank. When a two-shot foul is awarded it is customary to join the two circles with a curved line above the circles. If a bonus free throw is awarded, the circles are connected by a curved line below the circles. If the one and one opportunity is in effect and the first free throw is missed, it is customary to put a tag at the bottom of the circle, and the second circle is omitted. In this way, an accurate account can be made of the fouls and attempts. At the end of each half, a check should be made to see that the number of free-throw attempts awarded is equal to the number of circles.

The details of keeping score in this manner are recorded here in the interest of a uniform method of accurate bookkeeping and accounting. The referee will not explain all of these details.

The referee should, however, insist upon two procedures in scorekeeping. First, if at any time the scorers find a discrepancy in their records, they should notify the referee the next time thereafter that the ball is dead. And second, they should make no entry in their books that is based on their own judgment. If they do not get the signal for decisions clearly noting who is charged with a foul, they should sound their horn. The official should designate the violator for them, so there can be no question about the accuracy of the records.

Notify referee of errors—Be sure, don't guess

To indicate a substitution, the scorers may sound their horn at any time when the ball is dead, time is out and no change of status of the ball is about to take place. The officials, however, should call to their attention the fact that when the ball is awarded to the free thrower at the free-throw line, it is alive. The scorers may sound their horn while the official has the ball in his possession, but when it is given to the free thrower, they should withhold their signal until the next substitution opportunity, in order to avoid disconcerting the free thrower. This point is emphasized because it is the one that is misunderstood, and thus violated, by scorers.

The officials should always make sure that the scorers have a signal by which they can announce substitutes or get the attention of the officials at any time the ball is dead. In spite of the emphasis in the rules, the officials should be sure that there is a horn, klaxon, or gong, which is distinctly different from their own whistles.

6.   TO THE TIMERS

The officials should follow a similar procedure with the timers. It is even more important that the timers be properly instructed, because their decisions officially end each period. Consequently, the actions of the timers are of tremendous significance.

1. Designate the official watch.
2. Suggest method of cooperation for two timers.
3. Check signal devices for ending periods.
4. Check timing equipment.
5. Question concerning knowledge of time-in and time-out.

It is necessary to designate the official watch. If an electric timer is used, there is no problem; but if each timer has a watch, only one may be used as the official watch. If the referee should fail to designate an official watch and the game is close or tied, there is likely to be trouble. Each timer could claim his watch as the official one. The time of each would probably not be the same. Naturally, each would argue for his time if it were to the advantage of his team. It is easy to see that the results could be embarrassing. This is not a hypothetical situation. It has happened on numerous occasions. That is why it is so important for the official to assign one watch as the official one.

Did you instruct the timers?

The official should also make sure that the signal devices for announcing the end of a period have sufficient volume and that they make a type of sound that will penetrate the noise of rooters. A signal that fails to sound or is difficult to hear when pandemonium reigns places the officials in a position where they must accept the judgment of lay assistants.

In anticipation of such emergency, the referee should give the timers full instructions. However, if the signals are automatic and synchronized with an electric scoreboard and clock, there is little need for the following. Toward the end of a period, the timer who is operating the watch should count the last ten seconds aloud as he watches his timepiece. The other timer watches the action on the court and holds the gun or other signal. If play is stopped at any time during the last ten seconds, the timer watching the play calls time. As the ball is put in play again, he calls play. The other timer continues his count. As the time expires, he calls time and the other timer, who has picked up the cadence of the count, fires the gun or sounds the signal.

In anticipation of a shot or a foul at the end of a period and the fact that the signal may not go off or may not be heard, the referee should ask the timer who is watching the action to be able to tell him one thing: "Where was the ball when time expired?" On the basis of this information, the referee can make decisions concerning play at the end of a period.

This procedure is suggested because it tends to remove the element of suggestion, which may be planted by other comments. The significance of this procedure is indicated by the rule (Rule 2, section 12), which states in part: "If the timer's signal fails to sound or is not heard, the timer shall go on the court or use other means to notify the referee immediately. If, in the meantime, a goal has been made or a foul has occurred, the referee shall consult the timers. If the timers agree that time was up before the ball was in the air on its way to the basket, or before the foul was committed, the referee shall rule that the goal does not count, or in case of a foul, that it shall be disregarded unless it is unsportsmanlike. But if they disagree, the goal shall count or the foul be penalized unless the referee has knowledge that would alter the ruling."

By focusing the attention of the timer on the position of the ball at the moment time expired, the referee tends to remove the power

Decisions at the end of a period are vital

of decision with respect to a score or a foul from the timer. This decision is left for the referee who is the proper person to make such a decision. If a leading or suggestive question such as "Did the goal count?" or "Was the ball in the air?" is asked, one may get a reply influenced by the question. Also, if the timers follow the procedure in which one watches the timepiece and counts off the last ten seconds and the other watches the ball, any possibility of disagreement over the position of the ball is avoided.

From the foregoing rather exhaustive discussion of the duties of the timers and scorers and their relation to the officials, the importance of attention to these assistants before the game starts should be quite evident.

Basketball officials' manuals list instructions for scorers and timers. The International Association of Approved Basketball Officials distributes instructions to schools and its members on conveniently prepared cards, which may be posted in scorebooks where they are available for handy reference before each game. The instructions shown are typical. Some schools have adopted the practice of pasting these instructions in their scorebook so they are available for ready reference and study. They have been found to be very helpful. These instructions are reproduced herewith for the information of officials.

Meeting Coaches and Captains

The final act of the officials before starting the game is to meet the coaches and the captains. Many officials have formed the habit of never meeting the coaches before a game. This practice probably stems from professional circles. It has no place in amateur athletics. In the first place, the coaches are asked by many conferences and officials' associations to rate the officials. If it so happens that the coach has not met either official before (this is not an uncommon occurrence), it is a little difficult for him to distinguish between the two when he makes his report. And in the second place, there is usually the necessity of learning about the activities such as introductions, The National Anthem, etc., which are planned to immediately precede the start of the game, and discussing special rules and interpretations or explaining special court conditions. The

Did you inform the captains and coaches on special rules and regulations?

𝓔 Instructions to Timekeepers

ROUTINE
1. Consult Officials as to signals used to indicate a time out and resumption of time.
2. Keep eyes on the officials throughout the game.
3. Check on the duration of time outs, substitutions, time of periods, etc.
4. Note the position of ball when you signal end of any period or extra period. Timekeeper's signal ends these periods.
5. Check on duration of time between 1st and 2nd, 3rd and 4th periods, and between halves. Notify teams, Officials and Scorers the required number of minutes before the start of each half.
6. Seek designation from Referee as to which is Official Timepiece and its Operator.
7. It is strongly recommended that the operator of the official clock be an Adult.
8. When an electric clock is used, have a manual clock on hand in the event of failure of the electric clock.

START CLOCK
1. When ball is legally tapped on all jump balls.
2. When ball is touched in bounds, if resumption of play is by a throw-in after clock has been stopped. (Chopping motion.)
3. When ball is legally touched after a missed free throw and ball is to remain alive. (Chopping motion trail official.)

STOP CLOCK
1. When time expires at the end of a period.
2. When an official signals a foul.
3. When an official signals a jump ball.
4. When a violation occurs.
5. When an official orders time-out:
   a. To avoid unusual delay.
   b. To repair or adjust equipment.
   c. For an injury or other emergency.
   d. Upon request of a player whose team has player control or when ball is dead.

GENERAL
If timekeeper's signal is not heard the timekeeper shall go on the court and notify the official—noting the position of the ball when time expires.

Referee shall appoint one timer as operator of the Timepiece.

The Official watch or clock shall be placed on the table between both timers. Another timepiece shall be used to check duration of time outs.

LENGTH OF PERIODS
High School Games—8 minute quarters; 1 minute between quarters and extra periods and 10 minutes between halves; extra periods, 3 minutes.

College Games—Two 20 minute halves and 15 minutes between halves, 1 minute between extra periods; extra periods, 5 minutes.

All Games—Time-outs requested by players are for 1 minute. Time-outs to replace disqualified players are for 1 minute. Sound warning signal 15 seconds before end of time-out period. Time-outs for substitutions for injuries are for 1½ minutes.

Timers are urged to study Rule 2, Section 12 and Rule 5 of the Official Rule Book.

Do the time and the score affect your decisions?

Instructions to Scorers

1. Seek designation from Referee as to who is the official scorer and which is official scorebook and consult with him as to signals used to designate fouls and time-outs. The official scorer should wear black and white striped garment.

2. Obtain names and numbers of all players who may participate in the game at least ten (10) minutes before the start of the game. At least three (3) minutes before scheduled starting time, have each team designate its five starting players. Report any failure to comply to referee.

3. Record field goals made, free throws made and missed, running summary of points scored, personal and technical fouls on each player, team personal fouls per half and time outs.

4. Designate each goal and each foul thus:

Field goal	X or 2	tuted for original	O s	
Free throw attempt	O	Two shot foul	O O	
Free throw made	O	Bonus opportuunity	O O or Q	
Free throw violation	O v	Personal Foul	P1 P2 P3 P4 P5	
		Technical Foul	T1 T2 T3 T4	

(heading: Free throw substi-)

Field goals scored in wrong basket are not credited to any player but are credited to the team in a footnote. Points awarded for illegally touching ball or baskets are credited to the thrower. When a live ball goes in a basket, the last player who touched it causes it to go there.

5. *Notify official (a) when team has taken the legal five time-outs, (b) when a player has had five personal fouls, (c) after a team has been charged with six personal fouls in either half of a game played in halves or four in a game played in quarters, (d) when a team has used time outs in excess of the five legal. In (b), (c) and (d) if play is in progress at time of discovery, withhold whistle until ball is dead or in control of offending team.*

6. Check with fellow scorer on each entry in score book, such as score, fouls, substitutions, charged time-outs, etc. If any discrepancy occurs notify referee at once on next dead ball—time out situation.

7. Blow horn to stop game only when ball is dead and time is out.

8. When a substitute reports (must be ready and entitled to enter game), signal when ball is dead and time is out and before change of status of ball is about to occur. Allow substitute to go on court only when Official beckons. Do not signal after ball has been placed at the disposal of a free thrower. If ball is dead after a free throw attempt, a substitution may be made. If thrower is to be replaced, be sure that it is legal for another player to attempt that particular throw. A substitute cannot replace a player designated to jump or designated to attempt a free throw, he must wait until the next dead ball, time-out, situation. Score book of home team is the official book, unless referee rules otherwise.

Scorers should be adults when possible and be equipped with a sounding device unlike that used by the Officials or Timers to signal the Officials. Scorers should study Rule 2, Section 11 and Rules 3 and 5 of the Official Rule Book.

(Coaches are urged to paste these instructions in the front of their Score Book for future reference.)

Are you a "held ball" addict?

great variation in courts makes this latter point necessary. And third, an exchange of pleasantries is likely to establish much friendlier relations.

The meeting with the captains is partly social or sporting and partly for business pertaining to the game. The captains should know each other and the officials. More particularly the meeting is for instruction. Ground rules, court markings, and any special rules or interpretations, as previously mentioned, should be explained. Here is an opportunity for the captains to ask any questions or to make any requests in conection with the game or the practices of the officials that may have a bearing on the game. The officials may remind the captains that they are the official representatives of their respective teams in case any questions come up during the game.

It should be emphasized here that it is out of place for officials to caution the captains about rough play or playing clean. Neither should they warn them that they will call the game closely. It is to be expected that the game will be handled by competent men and played by well-trained sportsmen. The game itself will reveal the validity of both assumptions. No preliminary statement, challenge, or threat is likely to alter the outcome.

9. Center Jump and Tossing the Ball

At the beginning of the game the referee tosses the ball. He takes a position on the opposite side of the court from the scorers' and timers' table so he may face these assistants. His primary responsibilities are to toss the ball correctly and to see that the two centers play in accordance with the rules governing the center jump. The art of tossing the ball for a jump is discussed below.

The umpire takes a position along the side line near the scorers' and timers' table and to the right of the center line of the court. It is his primary job to watch the players other than the jumpers. He should see that they do not push, crowd, or otherwise violate the rules before the ball is tossed and until it is tapped. He is responsible for calling violations of the restraining circle by the eight players other than the jumpers.

If the umpire is fulfilling his duties in connection with the other

Cover ten players, not two, on all jump balls

eight players, he will not be able to make decisions with respect to the tossing of the ball or the action of the jumpers. A test of neglect of duty is to hear the umpire blow his whistle to call attention to a defective toss or a foul or violation by one of the jumpers at the center jump. His attention, if he is doing his job, will be focused on the other players.

Diagram 21 shows the positions of the referee and umpire before the toss at the beginning of the game. The umpire follows the play in whichever direction it goes. He becomes the leading official if the ball goes to his right. He goes right and then stations himself along the end line, with the referee following the play from behind and at the side of the court. If the play goes to the umpire's left, he becomes the lead official until the referee can get to his position along the end line; usually the referee and umpire perform a see-saw movement with the referee becoming the lead official and the umpire moving to the trail position. Occasionally it will not be possible for the two officials to carry out this interchange. When this happens the umpire will move along the end line to the opposite side of the court and remain as the lead official while at the same time the referee will cross to the side where the umpire was stationed and continue as the trail official at that end of the court. (See section on switching for further details.)

10. Tossing the Ball for a Jump

A common fault among officials is to toss the ball too low. As a consequence the art of jumping to tip the ball has been lost. Instead, players maneuver to tip the ball as it is going up. It is necessary to do this in order to get a chance to play the ball at all. The rule prohibits a player from tipping the ball before it reaches its highest point. But the rules also require that the official toss the ball higher than either player can jump. Since he fails to throw the ball high enough, the players must jump as the ball leaves the official's hand in order to get a chance to tip it at all. If the players waited until the ball reached its highest point, and then jumped, they would reach above the ball and consequently there would be no contest in jumping and each would be thrown off stride. To avoid this, the jumper has, in self-protection, formed the habit of

Toss too high rather than too low

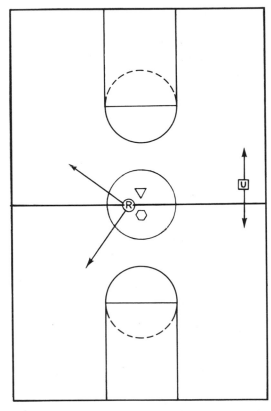

DIAGRAM 21.   Positions and movements of officials at the Center Jump
to start a period.

cheating by tipping the ball as it goes up. The contest then becomes
one of jumping first, and not one of out-jumping an opponent. This
is unfair to the better jumper.

This practice is so prevalent that when an official administers a
toss correctly, the players will usually not tip the ball at all. They
jump too soon and thus are usually coming down from the height
of their jump before the ball begins to descend. If the ball is tossed
high enough and the jumper happens to tip the ball as it is ascend-
ing, the violation will become very apparent.

The best advice to give to the young official is to toss the ball
too high rather than too low. Since the tendency is to undertoss,
this emphasis will usually produce a toss that is the correct height.
If the official will use the basket as his gauge and always toss the

A pause may calm excited player

ball considerably higher than the height of the basket (two feet above the basket is ideal), the jumpers will be able to time their jump properly and all illegal taps will be avoided. It is strongly recommended that the official use this uniform height to toss the ball regardless of the height of the players.

Tossing the ball midway between the two jumpers seems to be easier to control than regulating the height. The technique of tossing with one or two hands is largely dependent upon individual preference. Starting the toss from eye level is sometimes advocated over a toss which begins with an arm swing from the chest or waist to prevent the player from tipping the ball as it ascends. Here, again, the exact method depends entirely on habits of the individual official. None of these will of themselves guarantee a legal toss or jump. If the proper height is emphasized, the method is unimportant.

Players occasionally become spirited as the result of aggressive play preceding a jump. An official can allay emotional flare-up and prevent fouls by calmness, a slight delay, and even a fixed stare at the jumpers before tossing the ball. In cases where the players are crowding each other, they may be separated by stepping between them and spreading the arms. Such a maneuver is more effective than verbal directions. An excited or intense person seems to act more quickly as a result of physical contact. Likewise, players who are too far apart before the jump can be placed properly by pulling one into position.

When tossing the ball, an official should avoid two hazards. He should not hold his whistle in the mouth. He is so close to the jumpers that there is danger of having the whistle knocked out of his mouth by a swinging arm of a jumper. Grave dental injury may result.

He should not move back away from the jumpers after making the toss. To do so invites collision with a player who is charging for the ball. Officials have received serious injuries by stepping back into the path of a rapidly running player. The official who tosses the ball should always face the scorer's table. So important is the technique of properly tossing the ball that officials should spend time in practicing it so they become proficient and consistent at it. Since the height and ability to jump vary from player to player, one must develop expert judgment in order to make accurate tosses.

Don't move back after tossing the ball

FIGURE 36. Position of official when tossing ball for a jump. Note the height of approximately 12 feet.

Figure 36 shows an official making a proper toss. The ball is above the height that either player can jump. Also, the official has not moved back but is holding his position until after the ball clears.

To repeat, it is better to toss the ball too high than not high enough.

11. Front Court Play

a It is customary for each official to take certain positions on the court when the ball is in play and the players are moving in and out of the defense at one end of the court. b The leading official normally takes a position along the end line which is to his right as he faces the center circle from the side of the court when the

Be sure that no area is left unsupervised at any time

ball is at that end of the court. The trailing official takes a position behind and to the side of the play and on the opposite side of the court from the leading official.

The officials will reverse their positions when the ball is at the opposite basket. These relative positions always place one official ahead, or in front of, the play and the other behind, or alongside of, the play.

Both officials should move so they have a clear view at all times of the ball and the players contesting for the ball. Thus, the leading official working along the end line would move from a position behind the basket to the corner of the court farther from the trailing official. The trail official would move along the side line for the most part, but at times he would find it necessary to move over into the court in order properly to cover the play that goes toward the side of the court opposite from him. He will move from the center line along the side line up to, and sometimes beyond, the free-throw line extended as the ball penetrates the defense and moves toward the goal. The trail official should maintain a position back of and to the side of the player with the ball. The officials should avoid being directly across from each other at any time while the ball is in play.

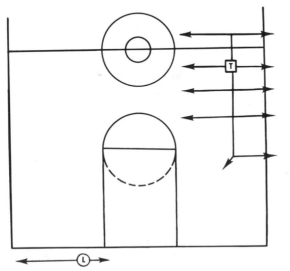

DIAGRAM 22. Positions and movements of the lead and trail officials when the ball is in play at one end of the court.

Erase ideas of sacred court areas for each official

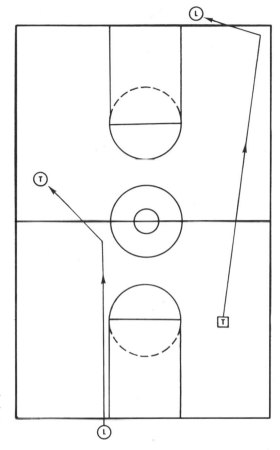

DIAGRAM 23. Movements and initial positions of lead and trail officials when the ball goes from one end of the court to the other.

The positions of the officials are always predicated upon an uninterrupted close observation of the play, and noninterference with the free quick movement of players.

Diagram 22 illustrates the positions and movements of the officials when the ball is in play at one end of the court. Diagram 23 shows their movements when the possession of the ball changes and play moves to the opposite end of the court. The movements and positions of the officials are now reversed. The trailing official now becomes the leading official at the opposite end of the court, and the leading official takes up the trail position.

This pattern of movement permits the officials to surround the

You need no passport to enter any part of court

play at close quarters from the front side and back side when it becomes congested around the goal, where decisions are difficult to make and yet where they are most important. This technique removes any semblance of a practice in which the leading official makes all the decisions at the goal at his end of the court. It eliminates any possibility of unequal calls at the two goals. Both officials will be on top of the play at each end and both will usually be making the same decisions at both ends.

There will be no such thing as a zone of influence or responsibility for each official. The reason for having two officials is that two can do everything done formerly by one official, and do it better. The assignment of two officials was not primarily to divide their responsibilities. Rather it was for the purpose of having a double check on the play. It must also be remembered that in spite of efforts to the contrary, an official occasionally has his line of sight blocked. Because this happens, each official should call everything (note exceptions in jump balls, try for goal, and out-of-bounds plays) he sees at any time. To do this effectively for under-basket play requires that he be close to the play.

Shaded diagrams have been developed to show the working area or positions of officials. Unfortunately, these have been misinterpreted. From them, many officials have drawn the erroneous idea that they were responsible for calling plays in these areas only. It is readily seen that if one official was more technical than the other or if he placed a different interpretation on certain plays, there would be quite different officiating in each area.

When the ball has been tipped after a center jump, the umpire follows the play closely, regardless of the direction, until the referee is able to assume his normal position. (Switching is described later in the text.) After the referee moves to his normal position, the umpire moves back to his regular spot if the initial move of the ball at the tip-off has required him to cover momentarily for the referee. This kind of team work guarantees that the play will always be covered closely by at least one official. This movement is indicated in Diagram 23.

As the officials maneuver with the play at one end of the court, they must be ready to handle fast breaks to the opposite end as a result of interceptions and recoveries. When situations of this kind occur, the official who was behind the play before the interception,

Anticipate the movements of the ball

now must keep in front of it as it speeds to the other basket. The official who was working along the end line follows the play from behind. Diagram 23 illustrates this movement. Usually the official who is back and to the side of the play can anticipate these reverses by seeing the situation develop. By means of his alertness he is able to move out ahead of the play without difficulty. There are times, however, when the situation changes so unexpectedly that he will be left behind momentarily. This fact should not discourage him from penetrating deeply to the front court to assist in handling the action around the goal. Fast-break play that results from interceptions or breaks of the game usually involves one or two players at the most. If such a play develops so quickly the official who should be ahead is behind the play, there is no difficulty in seeing all the action if he moves to the side so he has a clear view between the two players.

12. Jump Ball

Experience has decreed that officials shall be assigned specific duties in a few cases. Tossing the ball for jumps is one of the instances in which the duties for each official are designated.

The official who does not toss the ball will stand in the court near

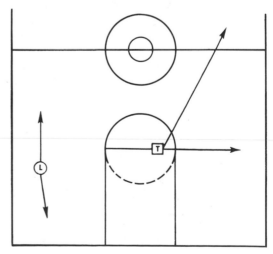

DIAGRAM 24. Positions and movements of the officials on a jump ball at the free throw line. Positions are the same at the opposite free throw line.

Are non-jumpers always observed?

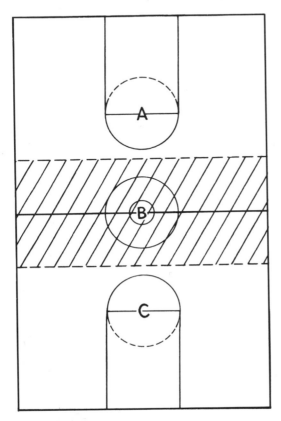

DIAGRAM 25. Areas from which play is resumed after a held ball. A held ball in area A, B, or C would be put in play by a jump at the circle in that area. In case of doubt, jump in area B.

the side line along which he is normally working. The responsibilities of each will be the same as described under the "center jump."

The official who does not make the toss must be ready to cover fast-break movements to either end of the court. If the end to which the play goes is not the end where he normally works, he will substitute for his fellow official until that official can take over his normal position.

Whether the ball is tossed at the center or at a free-throw line the official on the side of the court away from the scorer should make the toss. This permits the tossing official to face the scorer and then be able to see and be ready to respond to any signal from the scorer or timer. Each official will have the same duties and will

Co-operate—don't oppose

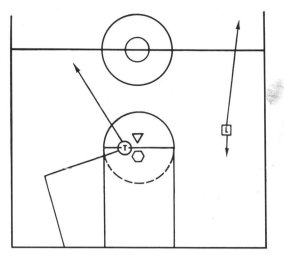

DIAGRAM 26. Positions and movements used by some officials for jump balls at the free throw line.

move the same, when the toss is at a free-throw line as when the toss is to be made at the center circle.

13. Out-of-Bounds

In order to call out-of-bounds plays correctly, it is necessary for the official to be close to the play, to be able to sight along the boundary line, and to be between the player and the boundary line. It is difficult to see the ball or a player in relation to a boundary line if the official has the player between him and the line. Shadows or the perspective from such a position may deceive the official and cause him to call a boundary violation when none has occurred. If one is not close to the play, it is difficult for him to see accurately and to tell who last touched, or who was last touched by, the ball before it went out-of-bounds.

Spectators are certainly not reliable judges in delicate out-of-bounds situations. This is evident when they voice their disapproval of boundary decisions where the ball has grazed a shoulder or a finger without being perceptibly deflected from its course. Except for the fact that the official who made the decision was right on the play, he too might have been in error.

It is because experience has shown officials that the one who is

Call out-of-bounds at your end and side line only

across the court from a boundary line play is not a reliable judge that a definite practice is now universally followed. Only the official who is working along a side line or an end line makes boundary line decisions on balls or plays that cross that side line or end line. The other official does not even blow his whistle. He does not even make a decision unless he is called upon to do so by his fellow official. The line of responsibility for each official is shown in Diagram 27.

The assumption here is that the decision of the official along the side line or end line is more reliable than that of his colleague. Therefore, it is better to have a few mistakes in the one case than many in the other. Also, it is bad practice for officials to be opposing each other in their decisions. Both would invariably make decisions on out-of-bounds plays, unless specific authority was delegated to each. It is especially bad for the official who is out of position, not near the boundary line and twenty or more feet away from the play, to make a contrary decision to the official who is in an advantageous position to determine with greater accuracy what has actually occurred. Here is one instance where spectators raise justifiable objections.

There may be cases where a ball is last touched by a player in the center of the court and then rolls out-of-bounds and that the official along the boundary line the ball crosses does not know who last touched the ball. There are also times when the official who is delegated to make a boundary line decision does not know who should be awarded the ball. He should in such instances look toward his colleague, who should be ready to assist. If the colleague saw the play, he should without hesitation announce the team that is to play the ball. If he is in doubt or did not see, he should immediately indicate a jump ball.

This type of cooperation between the officials on boundary decisions is preferable to dual responsibility. It is one of the exceptions mentioned previously.

In the administration of out-of-bounds play the rules admonish officials to make their decisions clearly evident to both teams. (Rule 2, section 9[b].) If there is any confusion, the official should obtain possession of the ball and withhold play until both teams have had a chance to recover their positions.

Two procedures are customarily followed for purposes of clarity.

Make your decisions clear

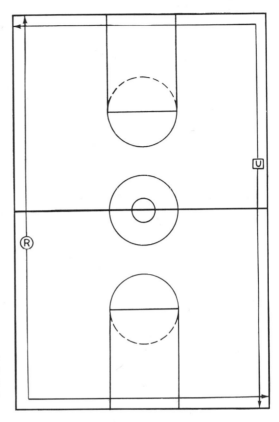

DIAGRAM 27. The lines between the arrows show the boundary line over which each official has jurisdiction for out-of-bounds balls.

The official indicates the team to which the ball has been awarded by calling out the color of the jersey that team is wearing, for example, "red," and at the same time pointing in the direction of the goal of that team. The official must, by rule, hand the ball to the player to whom it has been awarded.

There are times when an official must leave his normal position for covering the court in order to retrieve and handle the ball on an out-of-bounds play.

Two examples will demonstrate this situation.

1. The ball goes out-of-bounds on the side for which the trail official is responsible and near the front court end line. The throw-in is by the front court team. The trail official handles the ball for the throw-in. He is much nearer the end line than he usually stands. If an interception should occur on the throw-in, the trail official

How do you switch?

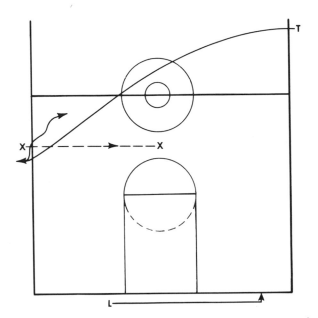

DIAGRAM 28.   Shows method of handling throw-in and subsequent play when ball is awarded to a team alongside in its front court and opposite from the trail official.

would be out of position. This is not considered serious because if there is a fast break play at the opposite basket, play is not congested because not more than two players are involved.

2. If, on the other hand, the throw-in is to be made by the back court team, the other official would handle the ball for the throw-in while his colleague moved to the end line at the opposite end of the court and to the opposite side from the spot of the throw-in. After the throw-in the official who handled the ball would cross to the opposite side from the spot of the throw-in and continue as the trail official. This move would be the signal for his colleague to move along the end line to the side from which the throw-in was made and continue as the lead official. These maneuvers represent a type of switching that is performed to place the officials in the areas in which they work most familiarly.

If the ball were to go out of bounds on the same side as discussed in the preceding paragraph but between the division line and the free-throw line at the opposite end of the court and the throw-in

Check all before awarding the ball

was to be by the same team as in the preceding paragraph, the same official would handle the ball but the officials would not switch after the throw-in. If the switch were made in this situation, the chance of missing an important play would be too great. These maneuvers are shown in Diagrams 28 and 29.

In administering the throw-in the official should stand between the spot of the throw-in and the goal of the player making the throw-in. This position prevents a player from committing technical

DIAGRAM 29. Shows positions and movements of officials during and following the throw-in when ball is awarded to a team at side in back court and opposite trail official.

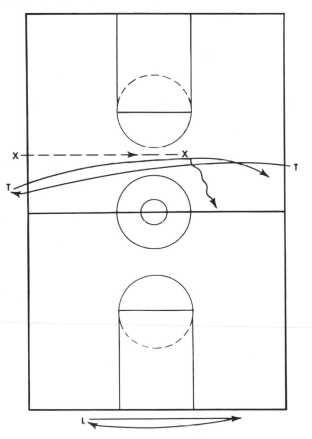

Stand between the thrower-in and his goal

infractions, which are usually inadvertent or are committed unconsciously and in haste. Some groups insist, however, that the official should stand on the opposite side so the play is always "boxed in" and so the official will not be impeded in case of an interception and a subsequent fast break. The author strongly supports the first procedure described because it prevents silly infractions and because the problem incident to being out of position in an interception and fast break are practically nonexistent, at least negligible.

H. Switching

1. There are two techniques practiced in connection with switching. In the one, the officials maintain their switched positions until there is a convenient time after a dead ball for them to switch back to their normal positions. A convenient time would occur after a foul, a held ball, or a substitution. It might occur after an out-of-bounds ball. It would not be convenient to switch back after a score.

2. In the other technique, the switch is only a momentary one. It lasts only so long as it is necessary for the official who was forced out of position because of a toss or out-of-bounds play to move into his normal position. As he moves to his end line, the other official simultaneously moves out to his normal position. This switch back is done without confusion or relaxation of vigilance.

This latter method is advocated by the author because it tends to hold the officials in their normal working positions to which they are conditioned. This plan of switching is much less confusing to young officials. They are always covering the end line to their right.

15. Free Throw

After a foul is called (see procedures when calling a foul), the following routine should be carried out before the ball is placed at the disposal of the free thrower:

1. The officials switch positions. Then the trail official moves to his position at the free-throw line immediately and the lead official

What do you watch during a free throw?

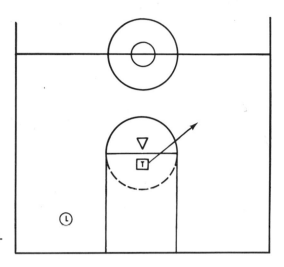

DIAGRAM 30. Position of officials during a free throw.

takes his position at the end line (see Diagram 30). The officials
should not saunter to their positions. For positions when administering the free throw for a technical foul, see Diagram 31.

b.2. The trail official handles the ball. His first duty after reaching
the free-throw line is to look toward the scorer to make sure that
the scorer has correct information concerning the foul and that
no substitutes are waiting or reporting to come into the game.
He should go to the free-throw line immediately in order to avoid
delay in putting the ball in play.

c·3. The official with the ball should stand between the free-throw
line and the basket until all is in readiness for the try for goal. He
should see that the players are properly distributed along the lanes.
Diagram 30 shows the position of the officials before and during
the try.

d,4. It is always necessary to indicate the number of free throws
that have been awarded. Regardless of where the foul occurred,
the official will be asked the number of throws unless he announces
the number each time.

e.5. Finally, he turns and hands the ball to the free thrower or
places it at his disposal at the free-throw line and steps out of the
free-throw circle, back and to the side of the thrower, so he is out

How many shots?

of the visual field of the free thrower. As he moves to this position he indicates to the timers the number of throws, so the timers will know how to operate the watch.

This routine, which consumes a small amount of time, is sufficient to permit players to station themselves properly along the lanes and for substitutes, if any, to report.

6. It is the duty of the trail official to watch the ball, the free thrower, and the players along the lane on the opposite side of the floor from him. The trail official is responsible for any violations that may occur in these three areas.

7. It is the duty of the lead official to watch the players along the lane on the opposite side of the court from him. He is responsible for any violations that may occur in their area. In order to administer these duties properly, he must be able to see when the ball touches the rim or backboard. He will be able to perform his duties best by assuming a position out-of-bounds along the end line at least two strides from the nearer free-throw lane line.

If a multiple throw is awarded, the lead official should quickly retrieve the ball after each throw except the last and pass it to his colleague at the free-throw line. The official handling the ball at the free-throw line will again hesitate momentarily to see that all is in order, to permit the teams to organize for the next throw, and to allow substitutes, if any, time to report.

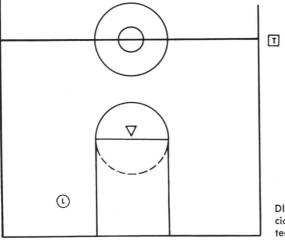

DIAGRAM 31.   Positions of officials during a free throw for a technical foul.

No need to watch a ball in flight—watch the players

In the case of a technical foul where the ball is to be awarded to the team throwing for a goal at mid-court after the throw, the opposite technique to that described above is followed. (See Diagram 31.) The lead official assumes possession of the ball and clears the opponents from the area between the free-throw line extended and the end line. The trailing official goes to mid-court where he is ready to hand the ball to the team that was awarded the free throw for technical foul, to play in from out-of-bounds. The lead official will throw the ball to him after the try.

If a double foul has been committed, each end-line official will handle the ball at his end of the court. This official also clears the area at his goal and rules on the legality of the play. The referee usually makes the toss at center after the last throw. In some sections, however, the official who administers the first free throw goes to the center circle to receive the ball from his fellow official after the last free throw. The purpose of this latter procedure is to avoid delay. The former method, however, permits the referee to check with the timer and scorer before the toss. It is consistent with the procedure at the start of each half and is recommended.

Try for Goal

When a team tries for a goal from a distance of 15 feet or more from the basket, it is usually necessary for the officials to concentrate momentarily on different areas before the ball reaches the basket. The official who has been behind and to the side of the play (the trail official) should focus his gaze on the shooter and the player guarding him. He must be sure that neither of these players interferes illegally with the other to the disadvantage of either. The shooter should not be permitted to charge, push, or jump into the guard. The guard should not illegally interfere with the shooter either before, during, or after the try leaves his hand. The fact that the players are aware that the trail official has not followed the flight of the ball but is watching them is a powerful deterrent to illegal tactics (the potential of presence). Figure 37 shows the trail official watching the shooter and his guard after the shot has been made. Note also that the end official is concentrating on the players near the goal.

Trailing official—move toward the goal after a shot

FIGURE 37. Position and attention of officials on a shot from out in court. Note that officials are watching players and not the flight of the ball.

After the trail official has assured himself that all is well between the shooter and his guard, he turns his gaze upon the basket. He must time this change of focus so that he can watch the ball as it approaches the basket. The trail official is primarily responsible for enforcing the rules covering goal tending and basket interference. He also rules on the ball and determines whether or not it has scored a goal or hit a support or the back of the backboard. Figure 38 shows the change of focus of the trail official as the ball nears the basket.

If, in addition to these duties, he can help to cover the play about the basket, he should do so. On long or medium long shots, he will not be able to assist in the under basket play as effectively as on short and lay-up shots. In the case of long or medium long shots there is not usually so much congestion under the basket, so that attention of both officials is not so necessary as it is on rebound-

End officials—where are you looking?

ing for the ball or on short shots. However, the trail official will move in toward the goal after a shot from the floor, so that he will be in a position to assist in any rebound play that may be subsequent to the original shot.

The lead official will devote himself to the maneuvering of the players close to the basket immediately following a floor shot. He must be sure that there is no blocking, tripping, holding, charging, or pushing as the players jockey for favorable positions in preparation for rebounding the ball if the shot is missed. (See Figures 37 and 38.)

Whereas, the trail official lingers with the players in the area of the shot, the lead official turns his gaze from the area of the shot to concentrate on the players in the vicinity of the goal. As the players converge on the goal, the attention of the two officials is again brought together. By this method of cooperation, the total court area is well covered for all important action.

FIGURE 38. Note that trail official watches ball as it approaches basket while lead official continues to direct attention to players.

Don't be timid—blow your whistle sharply

FIGURE 39.   Lead officials demonstrate a common error of watching ball on a shot. Note pushing on the court which is not detected
as a result.

Some officials have developed the bad habit of following the
flight of the ball when a shot for goal is made. Except in cases
where there may be overhead obstructions, no good purpose can
be served by focusing attention on the ball. The ball will come
down without human help. The trail official must see the ball
as it approaches the basket, and both officials will naturally keep
it in their visual field on rebounds. To watch the ball at any other
time in its flight is evidence of poor technique. Such practice invites
players to indulge in illegal tactics. Players are quick to sense when
officials' eyes are not directed at the players. The gaze of the lead
official should not be raised above eye level. Figure 39 shows
the lead official, eyes upward, watching the ball instead of the
players.

A study of pictures taken of games will reveal the fact that this
habit is a common one, the rule rather than the exception. For this

Pause after blowing the whistle

reason, officials should make deliberate efforts to develop correct court tactics in this respect.

As previously stated, the trail official must see the ball as it approaches the basket. He is primarily responsible for determining a score. He must be in a position to rule on possible infractions of the goal-tending and basket-interference rule. If a foul is called during a try, he must notice whether the ball went through the basket on the try or whether the ball was tapped or touched by another player either before or after the foul, before going through the basket. The trail official does not have to follow the ball through its entire flight to administer these duties. Only as the ball approaches the basket is it necessary for him to focus his attention on the ball. If he develops a wide vision, he will also be able to watch the players around the basket.

Responsibility for 3- and 10-Second Rule

The official who is working along the end line or the official who is in front of the play, by reason of his position on the court, is in the most logical position to govern the area of the court affected by the three-second rule. He is so close to this area that he can easily see and evaluate the movements of the players in this area, while, at the same time, he is watching the movement of the ball in the front court. By the same reasoning, the official who trails the play takes the primary responsibility for the ten-second-rule violations. This same official is the logical one to rule on center-line violations. This official is closer to the play that is near the center line and is, therefore, better situated for observing violations of this phase of the rules.

Specific duties or responsibilities have been assigned to each official for the court situations described in this chapter. This is done because it is felt that the position of the official in each case gives him a particular advantage that should permit him to see more easily and therefore to rule more equitably on the action incident to the situation. It is intended to show a way for cooperative effort, so more effective administration of a game can be attained.

It is not intended, however, to infer that the other official may

Are you a literal second counter?

not make decisions on any of these play situations. In all these cases, except the two specifically mentioned, both officials should feel at liberty to make any decision on any of these play situations that they can see.

There are times when the trail official will have the responsibility of watching the three-second area. Such an occasion would be when the ball has penetrated beyond the top of the free-throw circle and along the side line farther from the trail official. In this situation the lead official would have primary responsibility for the ball while the trail official was watching the players on the other area of the court.

Time-Out

During time-out, the officials have three responsibilities. They should, first of all, administer to the wants of either team and be ready to recognize substitutes. They should also use the opportunity to check with the scorers and timers on any points that may be pertinent, such as the amount of time left to play, checking score, and reiterating instructions concerning failure of signals to sound at end of period. Such precautions often avoid problems in close, exciting contests.

During time-out, the officials should confer on any phases of the game that are questionable. If they are not in tune, a brief conference may clear up moot points so they will work more smoothly together.

In order to carry out their duties most effectively, the official who is to handle the ball when play is resumed will hold the ball and take a position near where play is to be resumed. The other official should station himself near the scorer's table.

.¡ ₵PROCEDURE WHEN CALLING A FOUL

Each time an official calls a foul he should follow a definite pattern that will convey his decision clearly to the players, the scorers, and all others. The following procedure is recommended for this purpose.

When does trail official call 3-second violation?

1. Give a sharp, strong blast with the whistle. At the same time give the signal for time-out foul.

2. After blowing the whistle the official should pause momentarily while continuing to signal "time-out-foul."

3. Then before leaving the player who committed the foul, inform him of his decision by looking directly at him and by announcing his number and the color of his jersey, signaling the type of foul, and see that he raises his hand clearly above his head so the scorer may identify him.

4. Next, turn and if necessary move toward the scorer to repeat your decision, to make sure the scorer gets or has gotten accurate information. A nod or a wave from the scorer is an excellent means of confirmation.

5. The official who did not call the foul should retrieve the ball if necessary, and be ready to cooperate with his colleague in identifying the offended player or giving information about the location of the ball or about a goal when these are involved.

6. If both officials signal a foul or violation at approximately the same time, they should check with each other before announcing the decision.

7. After the above procedures are carried out the officials should move without delay to resume play.

17. PROCEDURE WHEN CALLING A VIOLATION

Each time an official calls a violation he should follow a definite pattern that will convey his decision to everyone present, particularly the players, so all can have a clear understanding of what took place. In order to accomplish the desired results the following procedure is recommended.

1. Give a sharp, strong blast with the whistle. At the same time give the signal for "time-out (no foul)."

2. After blowing the whistle, pause momentarily while continuing to signal "time-out (no foul)."

3. Then signal the violation which occurred and point in the direction toward which play is to be resumed.

4. Next go to the designated spot for the throw-in and call for the ball. Repeat the direction signal.

Practice the procedures for calling fouls and violations

e ·5. Take a position between the thrower-in and his goal and hand him the ball for the throw-in.

6. After handing the ball to the thrower-in or placing the ball at his disposal begin a silent count as prescribed by rule.

S 7. If both officials signal a violation at about the same time, they should check with each other to determine the sequence of the violations before announcing their decision.

Three-Man Team

Three officials have been used experimentally to officiate basketball games before 1950. Several plans for the officials to cooperate and coordinate their actions have been tried. At the moment no single plan has been acclaimed as the best. A recent revival of interest in the use of three officials suggests the desirability of discussing the three-official system.

The purpose behind the plan of the three-official system is to get full court coverage at all times by reducing the area for which each official is responsible. The speed up of play and the increase in the complexity of play have multiplied the duties of the officials to the extent that it is very difficult for two officials to cover all areas on the court with the proper concentration on each area at all times. As a consequence, rule infractions that should be called are not observed and therefore are not called. It is felt that the addition of the third official would correct this weakness. It is further reasoned that the addition of the third official would cause players to be conscious of the more complete coverage of play and that this fact would act as a deterrent to rule violations. Although the amount of data is limited, there is some evidence to indicate that games are freer from infractions when three officials are present. If this becomes an established fact, there will be a greater willingness to incur the additional expense for the extra official.

The diagrams that are presented to show one plan of operation may help the reader to a clearer understanding of the three-man system. The following discussion covers just one plan, which has been selected because it is the simplest and therefore the best for introductory purposes. The following are the salient features of the plan:

Three cover better

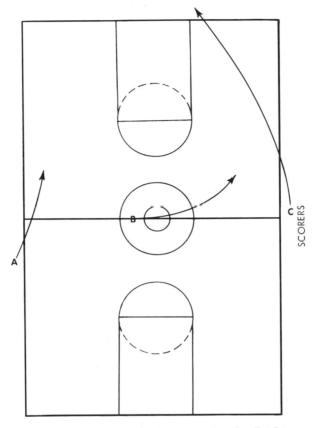

DIAGRAM 32. Starting positions and movements of each official in a 3-official game during a jump ball and as play moves to one end of the court. The positions and movements are relatively the same for a jump ball at either free throw circle.

1. The officials will be designated as A, B, and C in the diagrams.

2. For all jump balls, the official who makes the toss will face the scorers. The other two will be at the side lines, one on each side. As the side officials face toward the jumping circles, they will cover the play to their right. Therefore when the play goes to an official's right he will become the lead official at that end of the court. The other side official becomes a trail official on his side. The official who tosses the ball will become the trail official on the opposite side of the court.

Movement of three is simple to see

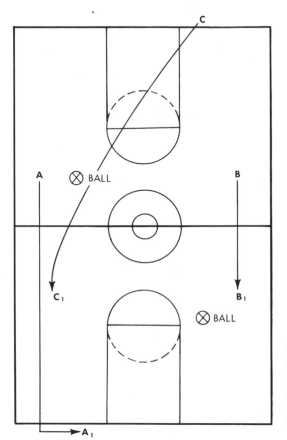

DIAGRAM 33. Positions of officials after tip to cover play in front court. Lines show the movement and A1, B1, C1 show the new positions of the officials when play moves to the opposite end of the court.

For any jump ball after the opening jump for a period, the official who makes the toss will be the trail official who is on the opposite side of the court from the scorers. (See Diagram 32 for the starting positions for a jump ball.)

3. The officials will work in a triangle at all times. (See Diagram 33.) One will be a lead official at the end of the court. The other two will be trail officials who will work along the side lines and back of the ball. The player with the ball will be covered by the trail official nearer to him. If a play starts from one side and then goes down the center, the trail official who covered the play on the side will continue to cover it.

Floor positions for three never vary

On a try the trail official who was covering the ball will stay with the shooter and his guard. The other trail official will move toward the end line to watch the ball at the basket. The lead official will concentrate on the players about the basket and the lane area at all times.

4. When the play moves from one end of the floor to the other, two officials switch positions by rotating counter clockwise and one official works from the same position. For example, the trail official covers the end line to his right, the lead official takes over the duties of the trail official who has switched to the lead position and the other trail official continues as a trail official. (See Diagram 33.)

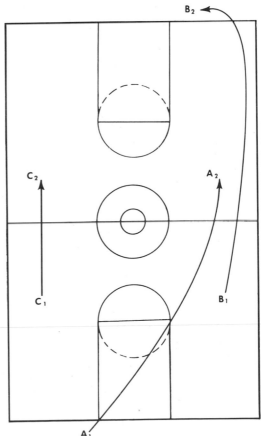

DIAGRAM 34. A continuation of play from diagram 33 to show how officials rotate positions when play moves back to end of court as shown in diagram 32. This play of rotation continues throughout the game without any variation as play continues to move from one end of the court to the other.

Rotate counter-clockwise

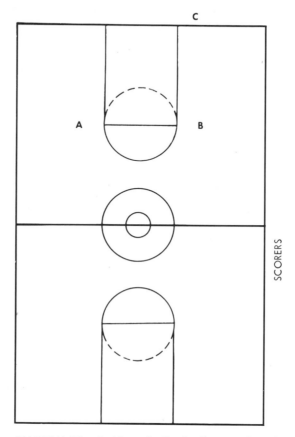

DIAGRAM 35. Position of officials during a free throw. The lead official watches the lane across from him. The trail official opposite the scorers handles the ball and thereafter watches the lane opposite him. The other trail official watches the free thrower and the ball.

When the play next changes ends, the trail official who did not switch now becomes the lead official to cover the end line to his right. (See Diagram 34.)

5. On free throws, the trail official opposite the scorers will always handle the ball and then watch the players along the lane farther from him. There is no switch before the free throw. The other trail official will watch the free thrower and the ball. The lead official will watch the players along the other lane. If a free throw

Three cover better on free throws

is missed and the ball is to remain in play, the officials will operate as indicated in 3 and 4. (See Diagram 35.)

6. Each official will be responsible for the boundary line along which he is working. He will make all calls and handle the ball for throw-ins from his boundary, except when the throw-in is from the side, and the subsequent play will require a switch by that side official. In this case the switch will be made before the throw-in, so

DIAGRAM 36. Positions of officials for a throw-in when play is to move to opposite end of court. In all other situations, the official who is responsible for a boundary line will handle the ball for the throw-in.

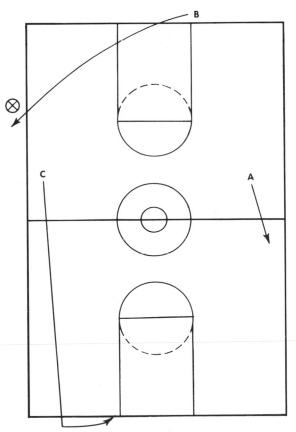

Each official has one boundary only

the official who would normally handle the ball can move to his duties as the lead official. (See Diagram 36.)

Signals

No treatise on officiating would be complete that did not include a presentation of the signals, which are used to interpret for the spectators, coaches, and players the decisions of the officials. The signals, reproduced here, have been adopted by all associations and are included as an official part of the rules. Every official should learn these signals. Each is obligated to use them as a means of relaying his rulings.

The voice, if the official has a strong one, may be used to supplement his body signals. It must be pointed out, however, that the use of the voice alone can be adequate only when the audience is quiet.

The official must have a sense of timing and the art of an actor to get across either by use of voice, pantomime, or both, his decisions to the public. There is always noise attendant upon exciting play near the basket or for that matter anywhere else on the court. Quite often the official's whistle evokes a response from the crowd. Consequently, a moment's pause before announcing a decision tends to create a hush of expectancy and draws attention to the official. At that point the official should go into action to tell his story and explain by pantomime the reason for his action. This is the surest way to satisfy a crowd and win their agreement even though they are partisan.

It must be repeated here that there is no place in basketball for the official who has the attitude that the game was created for him to perform and show off. Since the "grandstand" official is in the minority, the author has no fear of being misunderstood when he emphasizes the necessity for conveying decisions clearly to the crowd. The crowd is entitled to this consideration. It is a way of educating them in the technical aspects of the game. Too many officials through timidity or fear of being conspicuous, neglect this part of their job. By such neglect they weaken their effectiveness as officials. (See Figure 40.) The bonus rule requires a signal that

Clear signals educate the spectators

4. Beckon substitute when ball is dead and clock stopped

1. Start clock

2. Stop clock or do not start clock

3. Stop clock for jump ball

5. Stop clock for foul

6. Holding- follows Signal 5

7. Pushing or charging -follows Signal 5

8. Illegal use of hand -follows Signal 5

9. Technical foul

10. Blocking -follows Signal 5

11. No score

12. Goal counts or is awarded

13. Point(s) scored (1 or 2)

14. Bonus situation (for second throw drop one arm)

15. Traveling- Follow with Signal 18

18. Other violations also designates out of bounds spot and direction ball will go

16. Illegal dribble -follow with Signal 18

17. 3-seconds violation -follow with Signal 18

19. Player control foul

For free throw violation: Use Signals 2 and 18

For basket interference: Use Signals 11 or 12 and 13

FIGURE 40. The official basketball signals which should be used by all officials to convey decisions made by them.

Be dramatic—but not a show-off

does not appear in the official book. Extending the arms horizontally to the side and pointing the forefingers is recommended.

18. After the Game

After the final signal ends the game, the referee should check and approve the score. His approval terminates the jurisdiction of the officials. They should go to their dressing room immediately. They should avoid making any statements with respect to the game. Under no circumstances should they issue statements regarding the game or their officiating of it for publication. The official position is always a neutral, impersonal, and detached relationship. They must always maintain that relationship.

Maintain a neutral, impersonal, detached relationship to game

c h a p t e r   1 8

BASKETBALL: GUIDES
FOR ADMINISTERING
THE RULES

The purpose of this chapter is to lay groundwork which will help officials, coaches, and players develop a pattern by which a more uniform and realistic application of the rules can be attained. To reach this goal, there must first of all be an understanding of the intent and purpose of the rules. Next, definite guides must be established to help the official develop consistency and uniformity in administering the rules throughout each game. The following discussion is presented with the aim of accomplishing this goal.

Do you know the intent and purpose of each rule?

General Principles

At the outset it must be understood that most of the basketball rules that govern the limitations of action are stated in general terms in order to include all possible situations related to the rule. A rule may have been inserted into the guide because of a specific undesirable development, but its general coverage protects against unforeseen situations and technicalities that might develop later and avoids the necessity of too many rules and a bulky book.

The primary purposes of the rules are to maintain a balance between the offense and the defense, to provide an equal opportunity for the small as well as the tall player, to protect players, to encourage sportsmanship and fair play, and to emphasize cleverness, quickness, and skill as opposed to physical strength. As trends develop that are observed to threaten any of these purposes, legislation is adopted or changes in the interpretation of rules in force are made to stop the trend. For example, the "bonus" rule, which increased the penalty for fouling, stopped the trend to foul for profit and reduced the number of fouls by 20 per cent; a restatement and reinterpretation of the rule on personal contact has created a better balance between the offense and defense; the goal-tending rule and widening the foul lane curbed the great advantage the tall player enjoyed over the short player.

It is evident that the rules are to be administered in a manner to prevent a team from gaining an advantage not intended by the rules. Therefore the rules cannot be administered with mechanical blindness. Each situation in each game must be administered in terms of the effect of the situation at the time it occurs in the game. The type of play, the caliber of the teams, and the emotional and psychological factors involved will tend to determine the judgments made by the officials. The job of the officials is to interrupt as little as possible or as often as is necessary to keep the game within the bounds of the intent and purpose of the rules. It is because of this fact that officiating is a human art, and not a mechanical procedure.

1. *A player must make or cause personal contact to commit a personal foul (Rule 4, section 8d).*

At one time the rules prohibited a player from turning his back on the ball, completely disregarding it, facing his opponent, and moving as his opponent moved. This was a personal foul. No per-

Most rules are general

sonal contact was necessary. Now that this rule has long since been deleted from the book, no situation exists whereby a personal foul may be called unless there is personal contact. Even though a player takes an illegal position, which may cause contact, no foul can occur unless personal contact results therefrom. A screening position so close to an opponent that, in the opinion of the official, the opponent had no chance to avoid contact, is an example of this situation.

2. *Contact may occur, even violent contact, without a personal foul being committed.*

This statement implies that the official must not only see the end result of movement which causes contact but that he must see the action that leads up to the contact. As a matter of fact, his decision will be based largely on the movement of the players, their relative positions, and the direction of their movement, rather than upon the fact of contact. The comments on the rules that refer to personal contact state and imply this principle.

There are several situations that may be used to illustrate this. Two players are charging for a loose ball. They come from different directions. Each has an unimpeded path to the ball. They reach the ball at the same time and collide with terrific impact. If both have played the ball but, in spite of this fact, contact occurs, neither is guilty of committing a foul. Players 1, 2, 3, and 4 in Diagram 37 represent this case very clearly.

If, on the other hand, one player is between his opponent and the ball and this opponent charges into the player from behind as he dives for the ball, a different situation prevails. In this case, a foul has been committed. Also, even though both players are approaching from opposite directions, if one dives beyond the ball and into his opponent so he blocks his opponent from the ball, a foul has been committed. In this case, the player is not playing the ball but rather is blocking his opponent. Players 5, 6, 7, and 8 in diagram 37 indicate movements that produce illegal contact.

These diverse examples are given to avoid the conclusion that in all cases of loose balls, there is no possibility of committing a foul. Judgments must be based on the action. The accompanying diagrams will clarify this.

Occasionally a player will attempt to dribble between two opponents when there is not sufficient space to permit free movement,

There must be contact to be a personal foul

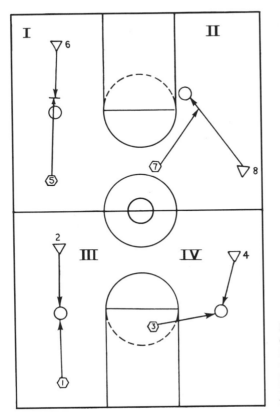

DIAGRAM 37. Legal and illegal contact in a contest for a loose ball. Illustrations I and II show illegal movements. Players 5 and 7 are not playing the ball. Illustrations III and IV are legal movements. Any contact here will be incidental.

or he may attempt to dribble between an opponent and a boundary line. As a result of his efforts, he trips over the legs of an opponent. The assumption here is that the opponents in each case are in a legal position. No foot has been extended nor movement made by the opponents to impede the progress of the dribbler. While the dribbler may take a terrific spill, it could not be charged that the defensive player has committed a foul in this instance. The dribbler actually suffered from his own folly.

In the case of a blind screen, a screen set behind an opponent, (outside of his visual field), the opponent may be chased into the screen while he is forced to move at a very rapid rate. The contact may be with considerable force. Since in screening action the objective is to impede the progress of any opponent by causing him

There may be contact and yet no foul

to make contact, the contact described above is not a foul provided the opponent stops on impact and then changes his path of movement to get around the screen. It is considered to be incidental contact. If the player who sets the blind screen has the ball and the impact by the opponent causes the screener to violate the running rule, a foul must be called.

3. *Blocking applies only to a player who does not have the ball.*

By definition, blocking is personal contact that impedes the progress of an opponent who does not have the ball (Rule 4, section 2). Conversely, it should be remembered that in no case may a defensive player block the player who has the ball. If a defensive player moves into the path of a player with the ball (usually a dribbler) and assumes a legal guarding position (Rule 10, Section 8) he cannot commit a foul for blocking. The only possible way he could foul would be to charge, after assuming a legal position, or he could fail to get into position and thus charge from the side, impede the progress of the player with the ball by contact, by means of an extended arm, hip, shoulder, knee, or foot, or by leaning into his path with his bended body. While it is not possible to block the player who has the ball, this player should not be assessed a foul for charging if he causes incidental contact when a defensive player suddenly appears in front of the dribbler in a legal guarding position.

Failure of officials to realize the full import of Guide Number 3 often causes the defensive player to suffer unjustly. The four examples that follow are typical. These are singled out because they represent situations in which the innocent player is penalized too frequently.

A player with the ball is dribbling toward the goal. An opponent places himself directly in the path of the dribbler. The dribbler catches the ball, jumps into the air to shoot. Either before or after shooting, he charges into the guard, who has not moved toward the dribbler, but who may have retreated slightly, jumped into the air in an attempt to block the shot, held his position, or ducked to avoid injury. Without question, the responsible person for the contact here is the shooter.

Under no circumstances could the guard be guilty of an illegal act under the conditions as described above. The shooter may receive a jarring fall as a result of his own overaggressive advance.

It is not possible to block the player who has the ball

The guard would still be blameless because he has first placed himself directly in the path of the shooter before the shot and he has not charged, pushed, held, or committed any other illegal act.

Many times it is necessary for defensive players to switch from one opponent to another. To illustrate: One player has the ball and a teammate cuts around this player to receive a pass and to displace his guard. The guard who originally guarded the player who first had the ball, now switches to guard the player who received the ball. As a result of this switch, he places himself directly in the path of the player who has the ball and is charged by him. If a foul has been committed it is committed by the player who has possession of the ball, not by the guard. The assumption here is that no other factors are involved except those described above.

A player gains possession of the ball as a result of a successful rebound attempt. As he returns to the floor after his jump, he turns and dribbles toward the side line. An opponent places himself directly in the path of the dribbler who makes contact with the body (torso) of the opponent. No other factors are involved. It is assumed that the opponent does not place himself in front of the dribbler in an illegal guarding position. If a foul has occurred here, it has been committed by the dribbler. The guard could not block because he is playing the man who has the ball.

A similar movement occurs when a player receives the ball with his back to his goal. He may be in mid-court, in the back court, at the free-throw line, anywhere. An opponent places himself directly behind this player. The player with the ball turns to move toward his goal and crashes into the body of his opponent. Here again no other factors are involved. This situation should not be confused with the guarding from the rear, which is covered completely in the next section of the chapter. If a foul has occurred, then the player with the ball is responsible. The guard could not be charged with blocking because he was impeding the progress of the man with the ball.

4. *When players are moving in exactly the same direction and path the responsibility for contact rests on the player who is behind.*

It is legal for a player to move in front of and in the same direction as an opponent for the purpose of impeding his progress. If the opponent runs into such a player, there is no foul for blocking. If any illegal act has been committed, it would be for charging by

Progress may be deliberately impeded legally

the opponent who is behind. The player who is in front may even slacken his pace or stop. This occurs in play where a player is running interference for a teammate who has the ball. In order to prevent an opponent, who is approaching from the rear, from overtaking his teammate, the player slows up or stops and thus causes the opponent to run into him. The responsibility is placed on the opponent who comes up from the rear.

It must be borne in mind that any deviation from the path that is in the same direction as the opponent is taking, introduces an entirely new set of conditions. Action under these circumstances must be judged and administered in terms of the criteria governing these new conditions (see 5).

Diagram 38 illustrates these two situations. Players 1 and 2 are offensive players. A is on defense. A and 1 are moving in exactly the same direction. 1 lets A run into him so that 2 may go to the basket unguarded. In the other part of the diagram, 3 and 4 are offensive players. B is on defense. 3 is not moving in the same direction as B. Here 3 has the greater responsibility, if contact occurs. Whether or not a foul occurs must be judged in the light of the principles stated under 5.

5. *When players are moving in different directions or even opposite directions, the greater responsibility for contact rests on that player whose team has possession of the ball.*

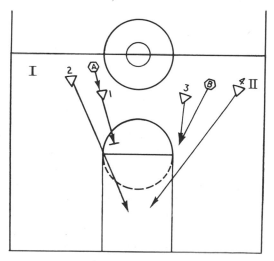

DIAGRAM 38. Legal and illegal screening movements. Illustration I shows legal action. A and 1 are moving in exactly the same path and direction. Illustration II is illegal. 3 is not moving in same path and direction as B. 3 would be guilty of blocking if he moved into B's path so quickly that B could not avoid contact.

Who reached the spot first?

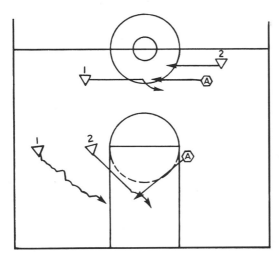

DIAGRAM 39. Offense is moving in a different or opposite direction to the defense. Offensive players 1 and 2 must stop or change direction to avoid contact with A or be guilty of charging or blocking if contact occurs.

If both players are moving so that their paths cross or if they are moving directly toward each other (see Diagram 39) and they continue in motion, then it behooves the player whose team has possession of the ball to avoid a collision. The defensive player will usually be following an opponent or cutting to intercept a play. The offensive player under these circumstances has no right to impede his progress. If he does, then he is guilty of blocking. This is in accordance with Rule 10, section 8, and the comment as contained in the official *Basketball Guide*.

Principles 4 and 5 are applied to some clever but complicated screening maneuvers that to be legal require perfect timing between teammates. The term "roll screens" is used to denote these maneuvers. A typical play is shown in Diagram 40.

In the diagram, player 1 (the team in possession of the ball) has moved up behind player A. Just as 2 starts to break by A, 1 reverses his direction. A runs into 2 when both are moving in the same direction. As described in Principle 4 above, this is a legal movement. The important factor here is timing. 1 must time his reversal so that he is moving in exactly the same direction as A when contact is made. If 1 is going in the opposite direction to A when they collide, then of course, he is blocking. It would be the responsibility of 1 in this instance to avoid contact.

Based upon the statement of General Principles, specific guides

Blocking or screening? It depends on relative position, timing, direction of movement

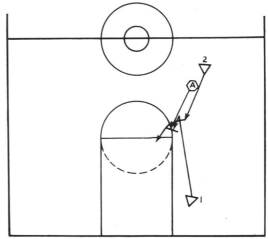

DIAGRAM 40. Roll screen movement. Player 1 moves toward ∧, but changes direction in time to move in the same path and direction as A without causing contact. This is legal play. Afterwards player 1 may stop or slow down to impede A.

will be presented to help the official in handling specific play situations. First, guides for contact situations and then noncontact situations will be presented.

Specific Guides for Contact Situations

The development and refinement of screen play to the point where it represents a major offensive weapon to combat the improvement in defensive tactics has necessitated a different set of guides outlining responsibilities for contact resulting from guarding situations and contact resulting from screening situations. It has also required a listing of guarding and screening situations to which the guides for each apply. The guides placing responsibility for contact resulting from guarding situations will be stated first.

Guides to Guarding Situations

1. A guard is entitled to any spot on the floor provided he gets to that spot first and provided he does not contact an opponent in taking such position. This guide is of primary importance to the official in determining responsibility for contact in all guarding situations. All others are secondary.

Was screener stationary and at a proper distance?

2. If a guard assumes a floor position in the path of an opponent a fraction of a second in advance of such opponent, he must be facing his opponent. After assuming a legal position he may turn his side or back to his opponent. If the guard assumes his position two strides or more before his opponent arrives, no particular facing is necessary.

3. It is not necessary for the guard to be stationary at any time. Movements of an opponent require offsetting movements of his guard if the guard is to maintain his guarding position. If the guard loses his guarding position by reason of the action of his opponent, it will be necessary for the guard to move in an attempt to regain his guarding position. Thus the important fact is whether the guard is in a guarding position when contact occurs. A guard may not, however, be moving toward his opponent when contact occurs.

4. Once a guard has established his position in the path of an opponent, he may turn or duck to protect himself when impact is imminent.

5. A guard may not move into the path of an opponent after the opponent has jumped into the air.

6. When a guard assumes his position a fraction of a second before contact is made by an opponent, the opponent is responsible for the contact provided contact is on some part of the front of the torso. This statement should be interpreted to mean that if only a small part of the guard is in the path of an opponent and if the front of the body is partially facing the opponent so contact occurs with the front of the torso, the guard is legally in the path of his opponent.

7. When a guard assumes his position well in advance of an opponent and has his feet on the floor, the point of contact is irrelevant provided there is no subsequent movement to cause the contact, such as leaning into the path of the opponent.

8. Both the guard and his opponent are entitled to erect (vertical) positions with the arms extended above their shoulders. If either leans or crouches over the other, he must not prevent his opponent from assuming an erect position.

9. If contact occurs by a player who violates any one of these guides, that player is responsible for the contact. The official must judge whether the contact is incidental or a foul.

A guard may move

Following are guarding situations to which the guides apply.

1. Guarding a player who does not have the ball.

This is a man-to-man situation. The guard may be dogging the footsteps of his opponent to prevent him from moving freely to a desired spot or he may be playing his opponent loosely or loosely and tightly alternately depending upon the position of the opponent on the court and with respect to his distance from the ball or the goal. It does not include switching tactics where a player without the ball is involved.

2. Guarding a player with the ball.

This may be a man-to-man situation, or it may be a double-teaming activity including pressing tactics. Each player is entitled to his position. In double-teaming tactics one guard is usually behind the opponent to prevent him from retreating, or the player with the ball pivots away from a single guard. The player who is behind may not impede the movement of his opponent by leaning over him and causing contact when the player with the ball attempts to pivot about. Neither is contact excusable from the rear even though the guard has a hand on the ball. This should be called closely in order to prevent rough play. If, however, the guard merely takes a position in the rear free of contact and without leaning over or reaching around his opponent, the opponent is responsible for the contact if he pivots into the guard.

3. Guarding the dribbler.

This is the situation that is most common and best administered. The guard has a right to shift to keep in the path of the dribbler. If, however, the dribbler is able to maneuver so he gets his head and shoulders by the guard, the guard may not charge into the dribbler from the side or impede the progress of the dribbler with outstretched arm. The guard must retreat then overtake the dribbler to reestablish his position in the path of the dribbler before the responsibility for contact reverts back to the dribbler.

4. Guarding the post player with or without the ball.

This is the situation where the erect position of each player is most often involved. If the guard is behind his opponent who is crouched with one foot in advance of the other, the opponent has the right to step back with his forward foot as far as his rear foot. The guard may not legally prevent the opponent from attaining this erect position.

Rules are the same for guarding players with or without the ball

On the other hand, the guard may not be displaced from his erect position by action of his opponent. If perchance the guard extends his arms directly above his head, the opponent has no legal right to push his arms or hands out of position in making a shot and certainly the guard should not be penalized, as is often the case, when this happens.

5. Guarding the rebounder.

Turning from a facing position to a position with the back to the opponent is a legal movement of the guard in rebounding situations. A guard may move into the path of or pivot to turn his back on an opponent at the last split second before the opponent gets opposite him in an attempt to run by to rebound. In this situation the guard must not charge the side of his opponent. If the guard is successful in this maneuver he would expect incidental contact from his opponent. However, the opponent may not charge through the guard nor push him out of position. The guard may not back up and into the opponent to move him away from the goal. (See Diagram 41.)

6. Switching to a player who has the ball.

It is perfectly legal to move into the path of a player with the ball (dribbling may or may not be involved), at the last instant even though the player with the ball is unable to stop without making contact. The player with the ball must keep his body under

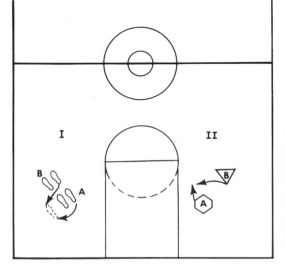

I   II

DIAGRAM 41. Preventing a player from gaining a desired position on rebounds. After a shot, A who is guarding and facing B pivots or steps into the path of B who attempts to go around him. This is a guarding situation and legal play. If after A pivots into the path of B, B runs into A, B is responsible for the contact. A may turn his back to B.

Learn the guide and the decision is easy

control, because he should expect that some opponent is likely to move into his path and impede his progress at any moment.

7. Guarding a player who is trying for goal.

The player who is trying for goal has no more rights than any other player. This statement is made because there is a tendency on the part of officials to give him greater freedom of action. The guard is entitled to his position the same as in any other guarding situation. If the guard, in an attempt to block a try, moves in a vertical direction, he may not be displaced by an opponent who is trying for goal either by being charged or having his hands or arms pushed aside. If the guard inclines forward from his vertical position, then he must be sure that he contacts the ball only.

Guides for Screening Situations

Because two or more players on the same team are involved in all screening situations, greater restrictions are placed on the movement and position of the screener than are placed on the guard in a guarding situation.

1. The screener must remain stationary after setting a screen or he is guilty of blocking when contact occurs except when he is moving in exactly the same direction and path of the player who is being screened. This is by far the most important guide for determining the legality of a screen. Any time the screener is moving and contact occurs, blocking takes place with the one rare exception that is stated. A roll screen is an example of this exception. (See Diagram 40.)

2. Facing is irrelevant when setting a screen. The screener may be turned sideways or have his back toward his opponent.

3. The screener may assume any normal basketball position. This rule eliminates extended arms, leaning the hips or shoulders, or moving a leg into the path of an opponent.

4. The distance of the screener from his opponent at the moment the screen is set is dependent upon whether the opponent is moving or stationary and whether the screen is set behind or in front of the opponent.

a. If the screen is set in front (in the visual field) of an oppo-

Screen must be stationary—with one exception

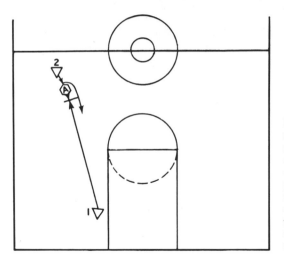

DIAGRAM 42. Legal screening movement. Player 1 assumes a position behind A and remains stationary when player 2 cuts around him causing A to run into player 1. 1 is far enough away from A to permit him to take one step without contact. A's contact would be incidental if he stopped on contact and deviated course around 1.

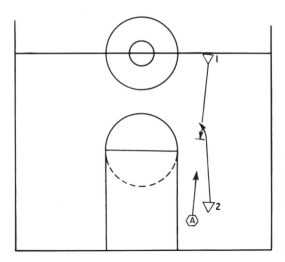

DIAGRAM 43. Legal screening movement. All three players are moving rapidly. Player 1 stops two strides from A who is attempting to catch up with 2. Since 1 is within the visual field of A there is no reason for A to contact 1.

nent who is stationary, the screener may be as close as he desires short of contact.

b. If the screen is set behind (out of the visual field) of an opponent who is stationary, the position is legal if the opponent takes one step (length not to exceed a normal distance for that opponent) before contact occurs.

The simple guide for the official is to note whether the player being screened is able to place his foot on the floor in concluding his step before contact occurs. If he completes the step, the position of

Running into a blind screen is not a foul if player stops on contact

the screener is legal. If before the step is completed contact occurs, the screener has committed a foul for blocking. (See Diagram 42.)

c. If the opponent is moving, the screener must assume his position in the path of the opponent in time to permit him to avoid contact. If contact occurs, the official must judge the legality of the time the screener took his position. This is the most difficult judgment for an official to make in screening situations. It has been determined by trial and error that, if the screener assumes his position so his opponent is able to take two strides before any contact occurs, the screen will be legal regardless of the speed of the opponent. A slow moving opponent will not need that much distance. The guide applies whether the screen is behind or in front. (See Diagram 43.)

The following play situations are classed as screening situations to which the above guides apply.

    1. Screening a stationary opponent from in front.
    2. Screening a stationary opponent from the rear.
    3. Screening a moving opponent from in front or the rear.
    4. Taking a position in the path of an opponent who is moving while looking back to receive a pass. This usually involves a pass-out on a fast-break situation. After such a player receives the pass, the situation changes to a guarding situation and the guides for guarding situations apply.

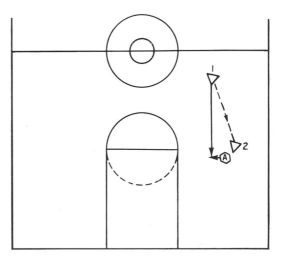

DIAGRAM 44. Blocking by the defense. A steps into the path of 1, who does not have the ball, so quickly that 1 is unable to avoid contact. This is a switching movement where the screening principles apply because 1 does not have the ball.

Switching to player without the ball is screening

5. Switching to an opponent who does not have the ball. Switching here may involve changing opponents or switching from guarding no one in particular (as in a zone defense) to specific coverage of an opponent. These are situations where the opponent is moving and the defensive player is responsible for complying with the guides for screening situations. (See Diagram 44.)

Specific Guides:
Noncontact Situations

The general principles stated at the beginning of this chapter apply with equal force to noncontact situations. Space will not permit an exhaustive analysis of all the rules that pertain to noncontact situations. Several will be discussed to show the application of the general principles; the official may apply the same philosophy in administering the others. Some guides to effect consistent judgment in administering those rules that seem to be violated more frequently than others will be presented.

At all times, the official should ask himself when administering the rules pertaining to noncontact situations: "Has an advantage not intended by the rules been gained?" If an advantage occurs, then a violation has been committed and should be called. With this principle in mind the following situations and guides are presented to carry out the intent and purpose of the rule covering noncontact situations.

THREE-SECOND RULE

The purpose of this rule is to prevent a player from camping in the restricted area, and thus to eliminate a difficult contact situation for the official. Therefore, if an offensive player moves without hesitation and without loitering across the lane, the official is not concerned about a literal three seconds. Also, if a player receives the ball before the count of three while he is in the lane, and then dribbles or pivots and dribbles to the basket and shoots, the official does not continue his count. In other words, if in the judgment of the official there is no attempt to gain an advantage, the official should not be too hasty in calling a violation.

It should be remembered that the three-second rule was passed

The philosophy for ruling on contact applies for non-contact situations

when the lane was six feet wide. The amount of time has no magic to it. When the lane was doubled in width the rules committee considered the desirability of increasing the time limit but made no change because it did not desire to focus attention on a literal number of seconds.

TEN-SECOND RULE

The ten-second rule was a compromise rule. Before 1933 when teams ahead in the score began to stand near the opponents' end line holding the ball and when the defensive team stood near its opponents' goal so that there was absolute inaction, it was evident that something had to be done to prevent stagnation. Half felt the offense was responsible for action and half were equally insistent that the defense was responsible. Since no acceptable solution could be found, a compromise was adopted: the division line and the ten-second limitation for play in the back court with a no return provision. This forced the offense to its front court, and it was hoped that the defense would be encouraged to push its defense to the back court. Thirty years later this hope was realized.

Therefore, the ten-second count or the division line violation becomes important when the defense is making a play for the ball by pressing or double-teaming tactics. If there is no opposition the official does not bother to count unless he feels that a team is delaying in the back court an unusual length of time, because there is no advantage to be gained.

When a player dribbles from the back court to the front without opposition it is possible for the ball to bounce in the front court and be touched while the player who is dribbling is still in the back court. Here no advantage is to be gained. It is not the intent of the rule that a violation should be called in situations like these.

DRIBBLE

While dribbling, players rarely tap the ball to the floor. Instead they literally keep their hand in contact with the ball as it rises from the floor, follow the ball by contact throughout its rise and fall, and at the last moment push it to the floor as contact is released. By this method the direction of the ball is changed. This

Was an advantage not intended by rule, gained?

action does not correspond to the exact wording of the rules. The intent is that the ball should not be held or carried by a player.

On the basis of the intent the official should use as his guide for legality *the facing of the palm* of the hand. *If the palm is facing downward, even at a very slight angle, the ball cannot be carried or come to rest on the hand in terms of the intent of the rules.* If the palm is facing upward, the ball is being carried when it comes in contact with the hand unless the ball is given a clear tap or bat. In this latter case a violation should be called, because the defense would be placed at a disadvantage if he acted on the theory that the dribble had ended.

Once during a dribble the ball may be touched twice before it hits the floor, and any time a ball is fumbled it may be recovered.

THROW-IN

The prohibition against the breaking of the plane of the boundary on a throw-in was intended to prevent interference by either team and to give the official a definite guide if problems arose. If there is no opposition to the throw-in, the prohibition has little importance unless an advantage is gained by a quick throw-in on a fast break. The other restrictions on the throw-in should be treated in like manner.

The five-second count on the throw-in was important at one time to prevent the undue consumption of time. Now the clock is stopped on all throw-ins except after a field goal. The five-second count is important now only in cases where pressing tactics are employed and after a field goal. In the cases where a delay would accrue to the advantage of the offense it must be strictly enforced. As in the other noncontact situations the matter of advantage is the determining factor. When pressing tactics are employed it should be remembered that the five-second count continues until the ball is touched on the court.

FREE THROW

The several restrictions governing the free throw are to prevent an advantage being gained by either team. Technical infractions such as mere touching of a boundary line may be ignored or play

Is the palm facing downward when dribbling?

stopped and a warning given. Here again actual procedure is based upon whether an advantage is gained. In no case should abuses be permitted that tend to make a travesty of the game.

HELD BALL

Held balls where two players are touching the ball should not be called too hastily with the idea of forestalling rough play. Rough play is controlled by calling fouls. A held ball should not be called until it is certain that neither player can gain absolute control. This suggests a delay for one tug or evidence of a stalemate. If one player is behind another, the player behind must release the ball when the player in front pulls the ball foward, in order to avoid a foul. In no case should a held ball be called when the ball is rolling on the floor and players are scrambling for it.

In a situation where the five-second count is involved, the official should be strict in administering the five-second rule when a team is employing extreme ball-control tactics and not attempting to score or where the defense is using aggressive pressing tactics.

Under other circumstances there is no need for strict enforcement of the rule nor was the rule intended for such purposes. Certainly no advantage is gained thereby. The specific references to pivot-post cutting movements in the comments to the rules is an indication of the intent of the rule.

Don't call a held ball to prevent a foul

chapter 19

SOCCER

Soccer, the world's number one sport, is nowadays played throughout the world; some 132 countries are members of the Federation Internationale de Football Association (FIFA). The same laws of the game meet with universal acceptance. Although it is the national game in about 70 of these countries, just as baseball is in the United States, its growth has been slow in America. It now appears to be one of the fastest growing sports in the U.S., probably because it has received much stimulation through improved methods of travel, which makes international competition possible, through television, which has created a new interest, and through the awareness by physical educators and parents of the many values gained through playing.

Soccer officiating has reached maturity

The Federation Internationale de Football Association is the governing body for soccer throughout the world. It makes all decisions pertaining to the laws of the game. The United States Soccer Football Association (USSFA) is our national association, which is affiliated with the Federation. Many soccer organizations, including the Intercollegiate Soccer Football Association of America (ISFA), which is the college governing body, are affiliated with the USSFA. In the United States, soccer is played at the professional, club, college, high school, and sandlot levels.

With the tremendous growth of soccer has come the increasing demand for competent and trained officials. As far as officials' organizations are concerned, soccer no longer lags behind some of the other sports because many local groups or associations are springing up, and there is a National Soccer Officials Association (NSOA). Through the efforts of these local groups, the NSOA, the USSFA, the ISFA, and college and high school soccer coaches' groups, many clinics are conducted to train new officials and to refresh the more competent ones.

At these clinics, demonstrations stressing proper positioning of the referees, game situations that require close attention, and interpretation of the laws by authorities designated as official interpreters, have been given. Written examinations are also given to test the knowledge of new officials. Some groups give written tests as refreshers to those considered competent. A practical test (actual refereeing of a game under observation) is a requirement of most officials' organizations.

Such clinics have helped to standardize officiating procedures and the interpretation of the rules. This has been a very important factor, because in few other sports is the referee concerned with "intent" when passing judgment on the legality of the play. These clinics have also upgraded officiating and made possible worthwhile financial remuneration to replace "interest" and "service" to soccer. To further upgrade officiating, reports are made on the work of each official after each game, either by the coaches or by appointed commissioners. A sample of these reports is shown in Form VIII.

There are two grades of referees, rated according to ability and experience as follows:

Grade 1. Referees who have attained and maintained the standard necessary to officiate at college games, according to the referees'

Referee—what is your popularity rating?

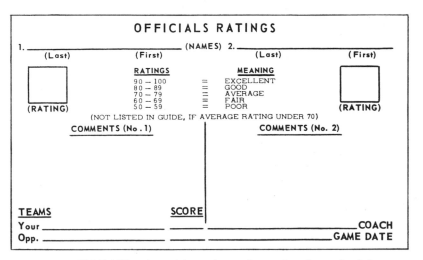

FORM VIII.   A card for rating and reporting the work of the soccer officials.

reports. A score of 70 or better is required to be rated as a Grade 1 official.

Grade 2. Referees who do not have the qualifications necessary for Grade 1, or new referees who need experience. This group is qualified to handle games at the high school level.

A listing of Grade 1 referees is published in the official NCAA Soccer Guide.

The Officials

The international laws which pertain to officiating vary in a few instances from the Collegiate-Scholastic laws. These differences will be discussed as the duties of officials and procedures for officials are presented.

According to FIFA laws the officials necessary for handling a soccer match are a referee and two linesmen. The referee has complete control of the game and makes all calls, as well as keeps time. He is assisted by two linesmen whose duties are to indicate when the ball is out of play and which side is entitled to the corner kick,

Agree on the working area with your colleague

goal kick, or throw-in. They also assist the referee to control the game, especially offside, in accordance with the laws. The linesmen should be equipped with flags for use in signaling the referee when the ball is out of play, or when there has been a violation.

In accordance with the official Collegiate-Scholastic Soccer Guide, the officials necessary to handle a soccer match are two referees with equal authority, two linesmen, and one timer from each team. The referees make all calls and are in complete control of the game. The two linesmen are appointed by the home team, but they are under the direct supervision of the referees. Each linesman should be dressed neatly and provided with an extra ball. When the ball in play goes out of play over the touch line, the linesman places the extra ball at the spot where the ball crossed the line. He then retrieves the other ball. Linesmen have no authority to call plays and might rightfully be referred as as "ball boys."

TIMEKEEPERS (NCAA)

Each school should appoint an official timer. It is recommended that a faculty member or the manager from each team be responsible for keeping the record of the playing time and notify the referee or referees at the end of each playing period. Because of the little scoring that is done, the timers usually act as scorers and record keepers. The timers should have one timing device visible at all times to both timers and a timekeeper's signaling device (any device such as a horn, gun, etc., but *not* a whistle). An extra clock and signaling device should be available for immediate use. Although timekeepers should know the rules pertaining to timing, the referee should instruct them as to their duties, and arrange an understandable series of signals to ensure cooperation. The expiration of playing time is indicated by the timekeeper's signal. Play stops the moment this signal sounds irrespective of the position of the ball or other considerations. The timekeeper should:

1. Keep track of playing time.
2. Take time out when signaled to do so by the referee.
3. Signal the referee when substitutions are to be made, signaling only when the ball has gone out of play for a goal kick, corner kick, after a goal, when an injury occurs, or between periods.

Consistency can be achieved through officiating under supervision

4. Keep track (on another clock) of the time-out between the second and third periods (half-time), and notify the referee and the teams two minutes in advance of its termination.

The clock is started when the ball is in play, not when the referee blows the whistle.

UNIFORM AND EQUIPMENT

The International Rules (FIFA) state that the referee should wear a blazer or blouse the color of which should be distinctive from the colors worn by the competing teams. There is, however, an accepted uniform that is worn by most referees throughout the world. It consists of a black blouse with white detachable collar, shorts of the same black material, stockings, plain black or black with white tops, and lightweight boots with clean white laces. Some wear a white, open-collar shirt and a suit-coat type black jacket. Since the referee is also the official timer, he should have two watches (one a stop watch) and two whistles. The linesmen wear the same uniform as the referee.

The referee's uniform (*NCAA Guide*) should consist of a white cap, black and white vertical-striped shirt, white knickers, and black stockings, *or* black shirt, black shorts, and black stockings. In order to maintain a good footing on the field, cleated shoes should be worn, preferably regular soccer shoes. Each referee should be equipped with two whistles, the second to be used in case the first fails, and a coin to flip for choice of goal.

The Diagonal System of Control
(One Referee—FIFA)

The recommended method of controlling the game when only one referee is appointed is the diagonal system as shown in Diagram 46. The referee moves along this diagonal after the kickoff. He is usually slightly behind and to the side of the ball. This method offers good coverage, but it fails when the linesmen do not cover as they are supposed to, or when the referee restricts his movement to the center circle.

Use the diagonal system if there is only one referee

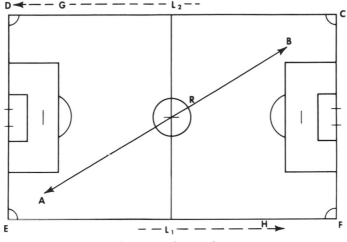

DIAGRAM 45. The diagonal system of control.

The imaginary diagonal used by the referee is the line A—B. Each linesman is responsible for the goal line and the touch line to his right as he faces the center circle. He tries to stay ahead of the play, and seldom goes into the back half of the field. When the referee is at A (Figure 2), Linesman 2 will be at a point between D and G, and when the referee is at B, Linesman 1 will be between F and H. This gives two officials control of the respective "danger Zones," one at each side of the field.

At the start of the game, the referee stands facing the timer's table in the center circle near the center line and moves to the diagonal behind and to the side of the ball after the kickoff as shown in Diagram 47. Both linesmen start at midfield.

During the taking of a corner kick (Diagram 48), the referee takes a position near the goalpost close to the diagonal, no matter at which corner area the kick is taken. Linesman 2 (L_2) is at midfield in position for clearance, while Linesman 1 (L_1) stands at the junction of the penalty area and goal line to observe incidents hidden from the referee.

During the taking of a penalty kick (Diagram 49), the referee takes a position in the penalty area opposite the penalty-kick mark from where he can see that the kick is properly taken and that no

On corner kicks referee is at goalpost nearer diagonal

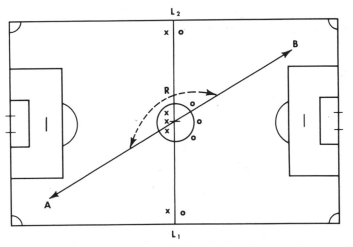

DIAGRAM 46.   The position of the referee at the start of play.

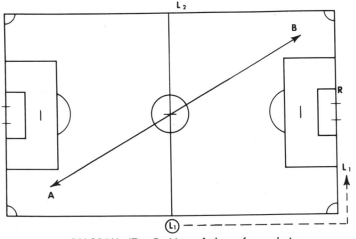

DIAGRAM 47.   Position of the referee during a corner kick.

encroachment of the yard rule takes place. L₁ watches the goal-keeper and acts as goal judge. L₂ is in position for possible clearance and counterattack, should the goalkeeper save a goal.

The dual-referee system gives better coverage

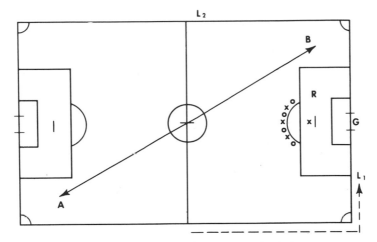

DIAGRAM 48.   Position of the referee during a penalty kick.

The Dual Referee System
(Two Referees—NCAA)

Although it is not mandatory, the NCAA rules recommend that the dual referee system be used. It has been so successful in providing a more adequate coverage of the field, a better controlled game, and a faster game, that nearly all secondary schools and colleges use two referees. Both officials have equal authority and responsibility in the calling of fouls and violations on any part of the field at any time.

It is absolutely necessary, however, that the two officials get together, so each will have a clear understanding as to how they will operate, and cooperate, in covering the play. This will save much embarrassment when one official calls a violation not seen by the other in his area. The success of dual officiating depends upon each man working well with the other, but to do this, each official must call a consistent game.

The field may be divided longitudinally or laterally with each official covering one-half of the field, but the most effective method is to divide the field diagonally. Each official is responsible for one touch line and one goal line. He should work near the touch line

The dual system is not mandatory

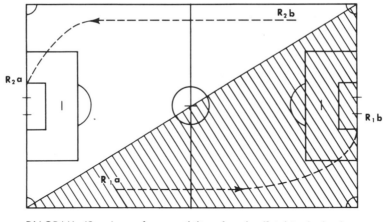

DIAGRAM 49.   Area of responsibility of each official in dual referee system.

and be responsible for this touch line and the goal line to his right as he faces the center circle. In the diagram above (Diagram 49) one official will be primarily responsible for the shaded area and the other will administer the play in the unshaded area. If they work correctly, the two officials should never be opposite each other. Thus there will be a *lead* official and a *trailing* official. As one of the teams moves the ball toward its goal, the official responsible for that goal must always be ahead of the play. He is the lead official. As the ball nears the goal, the lead official cuts toward the goal so he will be as near the play as possible. He calls all out-of-bounds play along his touch and goal lines. When R_1 (Diagram 49) is in position "b" (near the goal), R_2 should be in position "b" (about 20 yards beyond the center line, behind and to the side of the play). He is the trail official. When R_2 is in position "a," R_1 should be in position "a." They work in these relative positions to each other throughout the game. The trailing official should trail the ball up the field watching all backfield play, but he should also be alert to make decisions on any play when the lead official is screened from the play by the moving players. The trailing official, however, should allow the lead official to give the decision on a play (if he has seen it), because usually he is in a position to best observe the action.

The leading official makes the decisions

At the center kickoff, the referees should station themselves as illustrated in Diagram 49. R_2 should stand near the timer's table and signal the captains of both teams, the other referee, the timers, and the scorers that the game is about to start. It is this referee who blows the whistle to start play. R_1, the lead official, stands in a position well ahead of the play, where he will not interfere with the play. The positions and duties are reversed when the kickoff is in the opposite direction.

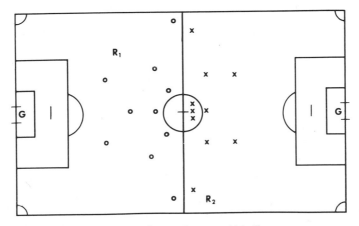

DIAGRAM 50. Position of the referees during a kickoff.

On corner kicks, the lead official, R_1, generally shall station himself near the goalpost on his side of the field. The trail official shall station himself as shown in Diagram 52. When the corner kick is on the side, the trail official has all the play within his visual field. When the kick farther from R_1 is taken from the corner nearest to R_1, it will be more difficult for him to see the play. The trail referee must be alert in this situation to assist in making calls for fouls and misconduct. The position and duties of the officials are reversed when the corner kick is at the opposite end of the field.

During a penalty kick, the two referees should take the same positions as shown in Diagram 52. The lead official, R_1, takes a position on the goal line just outside the near goalpost, out of the vision of both the goalkeeper and the kicker. R_2 takes a position as

The referees take same positions for corner kick and penalty kick

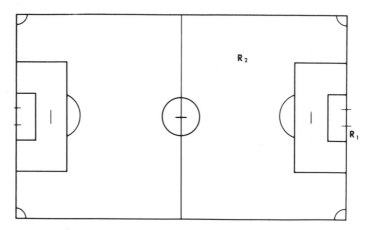

DIAGRAM 51.   Position of the referees during a corner kick.

shown, so he can observe any fouls and be ready for a counterattack should the goalkeeper make the save.

The NCAA rules calls for a referee to blow the whistle when the ball goes out of play and again before it is kicked into play (but not on a throw-in). Regardless of which referee blows the whistle when the ball goes out of play, the lead referee always blows the whistle to resume play. A minimum of playing time will be lost if the lead official blows the whistle as soon as the ball is set.

Pregame Responsibilities

Immediately after an assignment has been accepted by an official, he should acknowledge it confirming the date and time. The home team should send a reminder card one week before a game. It is recommended that the officials arrive at the site of the contest at least one-half hour before game time, and be on the field ready to work at least ten minutes before game time. Before going on the field, the referees (if there are two) should discuss procedures, system for covering the field, and any other items that will make for a well-officiated game.

Once on the field, the referee should inspect the markings of the field, check the nets for holes, secure the game ball and check it to

The rules give the referee discretionary power

see if it conforms to the rules, check with the timekeepers (if the referee is not keeping time) concerning the length of periods, signals for time out, and the proper methods for keeping of time, meet with the linesmen and instruct them if necessary, and check the players' equipment. Finally, he should meet with the captain of each team to give any final instructions and to dedide, by a flip of a coin, who wins the right to the choice of kickoff or choice of direction of play.

Game Responsibilities

According to the official rules, the duties of the referee, and guides to aid him in his duties are as follows:

1. To enforce the laws and decide any disputed point.

a. His decision on points of fact connected with play shall be final so far as the result of the game is concerned.

b. His discretionary powers commence as soon as he enters the field of play, and his powers of penalizing extend to offenses committed when play has been temporarily suspended or when the ball is out of play.

c. The referee should refrain from penalizing in cases where he is satisfied that by so doing he would be giving an advantage to the offending team. He must delay the whistle until the play is completed in order to apply this advantage rule. A good illustration of this is when a player who has been intentionally tripped or charged from the rear, recovers his balance and control and continues toward the goal for a shot. If the referee were to penalize the intentional trip or charge, play would be stopped. Stopping play would give the offending team time to set up a new defense and thus gain an advantage to which it was not entitled by rule. If the referee has decided to apply the advantage clause and allow the game to proceed, he cannot revoke his decision if the offended team fails to score.

2. To keep a record of the game, to act as timekeeper (if no official timekeeper has been appointed).

a. He should allow the full or agreed time, adding all time lost through accident or other cause to that period.

Do not penalize if the penalty hurts the offended team

3. To stop the game for any infringement of the laws.

a. The rules of the game are intended to provide that games are to be played with as little interference as possible, and in this view, it is the duty of the referee to penalize only deliberate breaches of the rules. Constant whistling for trifling and doubtful breaches produces tension and ill feelings on the part of the players, coaches, and spectators. A good official makes his presence felt and need not blow the whistle to gain attention.

b. He should, if possible, avoid waste of time in restarting the game. A wave of the hand may be used rather than the whistle.

4. To suspend or terminate the game whenever such action proves necessary.

a. A referee may suspend or terminate the game by reason of the elements, interference by spectators, or other causes, but if he does, it must be reported to the association under whose jurisdiction the match was played, within the stipulated time. Suspending or terminating a game because of the weather should be done only after very careful consideration.

5. To prevent any person other than the players and the linesmen from entering the field of play without his permission.

a. Trainers or coaches may enter the field only if called by the referee.

b. Substitute players (if allowed) must first report to the referee when coming on the field.

6. To caution any player guilty of misconduct or ungentlemanly behavior.

a. When cautioning a player, the referee should call him by, or inquire his name, and plainly state, using the word "caution," that if he is again considered to be guilty of ungentlemanly behavior, he will be ordered off the field.

7. To suspend a player from further participation if he is guilty of violent conduct, or if he persists in misconduct or ungentlemanly conduct.

a. If a player is ordered off the field, the referee should send the name of the offender to the association concerned within the time limit.

8. To stop the game if, in his opinion, a player has been seriously injured.

Know the rules but don't be technical

a. For a player only slightly injured, play should not be stopped until the ball is out of play.

b. A player who is able to go to the touch line or goal line for attention of any kind should not be treated on the field.

c. If the player is seriously injured, he should be removed as soon as possible and the game resumed.

9. To signal for recommencement of the game after all stoppages.

Further Aids for the Official to Interpret the Rules

THE FIELD

Because of the various levels of play (sandlot to professional) and because of the lack of space for adequate playing areas, the rules allow considerable variation in dimension for the playing area. It is stipulated, however, that in all cases, the length shall exceed the breadth. For greater uniformity, clubs should try to obtain a field that conforms to the dimensions required for international matches, i.e., 110 to 120 yards in length by 70 to 80 yards in width. College rules call for a field 110 to 120 yards in length by 65 to 75 yards in width. The field of play should be clearly marked with white lines, not V-shaped ruts. The line itself is the outer edge of the marking; thus all markings are within the area they enclose.

Touch lines, or side lines, are the lines marking the length boundaries of the field. When the whole of the ball passes over either of these lines, either on the ground or in the air, a player of the team opposed to the player who last touched it throws it into play.

Goal lines are the lines at each end of the field, joining at right angles to the touch lines. At the corners, where they join is a quarter-circle arc, 1 yard in radius, to mark the area from which a corner kick is taken. When the whole of the ball passes over either goal line (not between the goalposts or under the crossbar) either on the ground or in the air, the ball is out of play and the game is restarted by either a

1. Goal kick—when the ball was last played by a player of the attacking team.

The official can influence the sportsmanship

2. Corner kick—when the ball was last played by a defending player.

Goals are placed at the center of each goal line and consist of two upright posts eight yards apart (inside measurement), joined by a crossbar, the lower edge of which should be eight feet from the ground. The width and depth of the goalposts and crossbar shall not exceed five inches. It is recommended that nets be attached to the posts, crossbar, and ground behind the goal. They should be appropriately supported and so placed to allow the goalkeeper ample room.

Flag posts (a flag on a post) no less than five feet high and having a nonpointed top mark the corners of the field, and assist the officials in determining whether a ball passing close to the corner has gone over the goal line or the touch line. They must be firmly fixed, but not so rigid that they may cause injury to a player colliding with them. (NCAA rules allow corner flags of the pliable, coiled wire type to be used, even though they do not conform to the mentioned standards.) Similar flag posts may be placed opposite the half-way line on each side of the field, not less than one yard outside the touch line, but they are not essential.

A half-way line divides the field into two equal halves. It assists the referee at the kickoff, when all players must be in their own half of the field until the ball has been kicked, and for offside, when a player cannot be offside if he is in his own half of the field when the ball was last played.

The center circle with a ten-yard radius from the center of the field provides a visible mark during the kickoff for the opposing players who must be at least ten yards from the ball until the kick has been taken.

The goal area at each end of the field is enclosed by two lines drawn at right angles to the goal line, six yards from each goalpost, extending six yards into the field of play, and joined by a line parallel to the goal line. The goal area serves two purposes:

1. To indicate the area in which the goalkeeper has special protection. He can only be charged when in possession (actual contact with the ball), or when obstructing an opponent. (NCAA rules, however, allow no charging of the goalkeeper.)

The referee may overrule the linesman

2. To limit the area in which the ball is placed for a goal kick. For a goal kick, the ball may be placed anywhere in that half of the goal area nearest to where it crossed the goal line. The penalty area is enclosed by two lines drawn at right angles to the goal line, 18 yards from each goalpost, extending 18 yards into the field of play, and joined by a line parallel to the goal line. A suitable mark is made within each penalty area, 12 yards from the midpoint of the goal line, measured along an undrawn line at right angles thereto. These are the penalty-kick marks. From each penalty-kick mark, an arc of a circle, having a ten-yard radius, is marked outside the penalty area. This arc is not a part of the penalty area; it is only the marking to indicate the distance of ten yards away from the penalty-kick mark when a penalty kick is being taken. The penalty area serves the following purposes:

1. It indicates the area in which the goalkeeper may handle the ball.

2. It indicates the distance the ball must travel during the taking of a goal kick before it can be played by another player.

3. It indicates the area in which a penalty kick is given when any of the nine penal offenses are committed intentionally by a defending player.

4. It indicates the area outside of which all players, except the kicker and the goalkeeper, must stand during the taking of a penalty kick.

THE BALL

The ball must have a leather casing, must have a circumference of not more than 28 inches nor less than 27 inches, and shall not weigh more than 16 ounces nor less than 14 ounces at the start of the game. (NCAA rules add that the ball must be inflated to a pressure of not more than 13 pounds nor less than 12 pounds.) A plastic-coated leather ball is popular for wet conditions.

PLAYERS

The game is played by two teams, each consisting of not more than 11 players, one of whom is designated as the goalkeeper. One

The linesmen are usually lay officials

of the other players may change places with the goalkeeper provided the referee is notified (if this change is made without notifying the referee, the player will be penalized when he touches the ball with his hands). Although the minimum number of players on a team is not set, it is recommended that there be no fewer than seven players on either team.

Substitutes may replace players during a game, subject to agreement before a match. In many levels of competition, substitutes are regulated by the rules of the conference to which the teams belong.

If a player leaves the field during the progress of the game (except through the normal movement of play) without the consent of the referee, he is guilty of ungentlemanly conduct.

EQUIPMENT

A player is not allowed to wear anything that is dangerous to another player, such as rings, watches, spectacle guards, etc. There is no prescribed uniform, but the usual equipment for a player consists of a jersey or shirt, shorts, stockings, shin guards, and boots. The goalkeeper must wear a color that distinguishes him from other players. NCAA rules make numbers (six-inch minimum size) on the back of the jersey mandatory.

The rules do not insist that boots must be worn, but if they are, they must conform to the following standards:

1. All studs and bars must be made of leather, rubber, aluminum, plastic, or similar material (NCAA rules allow a molded sole with multiple cleats under the prescribed size).

2. Studs shall be solid and round in plan. They can be cylindrical or conical with a minimum diameter not less than half an inch. Bars shall be traverse and flat (not less than one-half inch wide) extending the width of the shoe.

3. Combined bars and studs may be used, but neither shall protrude more than three-quarters of an inch. If nails are used, they must be driven flush with the surface.

The referee should inspect the players' equipment, and if a player wears any article of personal equipment not conforming to the above requirements, he should be sent off the field to adjust his equipment. He shall not return without first reporting to the referee,

Charging is limited in college games

who shall satisfy himself that the equipment is in order. The player can re-enter the game only when the ball is out of play.

DURATION OF THE GAME

The duration of an international match is two equal periods of 45 minutes (running time) unless otherwise mutually agreed upon.

In college (NCAA rule), the game is divided into four equal periods of 22 minutes. In high school games, four 12- or 15-minute periods, and in junior high games, four 8- or 10-minute periods are recommended. An interval of one minute is allowed between the first and second periods, and between the third and fourth periods. The half-time interval is 10 minutes, except by consent of the referee.

In most competition, the time to be played is specified, and in case of a tie game, two extra periods of five minutes each are to be played, the score then standing as official. Time shall be extended to permit a penalty kick to be taken at or after the expiration of the normal periods or extra periods.

If the referee is the timekeeper, he should make allowances in either half of the game for time lost through accident or other cause and add it to the playing time for that period.

The Laws of Play

For the kickoff, the ball is placed in a stationary position at the center of the field. The game is started after the referee gives the signal and a player of the team kicking off takes a place kick. The following conditions must be observed:

1. Every player must be in his own half of the field, and all players of the team opposite to that taking the kickoff must remain not less than ten yards from the ball until it is kicked.

2. The ball must be kicked into the opponent's half of the field (forward) a distance equal to its circumference (27-28 inches), in order to be deemed in play.

3. The kicker may not play the ball a second time until it has been touched or played by another player.

The referee may be the timekeeper

4. A goal cannot be scored direct from the kickoff. For any infringement of this law, the kick is retaken, except in the case of the kicker playing the ball twice in succession; for this offense, an indirect free kick is awarded to the opposing team. After a goal has been scored, the game is restarted in the same manner by a player of the team against whom the goal was scored.

At the end of each period, the teams change ends, and on restarting, the kickoff is taken by a player of the opposite team to that who started the previous period.

BALL IN AND OUT OF PLAY

The ball is out of play when it has *wholly* crossed the goal or touch line, whether on the ground or in the air, and when the game has been stopped by the referee. It is out of play when a ball passes out of play during its flight, but curves or is blown so that it lands in the field of play.

The ball is in play at all other times from the start of the match to the finish including:

1. If it rebounds from the goalpost, crossbar, or corner flagpost into the field of play.

2. If it rebounds off either the referee or linesmen when they are in the field of play. *Note:* In NCAA rules, a ball that touches the referee is a dead ball, and the game shall be restarted with a dropped ball.

3. Until the referee makes a decision on a supposed infringement of the rules, or the ball has gone out of bounds.

It is the position of the ball that is important, because it is possible for the ball to be out of play even though the player plays it or the goalkeeper catches it when he is standing within the playing area. It is also possible for the ball to remain in play even though the player playing it is out of the field of play. The penalty will be a direct free kick if the goalkeeper handles a ball that is outside the penalty area, even though he is in the area. Play should not cease until the referee blows his whistle.

When play is stopped for an infringement of the rules or when

Ball may be in play even though the player is out of bounds

the ball has gone out of play, the game shall be restarted by an appropriate kick or throw-in, but when restarting the game after a temporary suspension of play from any cause not mentioned in the rules, the referee drops the ball at the place where it was when play was suspended (a drop ball). Such causes might be injury, interference by spectators, or when the ball becomes lodged between two or more players. (Under NCAA rules, there can be no drop ball in the penalty area. It is dropped at a point outside the area, nearest to the point where it was when play was suspended).

A drop ball is one the referee holds up and lets drop directly from his hand to the ground between two opposing players. It is not in play until it touches the ground. If a player touches the ball before it reaches the ground, it must be redropped.

METHOD OF SCORING

Soccer is a low scoring game, and often the result can be decided by a single goal. Therefore, the following conditions concerning the method of scoring must be clearly understood:

1. The whole of the ball must pass completely over the goal line between the goalposts and under the crossbar. *The referee must under no circumstances give a goal unless he is sure that the ball is completely over the line, and he is in a position to so decide.*

2. The ball cannot be thrown, carried, or propelled by the hand or arm by a player of the attacking side. However, if a defending player handles the ball, and it passes over the goalline into the goal, a goal is scored. Should a goal be prevented by a defending player (other than the goalkeeper) handling the ball, a penalty kick is awarded if it occurs in the penalty area.

3. Should the crossbar become displaced, the referee must decide whether or not the ball crossed the goal line below where the crossbar should have been.

4. A goal will not be scored if a player kicks an indirect free kick directly into the goal. A goal kick will result if it was an attacking player or a corner kick if it was a defending player. The team that scores the most goals is the winner. If both teams have a like number of goals, or no goals, the game is termed a draw.

The whole ball must be within the goal for a score

Fouls and Misconduct

FREE KICK

A free kick is given for any violation of the rules of play. Such free kicks are classified into two types:

1. Direct free kicks—given for "penal" or "personal" offenses (those where intentional personal contact is made that might cause injury to another player). A direct free kick is one from which a goal can be scored if kicked directly into the goal.

2. Indirect free kicks—given for "technical" offenses (those concerning method or administration of play). An exception to this is the corner kick, which can be scored direct. An indirect free kick is one from which a goal cannot be scored if kicked directly into the goal. The ball must touch another player other than the kicker before it can score.

DIRECT FREE KICKS

A direct free kick will be awarded if a player intentionally commits any of the following nine offenses:

1. Handles the ball. A player (other than the goalkeeper within his penalty area) is guilty if he intentionally handles, carries, strikes, or propels the ball with his hand or arm (fingertip to shoulder). Sometimes the ball unavoidably touches the hand or arm. The referee should rule it as unintentional, even if the player gains an advantage. Such unintentional handling should not be penalized.

2. Kicks or attempts to kick an opponent. This includes using the knee on an opponent.

3. Trips an opponent. This includes throwing or attempting to throw an opponent by the use of the legs or by stooping in front or behind him. The referee must notice the difference between an intentional trip resulting from normal play, or one that is feigned.

4. Jumps at an opponent. Jumping at an opponent is quite different from jumping to play the ball, which is jumping upward, even though contact with an opponent exists. A person must not jump when executing a sliding tackle (NCAA rules make all sliding tackles illegal).

The referee may extend the intermission

5. Charges an opponent in a violent or dangerous manner. A fair charge consists of a nudge or a contact with the shoulder when both the player and the opponent have at least one foot on the ground, and the arms held to the body. The man making the charge must be in an erect position. Charging is permitted only when the ball is within playing distance of the players concerned, and they are definitely attempting to play it.

6. Charges an opponent from behind unless the latter is deliberately obstructing. An opponent may be charged from the rear only if he is deliberately obstructing, but such a charge must not be violent or dangerous.

7. Holds an opponent with his hand or any part of the arm. Holding includes the obstruction of a player by the hand or any part of the arm extended from the body.

8. Pushes or attempts to push an opponent. A player may not place his hands or arms on an opponent in an effort to reach the ball, nor may he in any way use the hand, elbow, or arm to push him away from the ball.

9. Strikes or attempts to strike an opponent.

Note: A drastic difference in NCAA rules is the addition of a tenth penal offense for which a direct free kick results. This rule states that the goalkeeper may not be charged under any conditions unless he is obstructing. If he has possession of the ball, he may not be interfered with or impeded in any manner.

INDIRECT FREE KICKS

An indirect free kick, which cannot score directly, is given when a player commits any of the following offenses:

1. Playing the ball a second time after taking any free kick, before it has been touched or played by another player. These include the kickoff, a free kick, a corner kick, and a goal kick if it has passed out of the penalty area.

2. Dangerous play. Any play the referee considers dangerous and likely to cause injury (such as attempting to kick the ball while held by the goalkeeper, or raising the foot higher than an opponent's shoulder when kicking, or heading a ball that is lower than the waist).

Unintentional handling of the ball should not be penalized

3. Charging at the improper time. Charging when the ball is not within playing distance, the charge otherwise being fair.

4. Obstruction other than holding. When not playing the ball, a person is obstructing if he runs between the opponent and the ball to allow a teammate to get it, or uses the body so as to form an obstacle to an opponent. A player may be charged from the rear when he is legally shielding the ball while playing it.

5. Charging the goalkeeper when he does not have the ball inside the goal area, unless he is obstructing (not NCAA).

6. The goalkeeper carrying the ball more than four steps without bouncing it on the ground.

7. Ungentlemanly conduct. This includes such things as distracting an opponent as he is about to play the ball by shouting at him, leaving the field of play without the referee's consent, or showing by word or action his displeasure at a referee's decision.

8. Violent conduct. Using foul or abusive language or if guilty of serious foul play.

9. Offside.

In NCAA play, all sliding tackles are illegal, resulting in an indirect free kick. Also, a substitution or resubstitution made at an improper time; a substitution or resubstitution made without reporting to the referee; persons other than the players and linesmen entering the field of play without the referee's permission; and, persistent coaching from the sidelines after a warning by the referee, all result in an indirect free kick taken at the point where the ball was when the infraction occured.

COMMON RULING CONCERNING ALL FREE KICKS

Whether a free kick is direct or indirect, the following rules must be observed:

1. Opponents of the player taking the kick must be at least ten yards from the ball until it is in play, unless they stand on their own goal line, between the uprights (this applies only when an indirect free kick is given to the attacking team nearer than ten yards from the goal line). The referee should caution a player who infringes the rule.

2. The ball must be stationary when the kick is taken.

A goal keeper with ball may not be charged

3. The ball must travel a distance equal to its circumference before the ball is considered in play. The goal kick and a free kick for the defending team in their penalty area must travel out of the penalty area before it is deemed in play. If the ball does not go out of the area, the kick is retaken.

4. The player taking the kick may not play the ball a second time until it has touched or been played by another player.

5. Except on the kickoff and a penalty kick, which must be kicked forward, a free kick may be kicked in any direction.

OFFSIDE

In order to prevent players from standing near the goal waiting for an opportunity to score from close range, soccer has an off-side rule, which players and referees must thoroughly understand. This rule states that a player is offside if he is nearer to his opponent's goal line than the ball at the moment the ball is played unless:

1. He is in his own half of the field of play.
2. There are two opponents nearer to their goal line than he is.
3. The ball last touched an opponent or was last played by him.
4. He receives the ball direct from a goal kick, a corner kick, a throw-in, or when dropped by the referee (drop ball).

Offside should not be judged at the moment the player in question receives the ball, but at the moment the ball is passed to him by one of his own side. It should be remembered that as long as a player is behind the ball, he cannot be offside. A player in an off-side position should not be penalized unless, *in the opinion of the referee,* he is interfering with the play or with an opponent, or is seeking to gain an advantage by being in an off-side position. A player who is offside cannot put himself back onside, it can only be done for him by having points 2 or 3 above, occur.

For an infringement of this rule an indirect free kick is taken by a player of the opposing side from the place where the infringement occurred.

PENALTY KICK

A very severe penalty (a penalty kick) is awarded for the nine penal offenses mentioned previously, intentionally committed by a

Sliding tackles are illegal

defending player in his own penalty area. Regardless of where the foul occurs in the penalty area, the penalty kick is taken from the penalty kick mark, and when it is being taken, all players, except the player taking the kick and the opposing goalkeeper, must remain within the field of play, but outside the penalty area, and at least ten yards from the penalty kick mark. The players may stand along the side lines of the penalty area, if they so desire. A goal may be scored from such a kick.

The opposing goalkeeper must stand (without moving his feet) on his own goal line, between the goalposts, until the ball is kicked. If the ball touches the goalkeeper before passing between the posts when the kick is taken at or after the expiration of any period, the goal still counts. However, should the goalkeeper deflect the ball from the goal, it will not count if the kicker or any other player kicks it into the goal.

The player kicking the penalty kick must kick the ball in a forward direction, and it is in play when it has traveled the distance of its circumference. The kicker may not kick the ball a second time until it has been touched or played by another player (if the ball hits the goalpost or crossbar and rebounds to him, the kicker cannot play it).

For any infringement by the player taking the kick, an indirect free kick is given to a player of the opposing side from the spot where the infringement occurred. For any infringement by the attacking team, other than the kicker, the kick shall be retaken, if a goal has resulted. For any infringement by the defending team, the kick shall be retaken, if a goal has not resulted.

THE THROW-IN

When the whole of the ball passes over the touch line, either on the ground or in the air, it shall be thrown in from the point where it crossed the line, by a player of the team opposite to that of the player who last touched it (a throw-in). During the throw-in, the following points must be borne in mind:

1. The thrower, at the moment of delivering the ball, must face the field of play, and part of each foot must be on the ground, either on or outside the touch line.

Remember, there are three kinds of free kicks

2. The thrower must use both hands and must deliver the ball from over his head.

3. The ball is in play immediately after it is thrown, but the thrower may not play the ball until it has been touched or played by another player.

4. A goal cannot be scored directly from the throw-in.

If the ball is improperly thrown in, the throw-in shall be taken by a player of the opposing team. If the player plays the ball a second time before it has been touched or played by another player, an indirect free kick is given to a player of the opposing team from the place where the infringement occurred.

GOAL KICK

A goal kick is awarded to the defending team when the whole of the ball passes over the goal line (excluding that portion between the goalposts and under the crossbar) either on the ground or in the air, having last been played by a member of the attacking team.

A goal kick must be kicked directly into play beyond the penalty area from a point within the half of the goal area nearest to where it crossed the goal line. All opposing players must remain outside the penalty area until the goal kick is taken.

The ball is not in play unless it passes directly out of the penalty area. The ball may not be kicked to the goalkeeper so that he can kick it out of his hands, unless it first passes out of the penalty area.

The kicker shall not play the ball a second time after it has passed out of the penalty area until it has been touched or played by another player. If he does so, an indirect free kick is awarded the opposing team. If an opponent, the kicker, or any other player plays the ball before it passes out of the penalty area, the kick is retaken. A goal may not be scored directly from such a kick.

CORNER KICK

A corner kick is awarded to the attacking team when the whole of the ball passes over the goal line (excluding that portion between the goalposts and under the crossbar) either on the ground or in the air, having last been played by a member of the defending team.

There are four points common to all free kicks

A corner kick must be kicked from within the quarter circle at the corner flagpost nearest to where the ball crossed the goal line. The corner flagpost may not be removed when the kick is being taken.

Players of the opposing team may not approach within ten yards of the ball until it is in play (traveled the distance of its circumference). The kicker shall not kick the ball a second time until it has been touched or played by another player. For any infringement of this rule, an indirect free kick is given to the opposing team, taken at the point of the infraction.

A goal may be scored directly from a corner kick, and there is no offside.

HAND SIGNALS

In order to make decisions clear beyond all doubt to the players, coaches, and spectators, the collegiate rules make it mandatory that the referees use a series of signs and signals. These should be simple gestures, not overdone to draw attention to the referee, but to notify everyone what the violation is, and the direction of the play.

The suggested signals for referees are:

GOAL	Both arms raised overhead.
OFFSIDE	Hands on and off hips—repeat.
TRIPPING	Kicking motion with the leg.
STRIKING	Short throwing motion with clenched fist.
JUMPING	One arm raised with up and down motion.
HANDLING BALL	Stroke arm with hand, several times.
HOLDING	Grasp wrist with hand, several times.
PUSHING	Both arms extended forward, palms of hands facing forward.

A throw-in must be overhead with both hands

CHARGING VIOLENTLY CHARGING FROM BEHIND	Repeated moving of shoulder forward with opposite hand on shoulder.
GOALKEEPER CARRYING BALL	Rotating one hand over the other in front of body.
DANGEROUS PLAY	Raise arms sideward to horizontal.
BALL DEAD	Raise one arm aloft, open hand.
TIME-OUT	Hands criss-crossed over head.
CORNER KICK	Point to corner flag on the side kick is to be taken.
INDIRECT FREE KICK	Forward underarm swing with one arm pointing direction of kick.
DIRECT FREE KICK	Forward underarm swing with both arms pointing direction of kick.
PLAY ON	Hand raised (fist closed) over head with "play on" called out.

Suggestions for Referees

When a person accepts the responsibility of being a referee, he assumes a responsibility to the school or college, to the coaches, to the spectators, and to the players. Following are a few constructive points for the referee to remember:

1. He should not referee a game when he finds himself biased against one or both teams, any member or coach of the teams, or any member of the institution a team represents.

2. He should arrive, and notify the office of the director of athletics or the coach of his arrival, at least one-half hour before game time. Should his arrival be delayed, he should also notify

All officials must use the same signals

immediately the coach or the athletic director of the home team.

3. He should feel responsible for having a thorough working knowledge of the rules of the game and should strive to see that these rules are efficiently administered during the game.

4. He should enforce the rule that calls for him to order from the game a player using foul or abusive language or being guilty of serious foul play.

5. He should keep up to date with changes in the rules of the game by frequently reading the rule book and by attending interpretation meetings.

6. He should refrain from coaching players of either or both teams while a game is in progress.

7. He should be friendly with both coaches and players before, during, and after a game, but not fraternize with either in public.

8. He should call his own plays and not be influenced by coaches, players, or spectators.

9. He should not criticize another official with whom he may be working.

10. He should take complete charge of the game, showing the players he is "boss," without letting the tone of voice be antagonistic.

11. He should be on the play at all times, and when a violation is noticed, he should look at the player when he blows the whistle.

12. He should give the appropriate signal when applying the advantage rule so all concerned will know that he saw the violation.

Bibliography

National Collegiate Athletic Association, *The Official Soccer Guide.* National Collegiate Athletic Bureau, New York, 1967.

The Football Association, *How To Become A Referee.* The Naldrett Press, London.

Know The Game, Educational Productions Ltd., London.

Referees' Chart and Players' Guide to the Laws of the Game. The Naldrett Press, London.

Rule of the Association and Laws of the Game. The Naldrett Press, London.

United States Soccer Football Association, *Soccer Football Rules.* The United States Soccer Football Association, New York, 1966.

Be neutral—or don't officiate

Questions and Answers

The following questions have from time to time been submitted to the Referees' Association, and the interpretations have been approved.

LAW I

1. (Q) If the crossbar becomes displaced through breakage or faulty construction in a competitive match and there are no available means of repairing and replacing it, should the match be abandoned?
   (A) Yes. The crossbar may not be substituted by a rope in order to finish the match.
2. (Q) Is it necessary for flags to be placed at the halfway line?
   (A) No.

* * *

LAW IV

1. (Q) If a player, following doctor's orders, protects his elbow or any similar part of his body with a plaster bandage to prevent further injury, has the referee power to decide if the bandage constitutes a danger to other players?
   (A) Yes.
2. (Q) Should a player be permitted to take part in a game when he is wearing ordinary kind of boots instead of the normal football boots?
   (A) The laws of the game do not specify that a player should wear any particular type of boot; if, however, they are equipped with bars or studs, the bars or studs must conform with Law IV.

* * *

LAW V

1. (Q) Is the referee allowed to add time if a player deliberately wastes time?
   (A) Yes, and player should be cautioned.

Don't call a play on anticipation

2. (Q) A linesman signals that the ball has passed over the touchline, but before the referee has given the ball out of play, a defending player inside the penalty area strikes an attacking player. What action should the referee take?

(A) After having taken the appropriate action in relation to the offense, the referee should restart the game with a throw-in because the ball was out of play when the offence occurred.

3. (Q) What action should a referee take against a player who lights a cigarette during the game?

(A) Caution him for ungentlemanly conduct.

4. (Q) Can a captain send off one of his own team for serious misconduct?

(A) No. Only a referee can send a player off the field.

❋ ❋ ❋

LAW VI

1. (Q) May a referee ask a *neutral* linesman to give an opinion as to whether or not the ball crossed the goal line between the posts?

(A) Yes.

❋ ❋ ❋

LAW X

1. (Q) If a referee signals a goal before the ball has passed wholly over the goal line and he immediately realizes his error, is the goal valid?

(A) No. The game should be restarted by dropping the ball immediately outside the penalty area.

❋ ❋ ❋

LAW XI

1. (Q) Does a player infringe the law if he is in an offside position and moves a little way beyond the boundary of the field of play to show clearly to the referee that he is not interfering with play?

Follow the official interpretation

(A)   No, but if the referee considers that such a movement has a tactical aim or is in any way a feint, and the player takes part in the game immediately after, the referee should blow his whistle for offside.

2.   (Q)   Is a teammate allowed to stand in an off-side position at the taking of a penalty kick?

(A)   Yes, but he would be given offside if the kicker failed to score directly and the player attempted to interfere with the game. The player would not be offside if the goalkeeper had stopped the ball and the ball went to him.

* * *

LAW XII

1.   (Q)   Should a penalty be awarded, if while the ball is in play, a player intentionally trips or strikes an oppenent who is in an off-side position in the penalty area, but who is not attempting to play the ball or interfere with play in any way?

(A)   Yes.

2.   (Q)   If a player intentionally lies on the ball for an unreasonable length of time, is he guilty of ungentlemanly conduct?

(A)   Yes. He must be cautioned, and an indirect free kick awarded to the opposing team. In case of repetition of the offense, he must be sent off the field.

3.   (Q)   What action should the referee take if two players of the same team commit ungentlemanly or violent conduct toward each other on the field of play?

(A)   The referee should caution them or dismiss them from the field of play and restart the game by an indirect free kick.

* * *

LAW XIII

1.   (Q)   If a player takes a free kick and then intentionally handles the ball before it has been played by another player,

If you err and know you err—correct it

should the referee punish the more serious offense and if so, how?

(A) Yes, by a direct free kick or by a penalty kick if the offense took place in the penalty area.

2. (Q) A player is awarded a free kick in his own half of the field of play and he passes it back to his own goalkeeper, who misses it completely, and the ball enters the net. Is it a goal or corner kick?

(A) The referee should award a corner kick provided that, in the case of the free kick in the penalty area, the ball has already gone into play, otherwise the free kick inside the penalty area must be retaken.

3. (Q) If the ball from an indirect free kick touches an opponent and enters the net, should a goal be awarded?

(A) Yes.

*   *   *

LAW XIV

1. (Q) If a player intentionally goes beyond the boundary of the field of play at the taking of a penalty kick, should the referee caution him and if he repeats the offense, send him off?

(A) Yes.

2. (Q) If a penalty kick is retaken because the goalkeeper moved his leg, must the same player take the kick again or could another player do so?

(A) Another player could retake the penalty kick.

3. (Q) If a player taking a penalty kick backheels the ball to a colleague who scores, should the goal be allowed?

(A) No. The goal should be disallowed and an indirect free kick awarded to the opposing side.

4. (Q) Can a player taking a penalty kick push the ball forward for a colleague to run to it and score?

(A) Yes, provided all the players are outside the penalty area at the time the kick is taken, with the exception of the player taking the penalty kick and the goalkeeper. It will be in order for the player taking the penalty kick to push the ball forward for one of his colleagues to run to it and score, provided the penalty kick is taken in normal time. The ball must travel the distance of its circumference before it would be in order for it to be played by the second player.

5. (Q) Is a player taking a penalty kick allowed to place the ball elsewhere than on the penalty spot owing to the waterlogged state of the field?

   (A) No.

6. (Q) What action does the referee take if, at the taking of a penalty kick, the ball strikes the goalpost and/or crossbar and bursts?

   (A) (i) He asks for another ball and restarts the game by dropping the ball.
   (ii) If the penalty kick is being taken in extended time (see *Universal Guide*, Law XIV, decision 8) and the ball strikes the goalpost and/or crossbar and bursts, the game ends.

✿   ✿   ✿

LAW XV

1. (Q) The ball is out of bounds, but before it is thrown in, a player deliberately kicks an opponent, what action should the referee take?

   (A) He should caution the player or order him off the field and restart the game by a throw-in.

2. (Q) If a player taking a throw-in throws the ball so that it does not enter the field of play but passes outside the touchline, what action should be taken?

   (A) Throw should be retaken.

✿   ✿   ✿

LAW XVI

1. (Q) Should the referee award a penalty kick if a player other than the goalkeeper takes a goal kick, and the ball passes

Know when a free kick may score a goal

out of the penalty area into play but is blown back by a strong wind without any other player having touched it, and the back plays the ball with his hand within the penalty area?

(A)   Yes. If, in similar circumstances, the goalkeeper takes the goal kick, and he tries to stop the ball entering the goal and just touches the ball with his hand but fails to prevent it passing into goal, the referee shall award an indirect free kick.

2. (Q)   If, at a goal kick, when the ball has travelled the distance of its circumference towards leaving the penalty area, an opponent then enters the penalty area and is intentionally fouled by a defending player, can a penalty kick be awarded?

(A)   No, because the ball was not in play at the time the offense was committed. The offending player must be cautioned and/or dismissed from the field of play and the goal kick retaken. If the ball has passed outside the penalty area before the game is stopped, a goal kick should still be retaken as the player of the attacking side has entered the penalty area before the ball was in play.

3. (Q)   If a player is intentionally tripped before the ball passes out of the penalty area at the taking of a goal kick, should a free kick be awarded?

(A)   No, the ball is not in play until it has been out of the penalty area. The offender should be cautioned or sent off and the goal kick retaken.

A penalty kick is from a specific spot

chapter 2 0

THE TECHNIQUES AND
ART OF
WRESTLING OFFICIATING

Because of the fast action and the nature of wrestling as a competitive sport and due to the closely confined area of a wrestling mat and the rapidly changing situations thereon, the work of a wrestling official is one of the most arduous tasks of all officials. Decisions under such conditions must be instantaneous and without hesitation. Such exacting judgments and decisions can best be understood and made only by an official who is schooled and experienced through long and faithful study of the rules, of the best techniques, and of the proper manner of carrying out and enforcing the regulations.

Fast action + confined area = a most arduous task

In order best to equip oneself for such a task, it is suggested that the prospective official should become thoroughly acquainted with the written rules as published in the official wrestling guide.[1] This publication sets forth not only the rules and regulations for collegiate wrestling but is the official guide for high school wrestling as well. In fact, most amateur wrestling in the United States is now following the pattern and rules as set forth in this annual publication. Not only are rules contained therein, but summary reports and photographs on wrestling in the various districts of the United States and suggestions for coaches, participants, and officials have been included in order to acquaint officials with the total situation and problems surrounding amateur wrestling as a sport. Greater uniformity in the interpretation and carrying out of these rules and regulations should culminate in the development of a wholesome competitive occasion, which will be satisfactorily appreciated and enjoyed by spectators, participants, coaches, administrative organizations, and officials. Such a favorable situation can eliminate much of the confusion that all too often has been present in wrestling and can place this sport—one of the earliest of man's competitions —on the high pedestal where it belongs.

Satisfactory experience in competitive wrestling and in coaching, though not essential basically for the qualified official, by no means detracts from his better understanding of the sport and, in turn, his appreciation of the point of view of the other persons who are always concerned in spirited competition. The well-qualified official will seek every means to equip himself thoroughly to be the neutral arbiter between keen competitors. Suggestions from coaches, participants, fellow officials, the public, and even the all too often uncalled-for criticism of the press, should be noted and brought to use by the learning official. For the young and inexperienced but willing referee, many techniques can be learned (and included in his repertoire and officiating manner) by watching the work of well-qualified and recognized registered officials, and then adapting it, to meet his type and style, to the situations as they arise.

Before he continues too far in his officiating career, the young referee will come to see that the spirit as well as the letter of the

---

[1] The National Collegiate Athletic Association, *Official 1967 Westling Rules*, The National Collegiate Athletic Bureau, Box 757, Grand Central Station, New York 17, New York.

Coaching and wrestling experience are assets to the official

rule must be his guide in carrying out and enforcing the rules and regulations as they are written and interpreted. The good official must not only act the part but must look the part. To this extent he should be properly dressed to handle a wrestling meet. The wrestling official's uniform usually acceptable to most sections and officials consists of a knit black and white short sleeved striped shirt, black and white trousers, white sox and black rubber-soled shoes.

Set forth in the forms, which are included at the close of the material contained herein, are the reports on the wrestling official's duties, qualifications, techniques, etc., which should be studied, understood, and followed by the wrestling referee prior to and during the progress of a meet and the various matches. The official guide contains many suggestions and requirements for the work of an official operating under the different rules, in addition to the specific duties listed in Rule 13.

Premeet Duties of the Referee

CHECKING WITH COACHES AND PARTICIPANTS

In due time, and with allowance before the meet for the coaches' instructions to their teams, the referee should visit the dressing quarters of each team and inspect the participants and their uniforms. After carefully inspecting the hands of the men for rings (which should be removed), and the nails (whether smooth and clipped short), one should check the ears, neck, and shoulders for oily rub by running a hand gently over these parts, and advise against chewing gum. The belt is observed for a rough clip or buckle, which should be covered if worn (in order to prevent chafing or gouging of an opponent); and the shoes should be noticed to be sure that they have eyelets and not hooks. Shirts without buttons at the shoulder and long trunks and shorts over tights are also a regulation requirement. Inspection of contestants in championships is usually made at the time the men come to the mat to wrestle. At this time, the official should talk to the coach (or the coaches, together) to be certain that any changes or new interpretations of the rules are clearly understood by the participants before the meet begins.

Inspect the competitors with meticulous care

Five or ten minutes before the meet is to start, the referee, upon entering the gymnasium or wrestling area, should walk about the mat to observe whether the protecting mats are loose or tied down, the mat of official size and properly marked with circle and arrow, and the general conditions under which he will have to officiate the matches.

In championships it is usually the duty of officials to check the weights of the contestants. If a beam-weight platform scale is used, it is best to set the beam slide at the desired weight, before the contestant steps on the scale for his check. This will eliminate the tendency to quibble over the point of the check. If an automatic swinging-arm spring-balance scale is used, the exact weight is shown for each contestant as he stands upon the scale and he can more readily read it himself. Weight maintenance, weight reduction, and exactness in weight check are troublesome problems in wrestling. The official can avoid some of the pitfalls surrounding these problems by maintaining an unwavering attitude and adhering to strict compliance with rules.

INSTRUCTIONS TO TIMEKEEPERS AND SCORERS

A combined timers' and scorers' table large enough for them to work at should be placed at one side and sufficiently away from the protecting mats not to interfere with freedom of movement during the matches. The referee sees to the placement of the men in accordance with the regulations in the guide and in the instruction digest (shown on page 303). The referee should also make clear the signals to be used and each man's duty as provided by regulations.

Just before the meet is to begin, if a dual meet, the referee calls the two captains to the mat and tosses a coin for choice of advantage position in split matches. For championship matches, the toss is made following the first period of wrestling, if no fall occurs before that time.

INSTRUCTIONS TO WRESTLERS

At the time the match is to start, the contestants are called to the center circle on the mat cover, where they shake hands and are

Check the mats

given brief instructions to do as much of their wrestling as possible in or toward the circle, and not to stop wrestling until the referee blows his whistle. They then step back to opposite sides of the circle and await the signal to wrestle. Rule 18, section 3, makes this instruction clear.

Duties of Referee During Meet

TECHNIQUES WHILE CONTESTANTS
ARE WRESTLING ON THEIR FEET

When the match is to begin, the referee starts the men by the hand and whistle signals as illustrated and described under referees' signals in the official wrestling guide.

While the men are on their feet, the official should be constantly on the move in order to get the best view from the side of both wrestlers, and at sufficient distance not to interfere with their progress, but close enough to control any illegal situation that might arise. Because a wrestling official works alone on a mat, he should shift from one side to the other of the contestants occasionally, unless they, in maneuvering, bring a view from the other side to him. This should be done in order that one can get a full view of both contestants while the wrestlers are in the closed or contact position. This position is usually taken by wrestlers on their feet while working for an opening or a takedown.

Things to observe while the men are on their feet are their tendencies to "play the edge of the mat" or "intentionally go off the mat." These are common practices of a man who is pitted against a strong opponent. He does this in order to be able "to run off or back off" the mat to prevent his opponent from going behind or getting a takedown. The rules are clear as to punishment in such a situation. (See Rule 10, Section F.)

One maneuver "off the mat" could hardly be interpreted as deliberate. However, repeated retreats of this kind should be handled with strict enforcement. Failure by the official to warn and then penalize creates an unfair advantage. It is within the regulations and the best judgment of an official to make decisions as to whether a man is being "pushed off" or "intentionally leaves the mat." Either

Keep the wrestlers in the center of the mat

man can be at fault, and the referee should then bring the men back to center, and warn them of what is taking place, and mention the penalty for such an offense. Most men, it is found, will pay heed to minor suggestions made to them in the spirit of fair play and good sportsmanship—the others are to be penalized. Contestants and coaches should know the rules.

In calling each penalty the referee shall give the hand signal for the points or warnings and announce the penalty so contestants, scorers, coaches, and spectators are aware of it, except when warning the defensive wrestlers for stalling.

"Stalling" while on the feet, or making no attempt "to wrestle aggressively" is another offense that must be met promptly and within the letter and spirit of the rules. "Warnings" are provided for in the rules. Tired or indifferent attempts to wrestle while on the feet should be met with firm decision if wrestling is to attract interest and if officials are to help improve the sport.

FIGURE 41.   Positions of wrestlers and referee for starting or resuming a bout from standing position. The contestants, the Crider twins of Colorado State College, begin wrestling when the referee, Jack LaBonde, head coach, sounds his whistle.

Keep to the side of wrestlers on their feet

A good technique for a referee to acquire early in his officiating is to pass between his men, whether they are brought back to center or not, after a flurry off the mat. This forestalls any attempt on the part of a wrestler to take advantage of his opponent before the men are ready to wrestle and the signal is given. Such a practice will save embarrassment to the wrestlers and to the official. It will avoid unnecessary delay.

TECHNIQUES WHILE MEN
ARE ON THE MAT

Many of the techniques used by the referee when the contestants are maneuvering for position and holds while wrestling on the mat also apply when the contestants are on their feet. However, when the men are on the mat, fast action and rapid changes require extreme alertness on the part of an official. It happens occasionally that two contestants look so much alike and are dressed so similarly that it is very difficult for the referee and spectators to distinguish them. In all dual meets or tournaments, the home management shall have immediately available some provisions for clearly identifying the contestants. Such provisions may be colored anklets, numbers, or any other plan that will accomplish the purpose.

When starting a match from the "referee's position on the mat," the contestants take the official position as designated in the rules (Rule 8, Section 1) for the start of a period or situation. In order for the referee properly to observe the stance and positions of the two men, he should begin the match from this position by being "eight or ten feet in front of the wrestlers, facing the scorers' table in the squat position," as indicated in Figure 42. He should raise his hand, indicating "ready," and blow his whistle when both men are motionless and in the proper position for starting the match. The whistle starts the action. The hand signal is for the timer (Figure 42). He should observe such things as knee, hand, and body positions of both men, as indicated in the rules, and correct, with all fairness and calmness, the irregularities, until a fair starting position is taken. Moving before the whistle and hand starting signal, edging or tightening hold on waist or arm, and other advantages, should be met with firmness, one's best judgment, and decision. To many officials become "officious" at this point and are apt

Fearlessly penalize the wrestler who is stalling

FIGURE 42.   Referee's position to begin "wrestling on mat." The referee sounds his whistle to indicate the start.

FIGURE 43.   Referee in position to check a possible hold to prevent an injury.

Fast action and rapid changes require an alert official

to enforce unduly some minutiae of the regulations. It would be better to handle situations of this kind quickly and without stress, so that the match is not delayed to the disgust of spectators and the disturbance of contestants. Much practice by the young and learning official during scrimmage sessions will quickly indicate the most satisfactory manner for handling these situations, which are really the lesser evils of wrestling. The spirit as well as the letter of rules must be applied with one's best maturity of judgment. The official should ignore the criticisms of a coach who attempts to incite an official to recognize inconsequential technicalities and thus mar a creditable officiating performance.

While the participants are maneuvering on the mat for holds or counters, the official should at all times be near enough to observe and quickly check illegal situations—like the twisting hammerlock. Illegal holds can be blocked before they become dangerous by a warning from the official while the holds are developing. It is when the wrestlers are on the mat that the official must be most alert. He must concentrate fully on the work at hand and he must

FIGURE 44. Referee's position when wrestlers are on the edge of the mat.

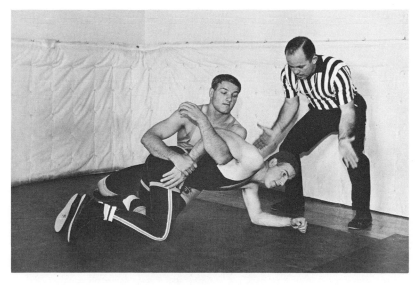

Permit no advantages before the whistle

FIGURE 45.   Referee's signal to indicate wrestler who has the advantage.

FIGURE 46.   Referee's signal to stop wrestling. He also blows his whistle.

Be quick to check illegal holds

FIGURE 47. Referee blows whistle and signals "stop wrestling" when all supporting parts of wrestlers are not on the mat.

permit no distractions. The alert referee will anticipate punishing holds or positions and act to prevent them and the possible injury which may result. (See Figure 43.) Of course, when violations occur, the regulations must be enforced and the concomitant penalties applied.

A referee can avoid many undue skirmishes or flurries at the edge of the mat by standing at the edge of the mat toward which the men are progressing and by directing them to "stay on the mat" or "work toward the center." (See Figure 44.) By this same tactic he can prevent them from going off the mat. He should not in any instance attempt to take hold of or push the men back onto the mat; neither should he be too quick to declare them off the mat. As long as "all supporting parts of one wrestler are on the wrestling mat proper" and both men not partly on the protecting mats, he should not declare them off the mat. (See Figure 45.) This procedure holds true in similar manner for takedowns from the standing position. Figures 46 and 47, on the other hand, show the referee signaling to stop wrestling because all supporting parts of the wrestlers are not on the mat.

Don't be too quick to declare wrestlers off the mat

FIGURE 48.   Referee awarding points with finger signal and up-raised arm.

FIGURE 49.   Referee points to player who has the advantage.

There must be distinct control before points are awarded

FIGURE 50.   Referee signals no advantage—neutral position.

AWARDING POINTS

The man behind must have full control and take opponent to the mat, before a takedown is declared and before points are awarded for having earned a "position of advantage." This does not mean necessarily that a wrestler must be "behind" his opponent to receive such an award, but he must have him in a position where he has an advantage and distinct "control" of his man in the down position. Figures 48 and 49 show official awarding points. In like manner, an official should refrain from declaring "reversal of positions" until and unless a man has secured full control of his opponent. There are many brief flashes, both on the mat and while coming to the feet, when a contestant has not lost control of his opponent, nor has his opponent gained freedom from the previous advantage. These instances must be met often, and in all their varied types, before one can always be sure that an advantage has been gained or an opponent has "escaped" to a *neutral position.* Figures 50 and 51 show an official indicating a neutral position.

If the man in the under position attempts to escape, comes to

Brief flurries do not necessarily mean an escape or reversal

FIGURE 51.   Referee indicates neutral position standing.

the feet, and earns the "neutral position" on the wrestling mat proper, he should be credited with an escape. However, if the men leave the mat proper while still locked together, the man who was in the "under position" must be placed in this same position in the "referee's position" in the center of the mat before wrestling is resumed.

It is in such situations as the foregoing ones that the skilled and qualified official shows his clarity of understanding of rules and his mature judgment, which is based upon his wide experience with these situations. The well trained and qualified official will find that he fails or succeeds at this point in his officiating. These are the instances when points are earned or lost, and match decisions are fairly or improperly rendered. It should be repeated that alertness and keenness in judgment are most vital during the rapid changes that take place in ground wrestling.

AWARDING FALLS

In like manner, when declaring or awarding "falls," the official can err or mark himself as a finished arbiter by the manner in

Make signals clear

which he handles himself and makes these close and important decisions. The official should not declare a fall unless he is in a position that enables him to see that both shoulders or area of both scapula are distinctly down for the full elapsed time of one second in college rules and two seconds in high school rules. Wrestlers in such situations are often in such tangled and intertwined positions that an official will find it difficult to take a position, even with the side of the face down flat on the mat, where he can "positively" see both shoulders. This is particularly true if he is to one side of the men. An arm, an elbow, a hand, or head may block the view of the official so that he is unable to see whether or not both shoulders are down on the mat. In such instances there are two things the official can do. He can jump over from one side to the other to make sure the unobserved shoulder is distinctly touching the mat, and at the same time look across from above to see whether or not the other shoulder has raised from the mat. (See Figures 52 and 53.) Or, better, he can go down to the feet position of one of the men and glance quickly from side to side in order to see if both shoulders are touching at the same time for the allotted count. (See Figure 54.) These instances are among the most difficult the official has to face. It is here that matches, even meets, are won or lost. It is not considered the best of technique in such situations to slide the hand under the shoulder to feel if it is actually down, as this may be a warning to the contestant to raise his shoulder because a fall is pending.

MANNER OF WARNING FOR STALLING,
FOR AWARDING AND DECLARING POINTS,
FOR INDICATING TIME ADVANTAGE,
FOR DECLARING TIME-OUTS OR STOPPING
MATCH BECAUSE OF INJURY

The referee shall indicate orally and by pointing in such a manner that all present may know whenever a contestant has earned the position of advantage. The regulations also indicate the manner by which points shall be declared and advantage announced during the progress of the bout when the match reverts to the "no advantage" status. The referees' code for signals also specifies the types

The escape must be complete before leaving the mat

FIGURE 52.   Position of referee to judge a near fall.

FIGURE 53.   Referee awarding points for a near fall.

The test of the official—the quality of his discriminating judgment

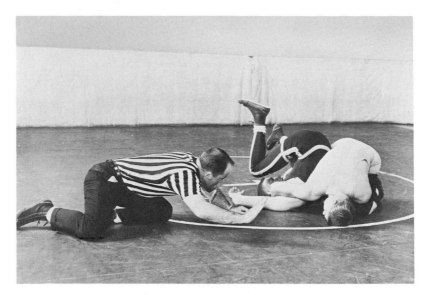

FIGURE 54. Referee in ready position to declare a fall.

of signals and the word or phrase used to announced all situations, such as, "Neutral Position," "Stop Wrestling," "Advantage," or "Time Out" and warning for stalling. (See illustrations of signals as shown throughout this chapter.)

The referee also makes sure by nod or glance at the table that the officials there have caught the awarded points and situation changes. Should any uncertainty arise as to the points awarded or the status at this instance, the referee or the head timekeeper should stop the match and straighten out the situation at once.

Likewise, the referee must make certain that the timers have observed his time-out signal. There are many brief flurries off the mat, when a wrestler's foot goes off or the contestant partly leaves the mat, with little or no time lost. In such instances the official does not ask for time-out. It is only for lengthy periods or for conditions that require time to bring the participants back to the center circle to begin wrestling, either on the feet or on the mat, at the referee's signal of "Wrestle!" that time out should be taken.

During injuries, or for other delays, the referee will check with

Be sure both shoulders are down for the full count

FIGURE 55.   Referee giving the warning signal for stalling.

FIGURE 56.   Referee declaring a fall by slapping hand to mat.

Be right—the results are in your hands

either the contestants, the officials at the table, and/or the coaches to see that all understand the situation. This provides an opportunity to care for the wrestlers when these emergencies arise.

The referee should advise the official timers not to take out time when he indicates a stalling warning by raising a clenched fist and pointing to the offending contestant with his other hand. If the stalling continues after such a warning, the whistle is blown, the match stopped, and one point is awarded against the offender. The match is then resumed in the center of the mat in a down position. It is the responsibility of both contestants to maintain action throughout the match and to wrestle aggressively. (See Figure 55.)

DECLARING FALLS AND NEAR FALLS

When the referee is in a position to see that both shoulders have been held in contact with the mat for the allotted one second of time, he declares and awards a fall by slapping the mat with the palm of his hand and at the same instant verbally announcing, "Fall!" (See Figure 56.)

In calling near falls, the referee must be in a position to observe that both shoulders are in contact with the mat for less than one full second or when one shoulder of the defensive wrestler is touching the mat and the other shoulder is held within one inch or less of the mat for two full seconds. Three points shall be awarded for these situations. Near falls shall be declared by "extending one arm vertically," but not until after the immediate situation is finished, no verbal announcement being given. Figures 52 and 53 show the sequences in declaring near falls and awarding points for them.

AWARDING A DECISION
OR DECLARING A DRAW

At the termination of a match, when a fall has not occurred, the referee goes through the following routine:

1. He checks with the timers and scorers in order to obtain the point score for the match.
2. He then calls the contestants to the center of the mat.
3. He raises the left arm of the winner to a vertical position.
4. In case of a draw, he raises the left arm of both wrestlers.

Announce decisions—scorers acknowledge

FIGURE 57. Referee awarding a decision.

5. If the match is terminated by a fall, he raises the left arm of the winner.

This method of awarding decisions leaves the right arms free and permits the contestants to congratulate one another by shaking their right hands.

It is recommended that the referee ask the contestants to shake hands as they approach him in the center of the mat. As they shake hands, he raises the arm of the winner. This technique tends to relieve any tension or embarrassment that the loser might otherwise experience. Referees who follow this procedure show consideration for the contestants. It is a means of fostering good sportsmanship.

The awarding of decisions is provided for in the rules. (See Figure 57.)

Mechanics of Working with the Timekeepers and Scorers (the Table)

At the beginning of the second and third periods and during the course of a match, whenever the wrestlers start from the down position, the referee shall be in a squat or kneeling position about eight

The raised left arm permits a right hand shake

or ten feet in front of the wrestlers and facing the scorers' and timers' table. (See Figure 42.) This position permits him to see both the contestants and the officials. It assures the scorers and timers a clear view of his starting signals. The position stipulated for the wrestlers in the "referees' position on the mat" is discussed under Rule 8, Section Ia, and should be enforced by the referee, as presented. The uninitiated official should remember that while he should live up to the rules as written, there is also a spirit behind them which he should abide by. It is not the duty of the official to attempt to coach the contestants regarding their position on the mat, either top or bottom man.

At all times during the course of a match, the referee should make clear to the table by signal and word the progress and changes in the match. In case of any uncertainty he should stop the match and check with the officials at the timekeepers' table. The timekeepers and scorers in turn should carry out their duties as prescribed under the regulations of Rule 13, Sections 4, 5, 6 and 7. The suggestions and digested summary of "Instructions to and Duties of Timekeepers and Scorers" on Form IX, may aid these officials in better understanding and carrying out their duties.

FORM IX

Instructions to and Duties of Timekeepers (Wrestling)

General Instructions: There shall be no communication between the timekeepers or representatives at the timekeepers' table and coaches, contestants, or spectators; and the time advantage shall be unannounced until the match is completed. This restriction is made to allow the timekeepers to give undivided attention to their duties. Timekeepers are directly responsible to the referee.

I. *Head Timekeeper*
   A. Sit between the two assistant timekeepers, and keep a check on their work.
   B. Check stop watches to see if they are in good working order, etc.
   C. Must have pistol, gong, or horn and rolled towel to toss at referee to indicate match time is over in event rooters' noise is so great, the official cannot hear.
   D. Record general time of the match.

In case of uncertainty, stop and check

FORM IX (*Continued*)

INSTRUCTIONS TO AND DUTIES OF TIMEKEEPERS (WRESTLING)

E. Notify the referee when the time limit of the bout has expired and when the time for intermissions has elapsed.
F. Start watch at signal of referee when:
  1. "Starting or resuming a bout standing."
  2. "Begin wrestling on mat (referee's position)."
G. Stop watch at signal of referee when:
  1. "Stop wrestling." (whistle)
  2. "Time out."
  3. "Declaring a fall."
H. Call the number of minutes remaining to be wrestled in the following manner:
  1. Three-minute bouts:
    a. 2 minutes! (at end of first minute of bout).
    b. 1 minute! (at end of second minute of bout).
    c. 45 seconds! (at end of 2 min., 15 sec., of bout).
    d. 30 seconds! (at end of 2 min., 30 sec., of bout).
    e. 15 seconds! (at end of 2 min., 45 sec., of bout).
    f. Sound gong or horn (at end of bout).
  2. Two-minute bouts:
    a. 1 minute! (at end of first minute of bout).
    b. 30 seconds! (at end of 1 min., 30 sec., of bout).
    c. 15 seconds! (at end of 1 min., 45 sec., of bout).
    d. Sound whistle (at end of bout).
I. Should have two extra stop watches for recording "time out" in case of injury to the contestants.
J. Should signal the referee immediately if any question arises between the timekeepers or scorers.
K. Should keep watches in plain view of all timekeepers.
L. Record time of each fall.
M. Record for referee the "choice of position" in each match.

II. *Two Assistant Timekeepers*
  A. "Home team" timekeeper
    1. Sit to right of head timekeeper.
    2. Record accumulated time advantage of "visiting team" wrestler.
  B. "Visiting team" timekeeper
    1. Sit to left of head timekeeper.
    2. Record the accumulated time of the "home team" wrestler.

Don't neglect pre-meet duties

FORM IX (*Continued*)

INSTRUCTIONS TO AND DUTIES OF TIMEKEEPERS (WRESTLING).

C. Report accumulated time advantage to referee at end of match.
D. Start watch at signal of referee when:
  1. "Advantage" for wrestler whose advantage he keeps.
E. Stop watch at signal of referee when:
  1. "Stop wrestling." (whistle)
  2. "Neutral position, standing" or "On mat."
  3. "Time-out."
  4. "Declaring a fall."
F. Should keep watches in plain view of all timekeepers.
G. When a multiple timer is used, such as the "Mohawk" timer, the timekeeper will sit at the right end of the table, the visiting scorer next to him, and the announcer and home scorer at the left end of the table facing the mat."

INSTRUCTIONS TO AND DUTIES OF SCORERS

General Instructions: Scorers are directly responsible to the referee.

I. In all matches there shall be two scorers.
  A. "Home team" scorer
    1. Record points awarded to wrestlers of visiting team.
  B. "Visiting team" scorer
    1. Record points awarded to the wrestlers of the home team.
  C. Each scorer shall record the various points awarded by the referee to the contestant whose record he has been assigned to keep.
    1. Each "takedown"—two points.
    2. Each "escape" from defensive position on mat—one point.
    3. Each "reversal of position" from defensive position on mat—two points.
    4. Each "near fall"—three points.
    5. Points for accumulated time advantage: one point for one full minute, and two points for two full minutes or more of net accumulated time advantage. Two points is the maximum to be awarded for a match, and these points shall be recorded on the final score.
    6. Predicament—Rule 8, section 13, two points.
    7. Penalties—(See Rule 11 and the penalty chart)

Time must be kept accurately; it may decide the match

FORM IX (*Continued*)

INSTRUCTIONS TO AND DUTIES OF SCORERS

D. Scorers should sit next to each other and check on the proper recording of scores in similar manner that the time-keepers check on each other.
E. Advise the head timekeeper immediately if there is a question about the score during any match.
F. Report total points of each contestant to the referee at end of match.

During the progress of a match, the head timekeeper shall be responsible for calling the minutes to the referee, contestants, and spectactors in each match. The last minute shall be reported at 15 seconds intervals (45-30-15 seconds).

The referee in turn will verbally convey the called times to the contestants, to keep them advised as to the time during the course of the match, and will stop the match with the "stop wrestling" and whistle signals, as indicated in the "Code of Signals." (See Figure 58.)

FIGURE 58.   Referee indicating time-out.

Check and recheck before announcing results

FIGURE 59.   Referee indicating rule infringement—interlocking hands.

Following this, the referee shall order the contestants to their corners, as indicated in Rule 18, Section 12. At the end of the match, the official will check with each scorer on the total points for each man. Next, he checks the watches for the time advantage for each contestant. He subtracts these to find the net time advantage. The accrued advantage points and time advantage points are totaled to secure the points for the winner of the match. Advising the officials at the table of this, he then goes to the mat, has the opponents shake hands, and awards his decision as indicated under "Awarding a Decision or Declaring a Draw."

The preceding section, "Instructions to and Duties of Time-keepers and Scorers," indicates the conditions under which the referee and other officials shall check with one another during the course of a match. Specific duties for each official in a wrestling meet are also indicated on this form.

Handle side line coaching with diplomacy

Techniques for Other Situations

There are many minor situations that the beginning official must learn to handle with dispatch and ease, in order not to draw undue attention nor detract from the smooth running of a wrestling meet. Time and experience will aid him in learning to solve disturbing problems.

Conferences with older and recognized registered officials on how to handle the many technical aspects of a match as well as the unusual situations will prove very helpful. For example, the learned referee turns a deaf ear to minor attempts of participants and coaches to aid a wrestler by comments, remarks, or exhortations. When these practices issue from the bench, they are called "sideline coaching" and are illegal under the rules. (Rule 12) Such situations can be deftly handled by the mere raising of a hand with the palm toward that team's bench to show those concerned that the official has taken note of their actions and that he disapproves. Procedures of this kind are effective and require no comments from the official. Should such conditions continue, it is within the right of the official to penalize the offenders by stopping the match and giving warning so that all may be aware of the situation. The better thing to do, however, is to go quietly to the coach of the team concerned, at the first time out or between matches, and acquaint him with the rules and the spirit of good sportsmanship and advise him to supervise his bench and boys according to the rules.

Another situation that can readily be handled by the referee without undue attention and delay is the occasional bulging of a mat cover upward when a wrestler is in a near fall or pinning position. As the official lies flat on the mat to observe the shoulders, he can pull upon the cover to flatten it and make the conditions proper in order to judge fairly a true fall or near fall. Of course, such bulging of covers can best be eliminated by the home management in seeing that the covers over the wrestling mats are tied or roped down to prevent slipping or bulging. A bulging or loose cover can also cause a contestant to trip or to slip. However, most high schools and colleges today use the plastic coated foam rubber mats, which have greatly improved the mat problem.

The official must provide himself with a whistle. While not required equipment, a stop watch may be found useful under many

Tie or rope down the mat covers

circumstances. Of course, the official always carries a silver dollar to use for the coin-toss choice. Other regular or unusual situations as they arise must be met and handled by the referee with the best of mature judgment.

Technique and Art in Officiating

The skilled and polished referee learns through practice and experience the manner by which he can best meet the requirements of his job. The job demands extreme physical and mental concentration. It requires tolerance for the unjust criticism that often accompanies officiating—even first-class work. However, if he is stimulated by the challenge offered, if he is interested in making a contribution to the sport, and if he is inspired to promote a true spirit of sportsmanship, he will surely receive great satisfaction from his efforts. He is most likely to attain the realm of the artist in his role as an official. Art in officiating, as in other things, takes the person beyond selfish motives and desires. It seeks to create a wholesome atmosphere in sports. Raising spirited competition to a high plane will make a real contribution to good citizenship. All connected with the sport—the participants, management, spectators, officials, coaches— are happier and better satisfied when the sport is conducted on this level.

Certification

Wrestling associations and conference organizations have taken a great deal of interest in training and developing qualified wrestling officials. There is a national association of qualified wrestling officials, along with the wrestling coaches' association, called the American Wrestling Coaches and Officials Association. The Association meeting is always held at the time of the NCAA Wrestling Tournament. Practically all states today have State Wrestling Officials Associations who certify wrestling officials for both high schools and colleges.

An excellent example of an efficiently organized group for certifying wrestling officials is the New England District Committee for

Spirited competition kept on a high plane marks the official as an artist

Approved Wrestling Officials. Organized since December, 1940, the New England District has been testing and certifying approved wrestling officials. This organization is a part of the New England Intercollegiate Wrestling Association, which is a branch of the National Collegiate Athletic Association.

The following is a brief recitation of the procedures under which this body operates. Annually, prior to the opening of the wrestling season in early December and at the meeting of the New England Intercollegiate Wrestling Association, the wrestling rules are interpreted. Coaches, officials, wrestlers, and college athletic officers gather to view films, discuss problems, interpret the new rules as they will be enforced in the district, and to examine new officials. The candidates are given a written test on the rules followed by a practical officiating test, at which time they officiate at a match. Three men must view and report on the outcome of the candidate's practical test. One member of the committee acts with a coach and registered official selected from those present. The prospective official must pass with a grade of 80 per cent on both the written and practical test to be approved for certification and included in the "Roster of Officials." (See *Wrestling Guide.*)

The form, "Report on Wrestling Official," included herein on page 311 is used as a checklist for rating the performance of the new officials. The composite rating the candidate receives forms the basis for his approval or rejection as a certified official. This checklist can also be used in contests during the regular season. By this record, tangible information can be recorded for use in reporting the work of officials. The candidates are given copies of the checklist prior to their examinations. In this way, they are able to learn the various factors that are used in the evaluation of their work. The checklist also acts as a guide to the candidate in his preparation for his practical test. The results of the test are discussed with each candidate. This is done regardless of whether the candidate is approved or rejected. By this process, each official is informed concerning his strength and weakness. Some officials who are not approved but who show promise are placed on a probationary list. These men are recommended for officiating at freshman, junior varsity, practice sessions, high school, preparatory school, or other less rigorous competition. By this means, they are able to obtain further grounding

Organize for quality, have a plan

and practice in the skill of officiating. This experience will be valuable to them when they present themselves for examination the following season.

Rating the Work of Officials
During the Season

Form X is used for rating the work of an official during a regular match. These reports are mailed to a central office and form the basis for rating the officials as a group. The information on these forms is passed on to the official so he may be advised concerning the caliber of his work. As indicated on pp. 313-15, the "Official's Check List" can be used during a regular contest for the purpose of facilitating the job of grading an official's work.

Signals

See Figures 41 to 59.

FORM X

A PLAN FOR RATING AND REPORTING THE WORK OF THE OFFICIAL

. . . . vs. . . . . at . . . . Date . . . .

Score of meet (V) . . . . (H) . . . . Referee . . . .

Remarks . . . .

. . . .

. . . .

Rating	Score	Coach's Numerical Score on
Excellent	90–100	Referee
Good	80–89	
Satisfactory	70–79	. . . .
Unsatisfactory	60–69	. . . .
		Coach's Signature

Know the official signals

FORM XI

WRESTLING REFEREE'S SIGNALS [2]

1. Starting or Resuming a Bout Standing—Extend *right arm* slightly above the horizontal to the front; verbally announce "Ready"—— pause——quickly lower arm and at the same instant blow whistle.

2. Stop Wrestling—Blow whistle; at same instant extend arm slightly above horizontal to the front, palm outward.

3. Neutral Position, Standing—Upper arms front, horizontal; both forearms vertical, hands extended.

4. Begin Wrestling on Mat (Referee's Position)—Referee should be eight to ten feet in front of wrestlers, facing timers' table, squat position. Give signal for number 1 above.

5. Advantage—One arm and index finger extended pointing to wrestler receiving advantage. At the same instant verbally announce "Advantage" and name the institution that offense represents.

6. Neutral Position (No Advantage) on Mat—Both arms extended sideward slightly below the horizontal, palms down; move hands back and forth with fingers spread and at the same instant verbally announce "No advantage."

7. Time Out—Give hand signal and blow whistle. (See Figure 58.)

8. Declaring Near Fall—Extend one arm vertically; no verbal announcement. (Award of near fall should not be made until the immediate "situation" is finished.

9. Declaring a Fall—Quickly strike mat with palm of one hand and at the same instant verbally announce "Fall." Do not slap wrestler on the back.

10. Awarding a Decision or Declaring a Draw—Referee shall call contestants to center of mat and raise the winner's left hand to a vertical position. In case of draw at end of match, referee shall raise left arms of both contestants to vertical position.

11. Award of Points—In connection with or immediately following the signal for change of position or advantage, the referee shall indicate award of points by pointing to the point scorer with the index finger of one hand and at the same time raise the opposite hand to or near a vertical position, extending one or two fingers of that hand to indicate the number of points awarded. Such signals must be clearly evident to the official scorekeeper and to the operator of the scoreboard (if such is used), and also so far as possible to coaches, contestants, and spectators.

12. Warning a Contestant for a Violation—The match is not stopped. The index finger of one hand is pointed to the violator. At the

---

[2] *Official Wrestling Guide 1966*, pp. 88-92.

Use the signals

FORM XI (*Continued*)

Wrestling Referee's Signals

same time, the referee verbally announces the warning and raises the opposite arm with his fist doubled to indicate the violation.

13. *Stopping the Match for Out-of-Bounds*—When the contestants are out of bounds, the referee stops the match and extends both arms horizontally to the same side toward the out-of-bounds.

14. *Awarding Predicament Points*—The referee does not signal a score for a predicament until the pinning situation is ended. He then extends one arm upward, indicating with the fingers the two points to be awarded.

15. *Interlocking Hands or Grasping Clothing During an Escape Maneuver*—When the bottom contestant is in the process of an escape or reversal and the contestant on top locks his hands or grasps the clothing to prevent the maneuver, the referee indicates the violation by grasping the wrist of one hand with his other hand, and holding it over his head. (See Figure 59.)

FORM XII

Official's Check List

.... vs. .... Place .... Date .... Time ....

Referee .... Score ( ) .... ( ) .... Reported

by .... Position ....

	Maximum Score	Check *	Total
	Maximum Score	Check *	Total
I. *PERSONALITY:* (15 points)			
A. Appearance			
1. Clean, attractive attire	5	....	
2. Well groomed	2	....	
B. Poise and businesslike attitude	4	....	
C. General—(Weak, antagonizing, uncertain, confident) (underline)	4	....	....

Signals guide the contestants

FORM XII (*Continued*)

OFFICIAL'S CHECK LIST

II. *INSPECTION AND INSTRUCTION:*
(10 points)
A. Before meet
   1. Wrestlers—(rings, nails, clothing, oil, etc.) .... 2 ....
   2. Equipment—(mats, watches, whistle or gong, etc. .... 2 ....
   3. Timers and scorers—proper instructions .... 2 ....
   4. Contestants and coaches—check relative to questionable situations ...... 1 ....
B. During meet
   1. Wrestlers—instructions and final inspection .... 2 ....
C. After meet
   1. Coaches (and contestants)—check for clarification of decisions rendered if questioned .... 1 ....

III. *RULES—KNOWLEDGE, INTERPRETATION, JUDGMENT, ENFORCEMENT:* (40 points)
A. Off-mat decisions .... 5 ....
B. Stalling .... 5 ....
C. Illegal holds .... 5 ....
D. Falls .... 5 ....
E. Near falls .... 4 ....
F. Takedowns, reversals, escapes and predicaments .... 4 ....
G. Decisions .... 3 ....
H. Time advantage .... 2 ....
I. Time-outs .... 1 ....
J. Miscellaneous (injuries, defaults, intermissions, penalties) .... 6 ....

IV. *TECHNIQUE:* (25 points)
A. Mannerisms on mat .... 3 ....
B. Use of voice .... 3 ....
C. Signals and awarding of points ...... 4 ....
D. Position and speed
   1. Starting bout .... 1 ....

How do you rate?

FORM XII (*Continued*)

OFFICIAL'S CHECK LIST

2. Wrestlers in standing position ..... 2 ....
3. Wrestlers on mat .... 2 ....
4. Referee's position .... 2 ....
5. Falls .... 2 ....
6. Anticipation of wrestlers' movements 2 ....
7. Near fall, predicament .... 1 ....
8. Tossing coin and choice of position 1 ....
9. Off-mat decisions and resuming in
   neutral position .... 1 ....
10. Declaring the winner .... 1 ....

V. *CONTROL OF MEET:* (10 points)
  A. Commanding respect and cooperation of
    all concerned
    1. Contestants .... 4 ....
    2. Coaches .... 2 ....
    3. Timers and scorers .... 2 ....
    4. Spectators .... 2 ....

TOTAL SCORE   100

Use reverse side for remarks

* Indicate weaknesses in "check" column by W.
  Indicate strengths in "check" column by S.
  Score value to be recorded also.

Where are you weak?

chapter 21

HOCKEY

The Rules Committee of the NCAA urges that officials for all collegiate games be selected from the lists approved by the National Collegiate Athletic Association and that they be members of the local Officials' Association. The following list of requirements must be met by a candidate before he can qualify as an NCAA ice-hockey referee or assistant referee.

General Qualifications

1. Honesty and fairness of judgment.
2. Ability to make quick decisions.
3. Firmness in abiding by decisions.

Jack be nimble, Jack be quick

4. Agility and speed on ice skates. Must be able to skate well forward or backward and to stop quickly.
5. Good eyesight.
6. Emotional control.
7. Knowledge of the 15 basic rules of the sport.

The duties of the officials for hockey are comprehensively covered in the officials' rule book.[1] Little can be added to the concise statements found in Rule 15. Likewise, in view of the fast action, the mechanics of working a hockey game are very simple. Diagram 52 represents the complete range of movement except for the mechanics of putting the puck in play by a face-off. The procedure for the mechanics of the face-off is covered in Rule 10.

General Information

All hockey officials should be supplied by the home team. Only the referee need be approved by both teams. Seven officials are needed for a match: referee, assistant referee, two goal umpires, timekeeper, assistant timekeeper, and penalty timekeeper. In an emergency, the timekeeper can do the collateral duties of assistant timekeeper and penalty timekeeper. However, five officials should be the minimum number to insure control of play. In college and secondary school games, the referees are usually the only professional officials. All others are laymen who volunteer their services because of their interest in the sport.

DIAGRAM 52.   Movements of referee and assistant referee along the boards in a hockey game. One official leads while the other trails. Arrows show limits of movements of each official in direction indicated.

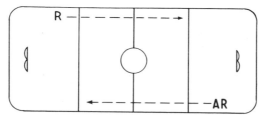

---

[1] *NCAA Official Ice Hockey Rules* (New York: A. S. Barnes and Co., 1949).

There must be a minimum of five hockey officials

Two important but seldom used rules that the referee should know are:

1. If a team refuses after three minutes to obey a decision of the referee, the latter may award the match on a forfeit to the other team by a score of 1–0.

2. If a team refuses to play an overtime period in the event of a tie game, the referee may award the match on a forfeit to the other team by a score of 1–0.

Note: This indicates that a referee is complete master of a hockey game, and he does not have to tolerate abuse or unsportsmanlike conduct. A hockey match will be clean and fair if a referee is alert and knows his job. A match can be rough-and-tumble if the teams realize the referee is careless and indecisive.

General Duties

The general duties for collegiate hockey officials are indicated in Rule 15 of the official NCAA ice hockey rules as follows:

RULE 15—OFFICIALS AND THEIR DUTIES

Number and Titles—Section 1. The officials of a match shall be: a referee, an assistant referee, two goal umpires, a timekeeper, an assistant timekeeper, and a penalty timekeeper.

Unless otherwise determined, the officials shall toss a coin to determine which shall be the referee in charge.

Note: It is recommended that linesmen be appointed to watch the zone lines and signal or report to the referee or assistant referee, all violations of the antidefense rule (Rule 11, Sections 2 and 4).

Referee and Assistant Referee—Section 2. The referee and, subject to him, the assistant referee shall have sole authority and control of the game and they are not required to confer with coaches during a game and its intermission periods. They shall see that the other officials are appointed and in their places, and that markings, cages and goalkeepers' leg pads conform to the rules. They shall start and stop play (except timekeepers' signal always stops play); enforce the rules; settle disputes; decide or interpret cases unpro-

Action is lightning fast—the speed of decisions must keep pace

vided for by these rules; appoint, and in their discretion remove the other officials; control the timekeepers; keep the score, announce each goal as scored; and at the conclusion of the match the referee shall declare the result. If, in the opinion of the referee, the playing conditions become unsatisfactory during the course of the game, he may call the game at any time. It shall be "no game" unless two periods have been completed. The puck shall be considered in play until the referee or assistant referee stops the play, which either may do at any time by sounding a whistle or horn, or by ringing a bell (except timekeepers' signal always stops play). They shall stop the play whenever either observes an infringement of the rules, except in the attacking or neutral zones upon commission of a foul to prevent a goal, the play shall not be stopped until the particular play or series of plays shall have been completed. The referee or assistant referee shall stop play because of the illness of any player, or for any other cause, which in the judgment of the referees justifies such action. They shall suspend the calling of a foul upon a defending player as provided in Section 6 (a) of Rule 14.

In case a player or players attempt to delay the game as stated in Rule 11, Section 5 (d), the referee shall order play to start and shall immediately resume play by a face-off, even though the offending player or players are not ready.

The decision of the referee on any question whatever shall be final and there shall be no appeal. He may change his own decision, or that of any other official, provided he does so before play is renewed following rendition of the original decision.

Note: The referee should skate along one sideboard and the assistant referee should skate along the opposite sideboard. One should watch, primarily, the play of the puck while it is being advanced toward one end of the rink and should follow the play if necessary to a point even with the crease. The other should primarily be concerned with the play not directly connected with the puck and should go as far as the attacking zone line. When the puck is being advanced toward the opposite end of the rink, the special attention of the officials should be reversed. See Diagram 52.

However, each official should call any infraction that he sees, regardless of its location or of the location of or direction of movement of the puck. Officials should change ends near the middle of

The official rules include the mechanics of officiating

the third period and at the middle of any overtime period. When play is stopped, the official who is to put the puck into play should always look toward the players' boxes to see if substitution is to be made, and he should not start the play if more than the proper number of players are on the rink. A signal—horn, or waving of the flag—different from that used by the referees, may be used to call the referee's attention that substitution is to be made, but only when play is stopped.

The referee or assistant referee shall see to it that teams are notified three minutes before play is to start after each intermission.

When an official rules a player off the ice, the official must designate the offense and any special amount of time to the penalty timekeeper and shall announce or have the offense announced. Play must be stopped whenever a penalty is imposed.

Timekeepers—Section 3. (a) The timekeeper and assistant timekeepers shall use one timer between them. They shall time the actual play, starting when the puck hits the ice on the face-off and stopping whenever the referee or assistant referee signals the play to stop and when a goal is made. They shall ring a gong or shoot a gun at the end of each regular period and of any other period designated by the referee, and this signal shall mark the absolute conclusion of play. They shall time intermissions and shall notify the referee (to inform the teams to be ready to play) three minutes before the expiration of each intermission.

Penalty Timekeeper—Section 3. (b) The penalty timekeeper shall keep a record of the offenses and the players penalized. He shall keep off the rink any player sent to him by the referee or assistant referee for the full time of the penalty in actual time of play, starting when the puck strikes the ice on the face-off and stopping whenever the referee or the assistant referee signals the play to stop and when a goal is made. He shall notify the referee, when play is stopped, if a penalized player went on the rink before his penalty time was completed. In case of a postponed time penalty, he shall see that no penalized player returns to the ice until there is a stoppage of play or until a substitute has been removed.

Note: If the penalty time is unexpired at the end of a period, the penalty carries over into the next regular or overtime period.

It is recommended that all except the penalty timekeeper and penalized players be excluded from the penalty box. Other officials, coaches, and spectators, alike, should be excluded.

Goal Umpires—Section 4. The goal umpire shall signal the referee when the puck enters the cage. The referee shall give the goal umpire an opportunity to inform him as to the manner in which the puck was caused to enter the cage and whether the conditions of the goal crease rule have been complied with. The final decision as to whether or not it shall be scored shall be made by the referee.

The goal umpire shall judge at the same cage during the entire match.

Note: The goal umpire should not talk to the goalkeeper.

Basic Principles for Hockey Officials

William J. Stewart [2] has pointed up the duties of the referee in six basic principles, which are listed below.

1. Officials should blow whistle loudly and more than once to make sure both teams hear it.

2. When teams are storming around the goal and players are all piled up around the goalkeeper, the official should blow his whistle the instant the puck is out of sight to prevent piling-on, to save injuries, and to protect goalkeepers, of whom most teams have only one.

3. Be very strict on any attempt to injure an opponent. Cross-checking, board-checking, slashing across the hands, etc., should call for instant and full penalties.

4. Officials should learn to skate backwards with players coming out of their defensive zone, not turning until the player has come out of his defensive zone. In this way the official always has the player in front of him.

5. If an offensive team is fouled, the official must make sure that they have no further opportunity to continue their offensive play before he blows his whistle for a penalty. Similarly the whistle should not be blown when an offensive player is offside in his

---

[2] William J. Stewart, "Hints on Officiating." In the *Official Ice Hockey Guide* (New York: A. S. Barnes and Co., 1948), p. 66.

When the puck is out of sight—stop the fight

attacking zone if the defensive team has a good opportunity for an offensive jump out of that zone.

6. To sum it all up: Be an official at all times. You will have to call plays that will hurt teams, but no coach likes a weak-kneed official.

Don't turn back on play

chapter 2 2

LACROSSE

Lacrosse [1] is advertised as the fastest game played on two feet. The very nature of the game requires that the officials be consistent and firm in handling it and that they be quick to penalize infractions of the rules in order to prevent the game from getting out of hand.

The game has an elite following, which has worked freely and unselfishly to promote its spread and to keep it on a high and dignified level. In this connection, much has been done to train and

---

[1] *Note:* The author is grateful to Nelson N. Cochrane, District Chief Referee of New England, who has generously furnished most of the material for this section of the book.

The nature of the game requires firmness

develop officials. In order to check on the work of the officials in regular games and in order to get composite ratings of them, each coach reports to the officials' association. A typical rating card for this purpose is shown in Form XIII.

The officials for the game consist of a referee, an umpire, a time-keeper, and a scorer. The referee and umpire are the professional officials, who are paid for their services. The timer and scorer are appointed by the referee. They are lay officials who are usually obtained from the manager of the home team. The procedures following are strongly recommended for lacrosse officials.

Personal Equipment

The referee and umpire customarily wear white-and-black-striped shirts, white knickers, black or blue hose and cap. They should carry a red handkerchief with a weight knotted in it. This is to be used to signal penalties. They both carry the same sounding whistle and a coin to be used for the toss.

Pregame Conference

Officials should get together in the dressing room at least a half hour before game time and discuss the important rules and situations that may arise and that will require prompt action on their part. The sides of the field where each is to work, how out-of-bounds balls are to be covered, and the mechanics that will be employed on attacking situations and fast breaks should be worked out at the pregame conference. It is even a good idea to go over the rules together and work for complete harmony during the contest.

Checking Equipment and Field

The officials should be dressed and on the field 15 minutes before game time. Officials should check goal nets and field markings im-

Coach—be objective

FORM XIII

RATING OF LACROSSE OFFICIAL

UMP. ☐

REF. ☐

_____

NAME OF OFFICIAL

KNOWLEDGE AND INTERPRETATION OF RULES	☐ NO ERRORS	☐ FEW ERRORS	☐ MANY ERRORS
ATTITUDE	☐ OVER-OFFICIOUS	☐ FIRM	☐ HESITANT
COVERAGE OF FIELD	☐ TOO CLOSE	☐ SATISFACTORY	☐ TOO DISTANT
CONSISTENCY OF RULINGS	☐ CONSISTENT	☐ INCONSISTENT	
OVER ALL RATING	☐ ABOVE AV.	☐ AVERAGE (FAIR)	☐ BELOW AV.

OTHER COMMENTS _____

_____

_____

_____

_____

VISITING TEAM _____   _____

SCORE

HOME TEAM _____   _____

SCORE

_____ DATE _____

SIGNATURE OF COACH

Inspect the crosses for safety and fair play

mediately upon entering the field. If nets are too taut or too loose, the home manager should be notified so adjustments can be made. All netting should be securely fastened to the ground and posts of the goal. They should arrange with the home team manager to have a spare man at each end of the field with one or two extra balls. When a ball goes over the end line an extra ball should be tossed to the proper player by this spare man who then retrieves the original ball.

The teams should be lined up at the center of the field for inspection of the crosses. The officials should look for small sticks, unlaced heads, anything that may hinder dislodging the ball by an opponent. This procedure is a safety precaution as well.

Instructing Timer and Scorer

Appoint a timer and be sure he understands rules about intermissions, time-outs, and notifications. If there is no pistol, have the timer secure a whistle to signal the end of a period and be sure he uses it only for this purpose. The referee in consultation with the coaches should determine the length of periods before the game.

Appoint a scorer and explain that all substitutes must report to him and that no substitute may run on the field until after he sounds his horn and has received a wave of the hand from an official. Be sure scorer understands how to keep the game record sheet and that a copy is to be furnished the referee at the end of the game. A sample of the Lacrosse Game Record (Form XIV) is shown on page 327.

Meeting of Coaches and Captains

A few minutes before game time the umpire should get the visiting team captain and meet the referee and home team captain on the field. Any local ground rules should be determined. At this time the captains are asked to instruct their squads on the following:

1. After retrieving an out-of-bounds ball, a player must step onto the field before he can expect the official to blow his whistle to resume play.

The timer is a volunteer—don't neglect him

FORM XIV

LACROSSE GAME RECORD SHEET

HOME TEAM_____ VISITORS_____

PLAYED AT_____DATE_____ REFEREE_____ UMPIRE_____

	1ST PERIOD	2ND PERIOD	3RD PERIOD	4TH PERIOD	OVERTIME	TOTAL
SCORE BY HOME TEAM						
PERIODS VISITORS						

HOME TEAM LINE-UP

G _____ _____ _____
P I _____ _____ _____
CP _____ _____ _____
1D _____ _____ _____
2D _____ _____ _____
C _____ _____ _____
2A _____ _____ _____
1A _____ _____ _____
OH _____ _____ _____
III _____ _____ _____

VISITORS LINE-UP

G _____ _____ _____
PT _____ _____ _____
CP _____ _____ _____
1D _____ _____ _____
2D _____ _____ _____
C _____ _____ _____
2A _____ _____ _____
1A _____ _____ _____
OH _____ _____ _____
IH _____ _____ _____

PENALTIES ON HOME TEAM

NAME	OFFENSE	MIN.	PER.	TIME

PENALTIES ON VISITORS

NAME	OFFENSE	MIN.	PER.	TIME

SCORING BY HOME TEAM

NAME	ASSIST	PER.	TIME

SCORING BY VISITORS

NAME	ASSIST	PER.	TIME

MANAGER'S SIGNATURE_____ REFEREE'S SIGNATURE_____

A complete record to be furnished referee at end of each lacrosse game. Referee to forward with comments
on reverse side to NELSON N. COCHRANE 138 Grand View Ave., Wollaston, Massachusetts.
DISTRICT CHIEF REFEREE NEW ENGLAND INTERCOLLEGIATE LACROSSE LEAGUE

2. Players for whom substitutes are entering the game should hold up sticks so the new players can find their positions quickly (especially when the entire midfields are substituted).

3. No one but the captains may discuss rulings with the official during the game.

Keep the record complete on the official sheet

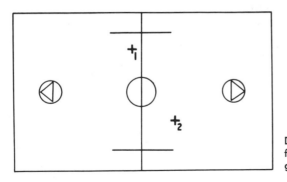

DIAGRAM 53. Positions of officials at face-off in a lacrosse game.

The visiting team captain will call his choice at the toss of the coin. After the toss, the game should be started promptly.

Positions of Officials
at the Face-Off

Each period starts with a face-off. Likewise, there is a face-off after each goal. The umpire who is on the opposite side of the field from the timer's and scorer's bench handles the ball. He also checks the position of the centers' sticks. To start play, the umpire backs out of the center circle and blows his whistle.

The referee, who is on the side of the field nearer the bench, is responsible for fouls and for watching for violations by players who may step into the center circle. The positions of the officials at the face-off are shown in Diagram 53.

Covering the Field

After the face-off, the officials assume positions so that one official is in front of the play and one is trailing behind the play. Each covers the end of the field to his right. This direction is determined as the official faces toward the center of the field with his back to the side line.

If the direction of play should change, the trailing official becomes the leading official. Thus, when the attack loses the ball, the

Know your duty at the face-off

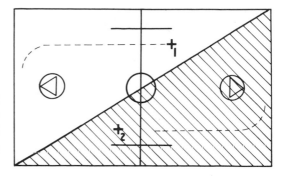

DIAGRAM 54. Positions and movements when ball is in play. One official always leads the play and one trails. The area of responsibility of each is also shown.

official responsible for the other end line must keep ahead of the play as it goes toward the far goal and be ready to call out-of-bounds play at the far end line. The other official should trail the play up the field and at the midfield stripe check for offside. However, when the play is close to him and near his side line, he should watch the ball and let the other official check the offside.

In general, each official is responsible for play close to the ball in his diagonal half of the field. However, cooperation is important. Neither official should hesitate to call a foul that may appear to be directly in front of the other. The attention of the near official may be turned to note a possible nearby interference, or an illegal check after a pass, or perhaps from his angle of vision he cannot detect the foul.

Diagram 54 shows the area of the field for which each official is generally responsible. The end that each covers is also shown by the direction of the line and arrow.

Positions and Duties of Officials at the Goal

When play is around the goal, the official responsible for the end line behind the goal should pay strict attention to the player with the ball and all shots. The other official should watch the general play around the goal and be alert for interference, players entering the crease, etc. Diagram 55 shows the positions of the officials when the ball is in the goal area. Note the end official is back of the goal.

Cover the ball when in your triangle

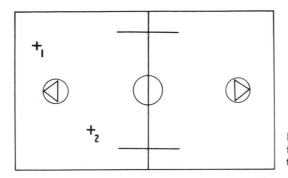

DIAGRAM 55. Positions of officials when the play is around the crease.

Procedure in Calling Fouls

Except in deliberately slow whistles, fouls should be called promptly by a loud blast. The official should point to the offending player, call his number, and announce clearly and loudly the type of foul and length of penalty. This should be supplemented by giving the proper signal to indicate the foul. The official must rule with firmness, as previously stated. He must not, however, be unpleasant, sarcastic, or overofficious. If, in spite of efforts on the part of the official to avoid antagonism, a player argues about his infraction of the rules, he should be given an additional penalty of one minute. Likewise, the official should not tolerate similar unsportsmanlike conduct from other players or from the bench. Penalties of one minute should be assessed without hesitation. If such infractions occur by the coach or players on the bench, the penalty should be assessed on a close-attack player.

It weakens the position of the official and tends to permit the game to get out of hand to give warnings. If it is a foul it deserves a penalty. Therefore, there is no place in lacrosse for such phrases as "If you do that again, I'll put you out" or "Watch that stuff" or "Quit moving after the whistle."

Guides to Specific
Play Situations

The following are guides to actual play situations. They refer to specific rules as indicated. They are so pertinent to the duties and

Call a foul where you see it

procedures of officials that considerable space is devoted to them on the following pages.

BALL OUT-OF-BOUNDS

Unless it is obviously accidental, rule that any ball kicked, batted, thrown, or pushed over the end line is deliberately caused to go over the end line. The ball is given to the opposing team.

SUBSTITUTIONS

If a substitute thinks the whistle has blown and runs on the field while play is still going on, the play is stopped and a technical foul is called for more than ten men on the field. If a player causes confusion by running out on the field before being waved on by an official, the same penalty is inflicted.

PRIVILEGES OF GOALKEEPER

If a goalie stops the ball with the hand and then puts the ball in his stick, this is sufficient evidence that he caught the ball contrary to the rule. A penalty should be inflicted.

INTERFERENCE

The defense player should be penalized for any shouldering, stick whacking, and shoving about of an attack player (note crease men carefully), except when the attack man is about to receive an actual pass that has been thrown to him. Careful watch should be made when a goalie yells "Check" to note any defense player who strikes at an attack player's crosse when the latter is not actually about to receive a pass.

Interference should be called on any defense player who hinders an attack player or steps in front of him when the attack player is making a cut toward the goal.

Block plays can be legal but are difficult to execute legitimately. A player may not step in front of a moving opponent who does not have the ball. However, he is entitled to a position on the field and may move or stand anywhere he desires provided that in the process

Don't warn—penalize

of reaching the desired position he does not hinder an opponent. Once he takes the position he thinks suitable for a block play, he cannot then move again after his opponent has started to move toward him. In other words, after he has assumed his block position, if he takes a step, turns his body, bends over, or does anything else to obstruct the path of his opponent as the latter approaches, he is then guilty of interference.

HOLDING

An attack player may ward off a blow at his crosse if he keeps his free arm stationary. If he pushes away or bats away a defense man's stick, he must be called for holding. (There should be a better rule to cover this situation, but this rule is the nearest thing to cover an obviously unsuitable act.)

A defense player may reach around the body of an attack player with his stick, or arm on his stick, to thrust at his opponent's crosse provided he does not impede the forward movement of the attack player. However, the instant the attack player's forward movement is checked, even momentarily, by the arm or stick across his body, this becomes holding and should be called promptly.

TRIPPING AND PUSHING

Most trips are probably accidental, but even if a player trips another by falling down in front of him, accidentally getting his foot in the way or unintentionally dangling his stick in the wrong place, the official must call this tripping and inflict a penalty.

When a player is legitimately reaching for a loose ball, and an opponent falls over his stick, this obviously is not a trip.

A defense player may hold off an opponent with his hand closed over the butt end of his stick, but if he punches or pushes the attack player around with this hand, he must be penalized for pushing.

LEAVING POSITION

When the whistle has blown, a player may not toss his stick to a more favorable position and then move to where his stick has fallen.

Develop a clear image for a legal block

When the ball goes out-of-bounds, the official should blow his whistle promptly as the ball touches the line. Any player who moves after the whistle is blown should be penalized. When a player is all alone, and there is no decision to make regarding who gets the ball, the player may continue running to retrieve the ball.

GENERAL CONDUCT

The officials should not tolerate any jeers, loud criticism, or other unsportsmanlike conduct from the bench. A penalty may be inflicted on a close attack player when that happens or the coach may be warned to keep his squad under control. On the second offense, penalty should be made on the offending team. It is more important that players learn self-control than that they score a number of goals.

STRIKING WITH CROSSE (SLASHING)

If a player strikes an opponent anywhere except on his stick (or on gloved hand on the stick), it is a slash. If the stick and player are struck at the same time, it is still a slash. All jabs at the stomach, hip, and elbow are called slashes. All follow-through swings that catch a man across the legs and feet are called slashes. Pushing at a man with the end of the stick should be called under this rule. The Rules Committee, the New England Association, and the chief referee have all ordered that officials adhere strictly to this rule. Therefore, all slashes must be called if they are illegal.

A player who just touches an opponent with his stick, or whose stick slides with no force along a helmet, arm, or shoulder is not committing a slash.

If a player, in order to protect his crosse, interposes his arm or shoulder in front of a blow which would not otherwise have struck him, this is not a slash.

If a player runs into a stick, the opponent may not be called for slashing (although in some such situations he may be called for holding).

Every one-handed blow at a crosse is not necessarily a slash if done expertly and with adequate control, but some one-handed swings may be slashes, just as some "wood chopper" two-handed swings may be slashes even though no one is hit.

Trips, even accidental, are illegal

PENALTIES

Personal Fouls

Most fouls are accidental and should receive only one-minute penalties. However, when a player deliberately trips an opponent, checks viciously from the rear, or otherwise flagrantly violates a rule in an intentional manner, two- or three-minute penalties should be inflicted.

Expulsion Fouls

Whenever a player deliberately strikes, kicks, or knees an opponent with intent to injure, an expulsion foul should be called. Whenever a player drops his crosse and starts swinging his fists, an expulsion foul must be called. Whether or not the offender fancies he has just been too roughly handled is insufficient excuse to void expulsion. Sometimes the offender has just been the victim of unnecessary roughness, and an alert official will have noted it and should call this foul in addition.

Execution of Penalties

The red handkerchief should always be carried so it will be easily accessible without fumbling. In slow-whistle situations the handkerchief should be tossed promptly and then the whistle blown after play is completed. Generally such situations occur when attack player is within 20 yards of goal and driving in for a shot, but sometimes, for example when a man is free in front of the goal, the whistle should be held on plays further out until the opportunity for a pass to the free man has occurred. Penalty should be inflicted after the play is completed, whether or not there was a goal.

Postgame Duties

The following postgame procedures are those that are in vogue in New England. They are recommended for all sections and particularly for college games.

When the whistle blows, see that the players freeze

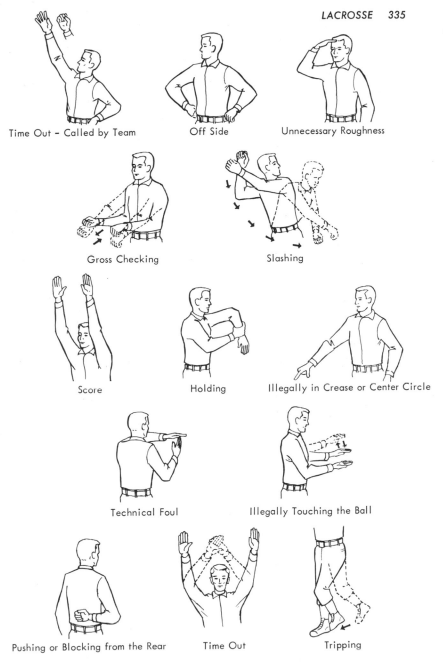

Time Out – Called by Team   Off Side   Unnecessary Roughness

Gross Checking   Slashing

Score   Holding   Illegally in Crease or Center Circle

Technical Foul   Illegally Touching the Ball

Pushing or Blocking from the Rear   Time Out   Tripping

FIGURE 60.   Official signals for Lacrosse.

Use the flag when there's need for a lag

A copy of the game record sheets should be secured from the official scorer. Before signing the sheet, it should be read over to be sure it is filled out completely and correctly. This should be mailed to the District Chief Referee, after writing comments on the reverse side. Comments are desired on the following topics:

1. Efficiency of manager in preparing field and handling game.
2. Attitude of players and coaches during game as judged by behavior.
3. Names of standout players.
4. Salient points of contest, type of play, and unusual occurrences.

After all college varsity games, the referee should send a collect wire, press rates, to the Associated Press, Boston, Mass., announcing place of lacrosse game and scores of each team.

Signals

Lacrosse like other sports has its system of signals to convey to those watching the game the actions taken by the officials. These are reproduced here for the convenience of the reader. No official is fully equipped to officiate a game unless he has a ready knowledge of these signals. (See Figure 60.)

Know the signals for your sport

chapter 23

ORGANIZATION
OF SKI MEETS

Organization of Officials

There are really two phases to the administration of ski competition: the organization for the meet, and the job of actually running off the meet. Because all preliminary work in preparation for a meet must be done away from the scene of competition, it seems pertinent to include a list of the duties of the officials who arrange for all the details of a ski meet. These officials include the following:

1. A director-in-chief
2. A director of officials

Make preparations away from the scene of action

3. A secretary, or clerk of office
4. The clerks of the various courses
5. An equipment director
6. A first-aid director
7. A transportation director

THE DIRECTOR-IN-CHIEF

He shall be the chairman of the committee and shall be responsible for the coordination and satisfactory conduct of the program. The director must keep constant check on the members of his committee to make sure that the work is functioning as smoothly as possible.

His duties begin long in advance of the actual running of the race. He must first consider the members of his committee, and he must choose them in light of their ability, responsibility, and willingness to do the work and make necessary sacrifices entailed in putting across a successful ski meet.

He must also prepare all budgets, and handle all financial matters connected with the meet. If it is within the province of the tournament committee to take care of such arrangements as housing and entertainment of the competitors, then this also should be listed as among the duties of the director-in-chief. However, it is advisable that this be left to separate committees, or at least to men subordinate to the director of the committee.

He should keep himself free from any particular job during the running of the races, so that he may be ready to apply himself to the ever-present, last-minute needs that will always crop up, no matter how well a race may be organized.

THE DIRECTOR OF OFFICIALS

It shall be his duty to secure all the officials necessary for the proper running of each event. A list of these officials, which will include such men as referee, judges, timers, starters, recorders, course setters, forerunners, and checkers, will be included in the detailed account of each event. However, a reminder is necessary that the more respected the name of an official in the ski world, the more respected his word becomes, so that any decision he makes

Two sets of officials are necessary

will be beyond question. Therefore the utmost care must be used in choosing officials.

THE SECRETARY OR CLERK OF OFFICE

His duties are mainly those of secretary and general office worker on the committee. He shall be responsible for mailing entry blanks to the competitors, for publishing lists of entries, distributing programs, compiling lists of officials, instructions sheets to competitors, etc. It should be his duty to see that all scoring cards for the various events be in the hands of the proper officials at the proper time, and that following the race they be brought to the scorer as soon as possible. He should also be responsible for posting the official results just as soon as possible after the finish of the race, and for publishing, in printed form, the final results of the race. These should be mailed immediately to all contestants.

He should also be responsible for all dealings with the press, all advance publicity, etc. In case of a large, important tournament, however, it would be wiser to appoint another man to handle publicity alone, for the job would become too large a one if much publicity work is entailed.

THE CLERKS OF THE COURSES

The duties of these men will be discussed in detail under the headings of the various races that they will run. It is necessary that there be a separate clerk of course for each event, because his duties are so numerous it would be almost impossible to be in charge of more than one race. It shall be his duty to be responsible for the satisfactory conduct of the event to which he is assigned, and he is subordinate to no one but the director-in-chief. He should organize a subcommittee, and assign to them the various jobs necessary for the running of his event.

EQUIPMENT DIRECTOR

It shall be the duty of the equipment director to collect and distribute to the various clerks of courses the equipment that they will need for the running of their events. Such articles as shovels, rakes,

Officials organize the meet

axes, ropes, slalom flags, cross-country flags, finish flags, communications equipment, timing and checking boards, pencils, watches, and number bibs are all necessary for the running of a ski meet.

FIRST-AID DIRECTOR

He shall be responsible for organizing and equipping a ski patrol competent enough to handle any possible accident that might occur during the conduct of events.

(Literature concerning the organization, equipment, and work of the ski patrol may be obtained by writing to the National Ski Patrol System, Eastern Division, 1416 Massachusetts Ave., Cambridge 36, Mass.)

TRANSPORTATION DIRECTOR

In a large tournament, and in a meet where not all of the courses are centrally located, it is advisable to have a director of transportation, who shall be responsible for the transportation of competitors, officials, workers, patrolmen, and all equipment to and from the race courses.

Meet Officials

The events that may be included in a ski meet are a) jumping, b) langlauf, c) slalom races, d) downhill races, e) combined scoring in either jumping and langlauf or downhill and slalom to count the combination as one event.

The officials needed for three events include: a referee, a scorer, a clerk of course, race committee, timing officials, communication officials, course police, first-aid patrol, forerunners, flag keepers, checkers and course patrol, judges, measurers, recorders. The duties of each and the techniques that each should acquire will be discussed in the order named and as they are required for each event. The nature of the ski meets requires quite different conditions for each. As a consequence, each event necessitates a separate course. While the various courses should be conveniently adjacent, it is obvious that in order to provide suitable terrain for each, there will

Meet officials supervise and run off the events

be some distance from one to the other. This fact and the extent of a course will obviously separate the officials.

All of these factors practically demand that only those with skiing experience and with an understanding of the characteristics of competition in an event should be appointed to officiate. In many respects, skiing is a specialized competition and requires officials who are expert in the activity. It is axiomatic that the extent to which a decision of an official is accepted, is dependent upon his standing and recognition in skiing society.

General Meet Officials

There are certain officials who serve in official capacity for the meet as a whole, instead of for individual events, and for that reason their duties are brought up now.

REFEREE

He is the general rule-maker or arbitrator of the tournament. He alone must decide upon all disputes arising before and during the race that must be decided at once on the spot. He should be present at the finish of each race course, and receive reports of the officials concerning offenses to the rules. He should make a list of all disqualifications and post it immediately following the completion of the race.

THE SCORER

This official is responsible for the computation of the results of each event, and the combined scoring, both team and individual. He must be something close to a mathematical genius, for this work is extremely complicated at times, and often a mistake in the computation of the results will cast a black shadow over an otherwise perfect race. It is obvious that he must be completely familiar with the methods of scoring. An adding machine and an assistant will be of invaluable aid in his work.

The methods of scoring a meet are complicated and detailed and

Only those with experience in skiing should officiate

will not be taken up here. There are specific instructions for the scorer in another section of this chapter.

RACE COMMITTEE

It will be necessary at this time to distinguish between the race committee and the tournament committee, for that question is sure to come up. As has been outlined, the tournament committee is in charge of the management of the meet. The race committee, on the other hand, has its greatest use in settling disputes that arise during the running of a specific event. Officially, a race committee shall consist of "a chairman and at least two other members of the organizing club." The referee and the clerk of course shall also be members. It shall deal with changes in the location of the course, and matters involving protests, rules, and penalties arising out of the race. Thus, under the system outlined above, the race committee need not function at all except under these specific conditions, and when it is needed, its personnel can be drawn directly from that of the tournament committee.

In a single event meet, the names "tournament committee" and "race committee" are synonymous, but in a large four- or five-event meet the job of the tournament committee is that of several race committees combined, and thus it must be given a separate title.

The Downhill Race

In commercial ski areas, where most meets are run, there is little need to worry over the conditions of trails and slopes as they are kept in the best of shape. There might be some corrections made in the various state ski areas that haven't been opened to commercial concerns.

SELECTION

Long before the race takes place, the clerk of course must make his selection of the proper course and alternate course that he intends to use for the competition. The degree of drop is a very

Scoring is complicated and detailed

important consideration, and usually the axiom that the more important the race, and the better the competitors, the steeper the course should be, can be followed. The race should be long for first-class competition, but in the East, with our limited altitude, "long" must necessarily be limited. A race should never be less than one mile in length, and anything over that is desirable. It is obvious that there should be no uphill stretches in any downhill race course. Usually a north or northwest or northeast slope is the one most suitable for a race course, for the sun has less opportunity to get at the snow, and the conditions will remain much more favorable, especially at low altitudes. If the race course is cut through the forests, as are most of the New England trails, then a few hints toward preservation of the trail might be found useful. Planting of any type of a tough grass along the trail will prevent some of the damaging erosion that is so prevalent on ski trails, and will also serve the double purpose of holding the early snows. The trail should be cut wide (30–50 feet, or more) to allow for sufficient checking space, alternate ways of running the course, and safety.

PREPARATIONS

As soon as the first heavy snow has covered the trail, it should be tramped, and this snow should be allowed to settle so that a good solid base will be covering the entire trail. At least two days before the race, the downhill course should be opened to competitors for practice, so the final tramping should be completed before that time. The course should be tramped to its maximum width, to allow plenty of room for checking, and to minimize the accidents that will occur when a racer gets off in the soft snow at the side of the trail. If at any time before the race itself the race committee should decide that further practice would spoil the condition of the trail they may close the race course to further practice.

CARE DURING THE RACE

There is little that must be done during the race other than that of tramping out the ruts that form on the corners. Rakes, and even gardeners' hoes, have been found very valuable in this task.

Selection and preparation of the course must match the class of the competition

OFFICIALS

1. Referee: His duties have already been discussed, for he serves in this capacity for all the events of the tournament.

2. Clerk of the Course: He shall have charge of all persons connected with the course, such as course police and flag keepers. He shall have charge of all preliminary preparations and selection of the race course already described. His duties may include those of course setter, but it is advisable to have this job handled by an expert skier, one who is held in respect as a skier by the competitors. As it is a rare occurrence when you can get so expert a skier to accept the other responsibilities of clerk of course, the two jobs are separated.

3. Course Setter: Prior to the race he shall set control gates (blue flags) at such points as he feels necessary for safety, or he may warn competitors by the use of flags of hidden rocks, stumps, etc. (yellow flags). He shall be responsible for setting direction flags (red flags). If in his opinion the course is unsafe to run, he shall have the authority to postpone the race.

4. Timing Officials: Enumeration of the necessary officials (Duties explained on page 353):

At least two timers. One to be known as the chief timer.
The starter and assistant.
Recorders for each timer and starter.

5. Communication Officials: There should be, whenever possible, some method of communication between the start and the finish of the race course. Telephones, either field sets or regularly installed phones in little wooden shelters, have been found to be the most satisfactory. Radio is almost as good but is not quite so dependable. The men who take care of this apparatus should be dependable, intelligent workers, able to make repairs to any part of their equipment at a moment's notice.

6. Course Police: It is their duty to keep the course in shape during the race, as has already been described. They can also serve to keep the spectators off the course, and as flag keepers at the control gates.

7. The First-aid Patrol: In a case where there is little manpower available this usually becomes another of the duties of the course

Mark the course

police, but it is much wiser to have a well-trained first-aid group, acting independently.

8. *Forerunners:* Before the start of the first contestant in a down-hill race, there shall be at least one forerunner who must run down the course in such time as to finish in front of the first contestant and his time relayed back to starting point as soon as possible. If on the day of the race there is a new fall of snow, there shall be at least three forerunners.

The Slalom Race

The general organization of a slalom race is very similar to that of the downhill. The position of the race course must be selected long before the time of the race. Preferably, it should be on an open slope, although several excellent slalom races have been held on trails, including the 1938 Nationals held on the Nose Dive trail on Mount Mansfield, Stowe, Vt. However, an open slope allows the course setter a great deal more freedom. The hill should have a *minimum vertical drop of 500 feet* for an important race. During the race the course police should be even more diligent than they are in the downhill, and no ruts or grooves surrounding the flags should be allowed to form.

OFFICIALS

The officials necessary for the slalom are almost identical to those of the downhill, with slight changes in their duties.

1. *Referee:* His duties shall remain the same.

2. *The Clerk of Course:* His duties remain the same.

3. *Course Setter:* Prior to the race he should set the flag combinations that make up the modern slalom. Large poles (preferably bamboo or tonkin reed) with red, yellow, and blue flags should be used. Each gate through which the competitors must pass should consist of a pair of these flags identical in color. There are all sorts of flag combinations (too varied to discuss here) open to the course setter. However, the importance of securing a capable, reliable, and respected course setter cannot be overlooked, for he plays a major part in the success or failure of any slalom race.

Provide adequate communications

4. Timing Officials: The same. Duties are explained on page 353.

5. Communications Officials: Their duties remain the same.

6. Course Police: Their duties remain the same, except that in the slalom a separate official serves as flag keeper.

7. The Flag Keepers:

a. *Flags:* Every flag keeper is responsible for the section of the course between his flag and the flag immediately above him.

The flags must be taken in their proper order. A competitor who has overshot a flag is not deemed to have passed through a lower pair of flags until he has reascended to the upper pair and until some part of his ski has crossed the upper pair of flags.

A flag keeper may direct the attention of a competitor to a pair of flags that he is in danger of missing altogether, but he may give no other information to competitors.

A flag keeper has the choice of two, and of only two answers, in reply to any question a competitor may ask. He may reply "Right" or "Back." He should reply "Right" to a competitor if any part of the competitor's ski has crossed the line between the flags he is keeping, even if a competitor has rendered himself liable to a single or double penalty. He should reply "Back" if, and only if, the competitor has rendered himself liable to complete disqualification.

b. *Penalties:* On a record card each flag keeper shall indicate in the proper place any penalties incurred by a competitor. Symbols for penalties shall be: the figure 1 for a single penalty, the figure 2 for a double penalty, and the letter X for disqualification. To avoid confusion no other marks should be made on the card.

Single Penalty. A single penalty shall be incurred if only one of the competitor's feet crosses the line between the control flags.

Double Penalty. A double penalty shall be imposed if neither of the competitor's feet crosses the line between the control flags, provided that some part of his ski crosses the line.

Disqualification. If neither of the competitor's feet and no part of either of his skis cross the line between the control flag, the competitor shall be disqualified.

At the end of each race the flag keepers will be notified by the starter when the last man has gone through. Flag keepers should then immediately surrender their records to the proper official who shall carry them to the chief timer.

The course setter may determine the success of the race

c. *The Penalty Time* in a slalom race shall be reckoned according to the following table:

If the shortest penalty-free time is
40 secs. or less, the single penalty shall be 4 secs.
40.1 secs. to 45 secs., the single penalty shall be 4.5 secs.
45.1 secs. to 50 secs., the single penalty shall be 5 secs.
50.1 secs. to 55 secs., the single penalty shall be 5.5 secs.
55.1 secs. or more, the single penalty shall be 6 secs.

The penalty shall be added to the contestant's time, to give his corrected time. The basis for reckoning penalties shall be arrived at separately for each part of the slalom. A double penalty shall be the equivalent of twice a single penalty.

8. *The First-aid Patrol:* Rarely are there any serious accidents incurred in a slalom race. However, it is advisable to have some first-aid equipment and men on hand throughout the event.

9. *Forerunners:* In a slalom race there should be at least two forerunners.

GENERAL REMARKS

No competitor shall be allowed to run any part of the course after the course setter has placed the flags in position.

A competitor may enter a gate or pair of flags from either side.

The slalom shall always be run on hard packed snow.

There shall be two runs to every slalom, but if necessary, in order to save time, only the best men in the first run may be allowed to enter the second.

Some sort of mark, preferably blueing or ink, should be used in placing the poles in the snow, so that when a flag is removed by a competitor's fall it may be replaced in exactly the same position.

The course setter has the option of altering the course for a second run.

The Langlauf or Cross-Country Race

Here again a great deal of the preparation must be done ahead of time. A trail must be chosen that can be divided into approximate

Flag keeper answers only "Right" or "Back"

thirds—uphill, downhill, and flat—so that as varied terrain as possible be given to test the competitors. The distance of the race must be determined only after careful consideration of the age of the competitors who will run it, their experience, the amount of training they have had, and the time of year.

OFFICIALS

The officials necessary for a cross-country race are very similar to those used in the slalom and downhill.

1. The Referee: His duties have already been covered.

2. The Clerk of Course: His duties shall be those of general supervision and management of the race. He should see that a warm room is provided for the competitors at the finish of the race, and that such refreshments as tea, oranges, and sugar are served. In the cross-country race there is a better opportunity for the jobs of the clerk of course and the course setter to be combined into one. The same differentiation that existed in the slalom and downhill race does not exist here. The course setter in the cross-country race must select his own course and mark it, which is a long and tedious job, and cannot be done just the morning of the race, as the course setter of a slalom would do. The duties of the course setter will be discussed below, but when planning a race it would not be a bad policy to combine both of the jobs into one.

3. The Course Setter: It shall be his duty to put the desired course of the race in shape several days before the actual running of the race, although no competitor shall be allowed to go over the course. All competitors shall be provided with a map. He should have a crew of experienced skiers who are willing and able to cover the entire race course several times in order to prepare the snow. Wide downhill skis should be used in this preliminary tramping, and the track should be at least three ski widths wide. Once again flags of three colors should be used: red for direction, yellow for warning, and blue for control, if, for instance, an open slope were encountered. Over a distance of 11 kilometers as many as 200 flags may be used. It is important that the trail be absolutely certain without forcing the skier to stop and look for directions, for a fatigued racer is likely to lose his way even on a trail that looks quite obvious to the course setter. This is extremely important, for even in major races contestants will frequently lose their way. If a trail

When the flags are set, no practice is let

should overlap itself in a loop, it would be advisable to have large direction signs posted. There should not be too many obstacles such as fences and logs on the course, nor should the trail cross roads frequently used.

4. *Timing Officials:* The same. Their duties will be explained on page 353.

In a cross-country race, if a competitor arrives at the start after his original starting time is past, he may enter the race at the discretion of the starter, but his time will be recorded as if he had started in his original position.

5. *The Checkers and Course Patrol:* The checkers should be placed at their stations by the clerk of course after consultation with the course setter, and after careful study of the course has been made. The purpose of the checker in the cross-country race is to make sure that each competitor covers the entire distance of the course; therefore the checkers should be placed so that it would be impossible for a racer to cut off any portion of the course and still pass each of the checkers. It shall be their duty to write down the number of each competitor as he passes the position, and to return that record to the clerk of course after the last contestant has passed him. They should try to prevent the course from becoming rutted, but this is rarely the case in a cross-country race, except in the downhill portion.

6. *Forerunners:* There should be at least one forerunner, though more men are preferred. This is important, for the first man is extremely handicapped if he has no one ahead of him upon whom he can pace his own gait.

The Jump

The selection and building of a jump hill, its degree of drop in the inrun and outrun, the position of the take-off, etc., are all technical questions and seldom, if ever, are the concern of any athletic director or ski coach.

OFFICIALS

1. *The Judges:* The judges are the men that do the actual scoring of the contestants' jumps on a point basis for form, distance,

The job of the clerk and course setter can be combined

take-off, etc. This is a job that can only be handled by experienced men who know jumping, and who have worked as judges before. The United States Eastern Amateur Ski Association has a list of accredited jump judges that is worth consulting before making out the judge personnel. There should be at least two, preferably three, judges for a jumping competition.

2. *Measurers:* Four or more measurers are usually necessary to take care of a 40-meter hill. The measuring is done with long poles (bamboo) from the side of the hill. A metal measuring chain marked in meters should extend down the side of the hill, and the measurers merely place their poles perpendicular to this chain, and read off the distances from it. Measuring is done from the outermost point of the lip of the jump to that point where the feet of the contestant touch the outrun slope. Measuring shall be done to the closest half meter.

3. *Director of Tournament:* He is actually in charge of running the competition itself. He is usually placed on the judges' stand. He instructs skiers when to start down the inrun, calls out their names, announces distances, etc. It is advisable, especially in a large tournament, to have a loudspeaker system for this man, so that he can be heard from all parts of the hill.

4. *Clerk of Course* (also known as the Chief of Hill): He is the man responsible for the condition of the hill at all times. He and his assistants must do the original tramping of the hill and must have it ready two days before the scheduled competition for practice.

5. *Flagman:* A man should be placed under the lip of the jump with a long flag that will extend over the tip of the take-off, and can be seen from the start of the incline. He shall raise the flag as a danger signal to those above, and lower it only after the hill is absolutely clear and ready for the next jumper.

6. *First Aid:* First-aid men should be present at all times during the jumping competition. They should be stationed at the bottom of the hill, and if any accidents do occur, the casualties will literally slide right into the arms of the waiting patrolmen.

GENERAL REMARKS

1. It might be advisable to split the job of clerk of course into two parts: that of the chief of hill (to take charge of the tramping and

The course must be prepared far in advance of the race

conditioning of the hill during the competition) and that of the clerk of course (to do all the preliminary work, and then to hold himself in readiness to do any one of the last-minute details that spring up during a jumping competition).

2. In case the hill is very icy, it should be broken up to a very rough surface with picks or axes or rakes or anything at all, and then new snow placed on it, and allowed to settle. Even very hard granular snow, or fine ice particles, if placed on the steep outrun of a jump and then allowed to settle for twenty-four hours, will congeal sufficiently to allow tramping and jumping thereafter.

3. A man should be stationed at the top of the inrun with a list of the correct jumping order of the contestants, so that he can get them in their proper order, and facilitate the job of the director of the tournament.

4. If the outrun of the jump is icy, crampons should be provided for the measurers.

5. The way the snow is tramped at the very edge of the take-off is of utmost importance. A slightly bad angle here may throw the jumpers entirely off. This is a job for some experienced impartial jumper to decide upon. A jumper is the *only one* who can tell if there is too much lift to the take-off.

6. If the snow is very fast and a jumper starting from the top is in danger of landing in the transition, or even out in the flat, the inrun must be shortened. Once again this can only be determined by an experienced jumper—a noncompetitor—and so it is advisable to have one or two "exhibition" jumpers who will determine points 5 and 6.

ORDER OF RUNNING
OF CONTESTANTS AND TEAMS

In an individual race there are two methods of selection. The first is that of a simple lot draw. All the contestants' names are placed in a hat, and then the order in which their names are drawn determines the order in which they run. The second is that of the selected group draw. The contestants are arranged in groups according to their previous records, the first group being the best, etc. Then the names of the contestants in each group are drawn from a hat, similar to the first method. Thus if there were ten men in each

Preparing a jump hill is the job of a professional

group, the last man drawn in the first group would race tenth, the first man in the second group would race eleventh, and so on.

The team-draw is that which is used in all competitions in which there is team scoring. The order in which the individual members of each team are to run is determined previously by their coach, manager, or captain. Then only the names of the teams are drawn, and the competitors' names are placed in their proper position. Thus if there are six teams entered, and team "A" is drawn first, then their men run 1st, 7th, 13th, and 19th, and the men on team "B" run 2nd, 8th, 14th, and 20th, etc.

If there is more than one event in the competition, the skiers nevertheless retain their same numbers and racing order throughout the meet. Thus, if in the cross-country event numbers 2 and 3 are not entered, the man wearing number 4 will be racing second.

Starting and Timing

TYPES OF TIMING

There are all sorts of methods used in timing a ski race, methods that have been in use since the beginning of racing, and methods just recently developed. Some are very accurate, elaborate, and complicated, and others are extremely simple, and usually inadequate. The most simple of these is known as the gun start. The starter fires a gun at the top of the course as the competitor starts his run. This is heard at the bottom of the course and the timers start their watches at the sound of the gun, and then stop them when the competitor passes the finish.

A more accurate method is used when the start of the race is within view of the bottom. The starter uses a flag which he waves or drops when the contestant starts, and this is recorded at the bottom by the timers. They stop their watches when the racer crosses the finish line.

The method most used today, however, in timing a downhill or slalom race, and even cross-country races, is that of the phone start, where radio or telephone communications are available. (Telephone communications are available at most ski areas for the conducting

Determine the order of competition in advance

of races.) The starter's assistant is at the top of the course and relays the start by phone to the timers at the bottom of the course.

Methods of electric timing have been developed and they have proved to be excellent, although sometimes quite costly. Western Union seems to be the leader in this field with a "Sports Timer" that clocks the competitors to one one-hundredth of a second. It starts by the opening of a gate by the competitor himself, and stops automatically as the competitor breaks a string stretched across the finish line.

SPECIFIC DUTIES OF
THE TIMING OFFICIALS

1. *The Starter:* It is his duty to see that the competitors leave the start of the race at the proper time and in the proper order. He is the man who gives the commands of 10 seconds, 5, 4, 3, 2, 1, Go! (in the same time intervals) that starts the skier off. These commands must simultaneously be given over the phone so they can reach the finish line, timers, and the racer himself. A good, clear, commanding voice is a great asset to the starter. In the case of flag starts he is also the one who drops the flag. If the starter is not present at the start, as in the case of phone starts, the assistant starter performs these duties as directed by the starter over the phone.

2. *The Timers:* It shall be the duty of the timers to get the time of each racer as he crosses the finish line. A racer shall never be considered to have finished a race until both of his feet have crossed the finish line.

3. *The Recorders:* There shall be a recorder for each timer and for the starter. It shall be the duty of the recorder to write down the time that the timer reads from his watch as the competitor finishes the race.

ACCURACY AND CARE OF WATCHES

In timing a ski race it is of the utmost importance that the watches used are accurate. A watch that behaves normally in a heated room may react in all sorts of ways when exposed to the cold for several hours. Thus it is advisable for all those officials handling watches during a race to keep them as warm as possible. This can be accom-

Use the most accurate timing procedure available

plished by keeping the watch in a bare hand, in a wide pocket, or against a heating pad that may be kept in a pocket.

The usual care given watches in other athletic events must also be considered in ski meets.

ISSUANCE OF RESULTS

No official times should be issued to the public at the race courses, and if any times are issued it should be emphasized that they are unofficial. The official times should only be issued after the complete results have been tabulated indoors, after all the checkers are in, and after all penalties have been applied.

Disqualification

The complete list of disqualifications can best be procured from the *FIS (International Ski Federation) Rule Book* and the National Ski Association *Official Rules for Downhill and Slalom Racing.* Enumerated below are some of the more common ones.

A competitor is disqualified if:
1. Both his feet fail to pass through control gates.
2. He runs the course after it has been officially closed.
3. He fails to appear at the start at the designated time.
4. He descends any part of the course without skis.
5. He replaces any of his equipment with things other than that which he carries (for example, borrowing from spectators in the case of losing a ski pole).
6. He toboggans down any part of the trail (that is, sitting on the skis).
7. He holds poles so that they will act as a brake, by placing them between his legs and sitting on them.
8. Uses a different pair of skis for the downhill and slalom in a combined downhill and slalom meet.
9. He alters the course.

Notes on Scoring Ski Meets

LANGLAUF

It should be the duty of the chief timer to come to headquarters with the cards immediately after the race, and it is desirable that the second timer or his recorder should also come.

Protect the watch

The chief timer's card should be the master card, the other being used as a check. As soon as the cards have been compared and the elapsed times properly checked and entered on the master card, the timers should be relieved of duty.

Meantime, two other men should be going over the station checkers' cards noting the number of any man missing a station. This can well be done by one man reading the numbers from the checkers' cards, while the other checks them off on a copy of the printed entry list. Any disqualification resulting must be entered on the master card, with a note of which station or stations he missed.

A frequent source of delay in past years has been in getting the checkers' cards to headquarters after the race. Everybody concerned should know where these cards are to go and be impressed with the need of getting them there at the earliest possible moment.

In case a man is scratched or disqualified, draw a line through his name and everything else clear across the card.

Next pick out the place of each man and enter it in the last column on the master card. *Write it plainly.* Two men (scorer and assistant) are required for this if the list runs over onto two cards as is usually the case. It is very easy to overlook someone, so time is saved in the end by doing this carefully the first time. When this is finished, check by counting the number of men to whom places have been given to see that it agrees with the highest number assigned.

While this work has been in progress a competent stenographer has loaded his machine with paper and carbons for four copies. He will type, as the scorer reads them to him from the master card, beginning with the winner, each man's place, name, number, college, and time. For example:

Place	Name	Number	College	Time
1	W. Smith	14	Boston U.	1-03-20

The reason for entering a man's number is that it saves a lot of time in checking that will be done by the stenographer reading back to the scorer after the list is complete.

While the list is being read to the typist, another man should be taking down the time of each competitor under the name of his college on a "team score sheet." Times need not be entered on this sheet. As soon as this is complete, he should cross off the slowest time under each college wherever one more time appears than the number of men to score for each team in the event.

After checking, team results should be taken down by the typist.

The scorer should keep *on his person* the original team score sheets, and a copy of the complete results for each event until the meet is over.

DOWNHILL AND SLALOM

The general procedure in scoring downhill and slalom will be essentially the same as for langlauf, the necessary differences being fairly obvious.

In the slalom there will presumably be only one timecard for each run. Corrected times, including penalties for the second run, and total times should be entered on the first run card, which will serve as the official record or "master card."

JUMP AND COMBINED EVENT

According to FIS procedure, it is the duty of the judges to compute scores for the jump and combined event. The scorer, of course, will offer any assistance desired and take over the final checking and recording of results and computation of team scores. Here again the procedure will be essentially the same as outlined for the langlauf.

SCORING JUMPING COMPETITION

The scoring of jumping competition is a complicated and specialized process. The reader is referred to the official rules for further information on scoring jumping.

The scoring of jumps is specialized—read the rules

INDEX

INDEX

A

Acting, dramatic, 11
After-game duties (*see* specific sports)
American League, 21
Anemometer, 87
Announcers, announcing:
swimming meets, 89, 90, 98
tennis, 107-9
track, 68-69
Anticipation, refraining from, 32-33
Appearance, physical, 20-21

B

Backboard (*see* Basketball)
Badminton, 130-34
during play, 132
during service, 132
general instructions, 133-34
pregame duties, 132
umpire in, 131
Ball (*see* specific sports)
Baseball, 10, 13, 14, 18, 37-57
balks, 56-57
batted balls hitting plate, 50-51
curve balls, 41

Baseball (*cont.*)
fumbles, 54-55
hit batsman, 51
interference by batter or catcher, 52
leaving base after caught fly ball, 55-56
low balls, 14, 40-41
physical condition for, 22
position, duties of field umpire covering bases, 45-49 (*see also* specific play situations)
position, duties on balls and strikes, 14, 40-44
what is a strike?, 52-53
position, duties on fair and foul balls, 44-45
and batted balls hitting plate, 51
pregame duties, 39-40
pregame preparations, 38-39
signals, 43, 44ff., 56
special play situations, 50-57
stepping out of batter's box, 51-52
striking at ball, 52-53
tagging situations, 53-54
touching all bases, 56
uniforms, 21, 38-39
Basic philosophy of officiating, 23-27

Basketball, 10, 12-13, 14, 18, 19, 179-247
after game, 228
backboard, checking, 184
ball, 184
basket, 184-85
bonus rule, 226-28, 230
center jump, 195-96
checking equipment and facilities, 183-87
dribbling rules, 245-46
free throw, 189, 210-13, 224-25, 246-47
front court play, 199-203
general principles, 230-37
    blocking and possession of ball, 233-34
    contact without personal foul, 231-33
    direction and responsibility for contact, 234-37
    personal contact for personal foul, 230-31
guides for administering rules, 229-47
guides for guarding situations, 237-41
guides for noncontact situations, 244-47
guides for screening situations, 241-44
held ball, 32-33, 247
jump ball, 203-5, 221-22
meeting coaches and captains, 192-95
need for total scene, 31
out-of-bounds, 205-10
and philosophy, 23-24, 25
pregame duties, 180-87
procedure when calling foul, 218-19
procedure when calling violation, 219-20
and restraint from anticipating decision, 32-33
scorers and timers, 187-92
screening, 232-33, 235ff., 241-44
signals, 226-28
substitution, 190
switching, 210, 225
10-second rule, 217-18, 245
3-second rule, 25, 217-18, 244-45
throw-in rules, 246
time-out, 218-19

Basketball (cont.)
tossing for jump, 195-99, 203-5, 221-22
    try for goal, 213-17
        guarding and, 241
    uniform shown, 20
    whistles, 185-87, 198
Batsmen; batters (see Baseball)
Benich, Tom, 20
Blocking:
    basketball, 233-34ff., 241ff.
    football, 18, 24-25, 152-53
    lacrosse, 331-32
Blowing whistle, 4 (see also specific sports)
    and confidence, 11
Bonus rule (basketball), 226-28, 230
Broad jump, 78-79, 81-83

C

Calmness and emotional control, 11-13
    and consistency, 15
Captains, meeting:
    basketball, 192-95
    lacrosse, 326-28
Center jump (basketball), 195-96
Certification:
    volleyball, 112
    wrestling, 309-11
Chainmen (see Football)
Charging (see specific sports)
Checkers (ski meets), 349, 355
Checking equipment (see Pregame duties and preparations)
Chief of hill (ski meet), 350
Clerk of office (ski meet), 339
Clerks of courses:
    ski meet, 339ff.
    swimming, 89, 90, 98
    track, 66-67
Clinics (see specific sports)
Close quarters, need for, 30-31
Clothing (see Uniforms)
Coaches (see also specific sports)
    and uniformity in rules, 29
Communications officials (ski meet), 344, 346
Completed acts, ruling on, 32-33
Condition, physical, 21-22
Conduct, players' (see specific sports)
Confidence, 10-11

Consistency, 13-15
Cooperation, 16 (*see also* specific sports)
any or all officials should decide on any play, 33
Corner kick (soccer), 253, 254, 257, 262, 267, 273-74, 280
Course police, course patrol (ski meet), 344, 346, 349
Course setters (ski meet), 344, 345, 348-49
Court play (*see* Basketball)
Cross-country ski race (langlauf), 347-49
  scoring, 354-56

D

Decisions (*see* specific sports)
Decisive action, 10
Direct free kicks (soccer), 268-69, 280
Director, ski tournament, 350
Director-in-chief (ski meet), 338
Director of officials (ski meet), 338-39
Discus throw, 78-79, 84, 85
  implement standards, 86
Distance from play, 30-31 (*see also* specific sports)
Diving (*see* Swimming and diving)
Downhill ski race, 342-45
  scoring, 356
Dramatizing, 11
Draw (wrestling), 301-2, 312
Dribbling (*see* Basketball)
Duties of officials, 19-20

E

Earnings, 22
Endurance, 21, 22
Equipment (*see* Pregame duties and preparations; specific sports)
Equipment director (ski meet), 339-40
Exercises, 22

F

Fair balls (baseball), 44-45, 51
Falls (wrestling), 296-97, 299, 300ff., 312

Field events, 77-87
  broad jump, 78-79, 81-83
  chief field judge, 77-79
  determining order of competition, 78
  discus throw, 78-79, 84, 85, 86
  hammer throw, 86
  high jump, 78, 80-81
  inspector of implements, 86
  instructions, 79-87
  javelin, 79, 84-85, 86
  judging legality, 79
  measuring results, 79
  pole vault, 78-79, 81
  recording and reporting results, 79
  shot put, 78, 79, 83-84, 86
  surveyor, 86-87
  35-pound weight, 79, 86
Field goal (football), 161-62
Field judge (*see* Field events; Football)
Field umpire (baseball) (*see* Baseball)
Finish judges (*see* Judges: swimming)
First aid officials (ski), 340, 344-45, 347, 350
Flag keepers (ski meet), 346
Flagman (ski meet), 350
Flag posts (soccer), 262, 277
Football, 13, 14, 143-78
  after game, 168-69
  and basic philosophy, 24-25
  between halves, 168
  between quarters, 164-65
  blocking, 18, 24-25, 152-53
  delay of game, 153
  enforcement of penalties, 174-75
  forward pass, 156-57, 178
  fumbles, 176-77
  goal-line play, 159-60
  guides to play situations, 173-78
  holding, 153
  kickoff, 148-50
  kicks from scrimmage, 157-58
    conditions surrounding ball, 158
    freedom of movement of kicker, 158
    illegal play against kicker, 157
    out-of-bounds kick, 157-58
  measuring position of ball, 166-67
  need for total scene, 32
  officials needed, 144
  offside, 14, 24, 152

Football (*cont.*)
  out-of-bounds, 157-58, 158-59, 178
  pregame activities, 144-48
  restraint from anticipating decision
    in, 33
  runs from scrimmage, 153-55
  safeties, 177-78
  scrimmage play, 150-53
  shift or motion plays, 151-52
  signals, 169-72
  time-out, 163-64
  touchbacks, 177-78
  touchdowns, 177
  try for field goal, 161-62
  try for point, 160-61
Forerunners (ski meet), 345, 347, 349
Forward pass (football), 156-57, 178
Foul balls (baseball), 44-45, 51
Fouls (*see* specific games)
Free kicks (soccer), 268-71, 279-80
Free throw (basketball), 189, 210-13,
    224-25, 246-47
Fumbles:
  baseball, 54-55
  football, 176-77
Fundamental principles, 3-33
  basic philosophy, 23-27
  general principles, 28-33
  the job, 3-7
  qualifications, 8-22

G

Gambling, 17
General principles, 28-33
Glasses, wearing, 21
Goal kick (soccer), 261, 263, 267,
    273, 281-82
Goals, goal line (*see* specific games)
Guarding (basketball) (*see* Basket-
    ball)
Guns, 65 (*see also* Starters; etc.; spe-
    cific games)

H

Halves, between (football), 168
Hammer throw, 86
Handball, 135-39
  hinders, 138, 139
  scoring, 136
  shorts, 138-39
  referee, 136-39
Heart power (endurance), 21, 22

Held ball (basketball), 32-33, 247
High jump, 78, 80-81
Hinders (handball), 138, 139
Hit batsman (baseball), 51
Hockey, 316-22
  basic principles, 321-22
  delay of game, 319
  general duties, 318-21
  general information, 317-18
  general qualifications, 316-17
  goal umpires, 321
  injuries, 321
  penalty timekeeper, 320-21
  timekeepers, 320-21
  whistling in, 321
Holding:
  football, 153
  lacrosse, 332

I

Inconsistency (*see* Consistency)
Indirect free kicks (soccer), 269-70,
    279
Influence (*see* Presence)
Injuries (*see* specific games)
Inspectors:
  swimming, 89, 90, 98-99
  track, 75-76
Integrity, 17
Interference (lacrosse), 331-32
Interference by batter or catcher
    (baseball), 52
Interpretation of rules (*see* Rules;
    specific games)

J

Javelin throw, 79, 84-85, 86
Job, the, 3-7
  official-player rapport, 5
  potential of presence, 3-5
  public relations, 6-7
Judges:
  football (*see* Football)
  ski jump, 349-50
  swimming, 89, 90, 92-93, 94, 95-
    97, 99
  track, 73-75
Judgment, 15-16
Jump ball (basketball), 203-5, 221-22
Jumping at opponent (soccer), 268
Jumps, ski, 349-52

K

Kickoff, football, 148-50

L

Lacrosse, 323-36
  ball out-of-bounds, 326, 331, 333
  checking equipment and field, 324-26
  covering the field, 328-29
  execution of penalties, 334
  expulsion fouls, 334
  general conduct, 333
  guides to specific play situations, 330-34
  holding, 332
  instructing timer and scorer, 326
  interference, 331-32
  leaving position, 332-33
  meeting coaches and captains, 326-28
  no warnings in, 330
  penalties, 334
  personal equipment, 324
  personal fouls, 334
  positions and duties at goal, 329-30
  positions at face-off, 328
  postgame duties, 336
  pregame conference, 324
  privileges of goalkeeper, 331
  procedure in calling fouls, 330
  pushing, 332
  rating officials, 325
  signals, 335, 336
  striking with crosse (slashing), 333
  substitutions, 326, 327, 331
  tripping, 332
Langlauf, 347-49
  scoring, 354-56
Leg strength, 21
Linesmen (*see* specific games)

M

Manuals for officiating, 19-20
Marich, Rudy, 20
Mechanics of officiating, 19-20
Michigan, University of, 21

N

National Collegiate Athletic Association (NCAA), 61, 316

Near falls (wrestling), 298, 301, 302
Nervousness (*see* Calmness)
Net play (volleyball), 121-22
Net umpire (tennis), 104
Neutral position (wrestling), 295-96ff., 312
Newman, Larry, 7
No advantage (wrestling) (*see* Neutral position)

O

Official player rapport, 5
Offside (*see* specific games)
Out-of-bounds (*see* specific games)

P

Pantomime, 11
Penalties (*see* specific games)
Personal appearance, 20-21
Personal fouls (*see* specific games)
Personal qualities (*see* Qualifications)
Philosophy, basic, 23-27
Physical condition, 21-22
Pistol (*see also* Guns)
  swimming starter's use of, 91, 92
Points, awarding (wrestling), 295-96, 297-99, 312, 313
Pole vault, 78-79, 81
Postgame duties (*see* specific games)
Pregame preparations, duties:
  badminton, 132
  baseball, 39-40
  basketball, 180-87
  lacrosse, 324-28
  soccer, 258-59
  tennis, 103
  volleyball, 119
  wrestling, 285-87
Presence, potential of, 3-5
Public relations, 6-7
Pushing:
  basketball, 10
  lacrosse, 332
  soccer, 269

Q

Qualifications, 8-22
  appearance, 20-21
  calmness, 11-13
  condition, 21-22
  confidence, 10-11

Qualifications (*cont.*)
  consistency, 13-15
  cooperation, 16
  duties, 19-20
  integrity, 17
  judgment, 15-16
  knowledge of rules, 17-19
  mechanics of officiating, 19-20
  reaction time, 9-10
Quarters, between (football), 164-65

R

Rapport, official-player, 5
Rating officials:
  lacrosse, 325
  wrestling, 311, 313-15
Reaction time, 9-10
Referees (*see* specific games)
Referees (Newman), 7
Reiff, Guy, 21
Reveille, Nick, 21
Rules, 14 (*see also* specific games)
  changes in, and consistency, 14
  knowledge of, 17-19
  official interpretations of, uniformity
    and, 29-30
Runs; running (*see* specific games)

S

Safeties (football), 177-78
Scorers (scoring):
  basketball, 187-90
  handball, 136
  lacrosse, 326
  ski meet, 341-42, 354-55
  soccer, 267
  swimming, 89, 90, 99
  tennis, 109-10
  track, 67-68
  volleyball, 115-18
  wrestling, 286, 302, 305-6
Screening (basketball), 232-33, 235ff.,
  241-44
Scrimmage play (*see* Football)
Secretary of ski meet, 339
Shorts (handball), 138-39
Shot put, 78, 79, 83-84
  implement standards, 86
Signals (*see* specific games)

Ski meets, 337-56
  checkers, 349, 355
  chief of hill, 350
  clerks of the courses, 339ff.
  communications officials, 344, 346
  course police (patrol), 344, 346,
    349
  course setters, 344, 345, 348-49
  director-in-chief, 338
  director of officials, 338-39
  director of tournament, 350
  disqualification, 354, 355
  downhill race, 342-45
    care of course during race, 343
    officials, 344-45
    preparations, 343
    scoring, 356
    selection, 342-43
  equipment director, 339-40
  first-aid officials, 340, 344-45, 347,
    350
  flag keepers, 346
  flagman, 350
  forerunners, 345, 347, 349
  general meet officials, 341-42
  issuance of results, 354
  judges for jump, 350
  jump, 349-52
    general remarks, 351
    icy hill, 351
    officials, 349-50
    order of running, 351-52
    scoring, 356
  langlauf or cross-country race, 347-
    49
    officials, 348-49
    scoring, 354-56
  measurers for jump, 350
  meet officials, 340-41
  organization of officials, 337-38
  race committee, 342
  referees, 341ff.
  scorers, scoring, 341-42, 354-56
  secretary or clerk of office, 339
  slalom race, 345-47
    officials, 345-46
    penalties, 346-47
    scoring, 356
  starting and timing, 352-53
  timing officials, 344, 346, 349, 353-
    54, 355

Ski meets (*cont.*)
  tournament committee, 342
  transportation director, 340
Slalom race, 345-47
  scoring, 356
Slashing (lacrosse), 333
Soccer, 248-82
  the ball, 263
    bursting of, 281
    in play, 266
    out of play, 267, 278, 282
  and basic philosophy, 25
  boots for, 264, 277
  charging, 25, 269, 270
  cigarette lighting, 278
  clinics, 249
  coaches and uniformity in rules, 29
  corner kick, 253, 254, 257, 262, 267, 273-74, 280
  crossbar, displacement of, 267, 277
  diagonal system of control (one referee), 252-55
  direct free kicks, 268-69, 280
  drop ball, 267
  dual system of control (two referees), 255-58
  duration of game, 265
  the field, 261-63
    waterlogging of, 281
  flag posts, 262, 277
  fouls and misconduct, 260, 264, 268-74ff., 278ff.
  free kicks, 268-71, 279-80
  game responsibility, 259-61
  goal kick, 261, 263, 267, 273, 281-82
  grading referees, 249-50
  hand signals, 274-75
  indirect free kicks, 269-70, 279
  injuries, 260-61, 277
  jumping at opponent, 268
  laws of play, 265-67
  officials, 250-52
  offside, 25, 270, 271, 278-79
  penalty kick, 253-55, 257-58, 271-72, 280-81, 281-82
  the players, 263-64
  pregame activities, 258-59
  pushing, 269
  questions and answers, 277-82
  scoring, 267
  substitutes, 260, 264, 270

Soccer (*cont.*)
  suggestions for referees, 275-76
  throw-in, 272-73, 281
  timekeeping, 251-52, 259, 277
  tripping, 25, 268, 279
  uniform and equipment, 252, 258-59, 264-65
  waterlogged field, 281
Softball, 58-59
Spectators (*see also* specific games)
  and public relations, 6-7
Sportsmanship (*see* specific games)
Starters:
  swimming, 89, 90, 91-92
  track, 63-66
Strikes (baseball), 14, 40-44, 52-53
Striking (lacrosse), 333
Surveyor, for field events, 86-87
Swimming and diving, 18-19, 88-99
  announcers, 89, 90, 98
  backstroke start, 91
  clerk of course, 89, 90, 98
  diving judges' duties, 95-97
  diving referee's duties, 95
  diving secretary's duties, 97-98
  false starts, 91-92
  forward start, 91
  inspectors, 89, 90, 98-99
  judges, 89, 90, 92-93, 94, 95-97
    take-off, 89, 99
  number of officials, 89-90
  referees, 89, 90-91, 95
  scorers, 89, 90, 99
  starters, 89, 90, 91-92
  timers, 89, 90, 92-93, 94-95

T

Tagging (baseball), 53-54
Technical fouls (*see* specific games)
Technicalities, 26
10-second rule (basketball), 217-18, 245
Tennis, 11, 18-19, 100-10
  announcing techniques, 107-9
  linesmen, 104-7
  net umpire, 104
  officials needed, 102-7
  referees, 102
  restraint from anticipating decision in, 33

Tennis (*cont.*)
  scoring, 109-10
  umpires, 102-3
35-pound weight, 79, 86
3-second rule (basketball), 25, 217-18, 244-45
Time-out (*see* specific sports)
Timers and timing:
  basketball, 187-88, 190-92
  football, 145-46, 147
  hockey, 320-21
  lacrosse, 326
  ski, 344, 346, 349, 353-54, 355
  soccer, 251-52, 259
  swimming, 89, 90, 92-93, 94-95
  track, 69-73
  volley, 115
  wrestling, 286, 302-5
Total scene, need to view, 31-32
Touchback (football), 177-78
Touchdown (football), 177
Touching bases (baseball), 56
Touching net (volleyball), 122
Tower, Oswald, 23-24
Track, 18, 19, 60-76 (*see also* Field events)
  announcers, 68-69
  clerk of course, 66-67
  and distance in viewing for decision, 31
  duties, instructions to officials, 62-76
  judges, 73-75
  officials needed, 62
  referee, 63
  scorer, 67-68
  starter, 63-66
  timers, 69-73
  track inspectors, 75-76
  uniform, 62
  written instructions, 61
Transportation director (ski meet), 340
Tripping:
  lacrosse, 332
  soccer, 25, 268, 279

U

Umpires (*see* specific games)
Uniforms, 20-21
  baseball, 21, 38-39
  basketball, 20

Uniforms (*cont.*)
  lacrosse, 324
  soccer, 252
  track (clothing), 62

V

Voice, 10-11 (*see also* Announcers)
  as basketball signal, 226
Volleyball, 111-29
  attitude in, 129
  ball in play, 121
  certification for, 112
  linesmen, 113-15
  net play, 121-22
  out of position on serve, 127-28
  over-the-center line, 126, 127
  playing the ball, 123-25
  point or side-out, 125-26
  referees, 118-29
  scorer, 115-18
  sportsmanship, 128, 129
  starting play, 119-20
  substitution, 126-27
  team of officials, 112-29
  technical foul, 128-29
  time-out, 126, 127
  timer, 115
  touching net, 122
  umpire, 118
  use of whistle, 129

W

Watches, use of (*see* Timers and timing)
Whistles, whistle blowing, 4 (*see also* specific games)
  and confidence, 11
Wrestling, 283-315
  bulging mat, 308
  certification, 309-11
  and close quarters for decision, 30
  clothing, checking of, 286
  coaches and uniformity in rules, 29
  decision, awarding, 301-2, 312
  draw, declaring, 301-2, 312
  duties during meet, 287-302
  falls, awarding, 296-97, 299, 300ff., 312
  giving instructions to timers and scorers, 286

Wrestling (*cont.*)
giving instructions to wrestlers, 286-87
illegal holds, 291-93
interlocking hands, 307, 313
mechanics of working with timers and scorers, 302-7
near fall, 298, 301, 312
neutral position, 295-96ff., 312
"off the mat," 287-88, 293
out-of-bounds, 313
points, awarding, 295-96, 297-99, 312, 313
position of advantage, 294, 295, 297

Wrestling (*cont.*)
premeet duties, 285-86
rating work of officials during season, 311, 313-15
sideline coaching, 308
signals, 288-307 *passim,* 312-13
"stalling," 288, 300
technique and art in officiating, 309
techniques while contestants wrestle on their feet, 287-89
techniques while men are on mat, 289-95
time-out, 299, 306, 312
warnings, 288, 297ff., 312-13